Where is my Bag?

After 24 hours of travel from my home in regional Australia, I have landed in Madrid on the evening of 15 April 2019.

I'm here to start a bicycle tour that will initially involve cycling in Spain for just over a month before making my way to France in time to attend a day at the French Open tennis, in late May.

Besides being tired from flying, I feel okay, so I make my way to the carousel to collect my bags.

Just as I get there, I'm told by a friendly staff member that one of my bags hasn't arrived. Presumably, my bicycle has been delayed since my first flight left Melbourne late, which meant there was only an hour between changing flights in Dubai.

However, my bicycle which is in a cardboard bike box has made it safely through. Instead, my black spotted canvas bag containing nearly all my camping gear, an Ortlieb bicycle pannier bag and my helmet is missing. Since I have been promptly told that my bag is lost, presumably it will arrive in 24 hours on the next plane.

My missing bag

Thankfully, I do have all my electronics, and clothing except my rain jacket, as they came with me as carry-on in my other pannier bag. Fortunately, I also still have my tent and Revelate Sweetroll handlebar bag, as they were in the box with my bicycle, along with my smaller bags, including a tool repair kit that goes on my bicycle's seat post.

For anyone who has read my book about cycling in Russia and Eastern Europe, *It's not about the Kilometres*; my gear is mostly the same except for a couple of items.

I am trying cycling sandals with bicycle cleats, so I won't need to carry socks.

After struggling on last year's trip to find books in English, I have purchased a Kobo ebook reader, which will allow me to read as many books as I want. Hopefully I will read more often rather than getting distracted by my iPhone. It's also smaller, so it takes up less room than a physical book.

Once I assemble my professionally designed touring bicycle called Vivente World Randonneur, it looks half empty with only one pannier bag on the back.

Thankfully, using a train it's easy getting from the airport to Madrid. As I leave the main railway station called *Estación de Madrid Atocha*, it feels strange riding in the dark without a bicycle light or helmet.

My Warmshower hosts Renata and Goncalo are located nearby, so it's easy finding their apartment. I'm welcomed in as I explain my situation with my bag.

They offer to help, including letting me use their phone to call Emirates, along with talking over the phone to Madrid airport staff in Spanish for me.

No one has any information on where my bag is, but I expect in the morning to get a positive update.

I will be referring to Warmshowers often. This is a website where people offer touring cyclists a place to stay at their home for free. Anyone can be a host and the host decides if they are available.

I awake, still tired from jet lag but at a decent time in the morning. Despite no news about my bag's location, I'm feeling optimistic that it will show up tonight. In the meantime, I will have a look around Madrid.

Last year, free walking tours were an informative way to learn about a city. So I join a small tour, where I discover Madrid is a relatively young European city as it only became the capital in 1561. Still, there are plenty of royal buildings and statues, with the main palace having long lines of tourists waiting to go inside.

Guided tour of Madrid, showed me pictorial street sign

On numerous street corners are murals explaining the name of the street, many with a religious connection. Some like *Plaza de Jesus* need no explanation as the picture is obvious.

After the tour, I briefly explore the former royal gardens, Parque de El Retiro. Now a public park it's busy with people out enjoying the sunshine, with many undertaking physical activities. In the centre of the park is a large lake with people boating, while on one side of the lake is a large semicircular monument with a statue of King Alfonso XII in the middle with stairs leading down to the water.

The well-tended gardens and buildings converted into galleries remind me of similar former royal parks I visited around St Petersburg in Russia last year.

Renata's apartment is not far from the park, so I return and once again ring Emirates.

I'm still getting the same message that they can't find the bag. I'm beginning to realise there is a possibility I may never see my items again, so I'm not in the mood for exploring much today.

I have been using most of the missing gear for more than a decade going back to university days, so they have nostalgic value, rather than just financial. Sure, my battered Trangia stove might not fit that well together anymore, and the two parts of the spondonicles are held together by a bobby hairpin (the tool that lifts the pots). Still, it has been on every significant cycling trip. Annoyingly the week before I left Australia, I purchased a new sleeping bag, which is now missing.

I keep thinking, *why didn't I put all my gear in the bicycle box, as I did last year when I flew to Moscow.*

It's another frustrating call in the morning with Emirates, as there is no more information on where my bag is. I'm not sure what to do as I was originally planning to start cycling tomorrow. To take my mind off this, I will continue exploring Madrid using the underground metro. Helpfully near the apartment are stairs leading down to a station.

Obtaining a ticket is easy because most machines have English language options, while the most straightforward ticket to buy is a tourist card which will allow me unlimited travel for a few days. Initially, the metro map is confusing, with numerous coloured lines criss-crossing all over the inner part of the city.

After closer inspection, I can see where I need to change trains to get between places of interest. With trains running every five minutes, riding the metro is relatively easy and comfortable. I have even seen a few people with bicycles on board.

The Museo del Ferrocarril de Madrid is a railway museum housed in an old station with a triangle shaped roof and a glass front. I'm hoping to learn about where railway lines went in Spain because this will help explain the history of the many rail trails I'm hoping to cycle.

It's a typical rail museum with rows of carriages and trains from various periods. The style of this former station building is of more interest to me than the trains on display as it shows a much older style, with wooden timetable boards and paper tickets on display. It's just what I imagine the old part of Atocha used to look like before it expanded.

Without English information, I'm trying to learn about each item on display using my limited Spanish, as I know some words, while others are just spelled a slightly different way to English. For example, train in Spanish is *tren* while station is *estación*.

The Museo Naval (navy museum) focuses on Spanish interactions with Asia, especially former colonies like the Philippines. I had been expecting the Americas to have been the focus instead.

It's a well-stocked museum with various artefacts, old maps, numerous portraits usually of Spanish men, and so many models and paintings of ships. With English information available I'm able to learn some history I didn't know about.

For most of Spain, the Thursday before Easter is a public holiday rather than the Monday afterwards as it is in Australia. We both still observe Good Friday. So on this Wednesday afternoon, I'm spending some time searching for bicycle and camping stores, just in case my bag doesn't show up. I have found some stores but few with items I'm after.

As I'm about to go on another free walking tour, Renate messages me saying the airline has just rung her to say they have found a bag. So I quickly return to her apartment to ring Emirates.

However, it turns out this bag contains items that are definitely not mine, including a tent, while they don't mention the obvious things I'm missing, like my helmet.

My original plan had been to leave Madrid on Thursday morning, especially as Renata and Goncalo are returning to their native Portugal for the Easter break. Thankfully, they are kind enough to let me stay at their place longer than planned, even while they are away. I will be eternally grateful to them for all their help.

This is why Warmshowers is such a valuable resource. If I had been at an Airbnb or hotel, it probably would have been an expensive and lonely experience trying to sort out my missing bag.

So at the moment, I will wait in Madrid until the weekend to see if my bag turns up. If it doesn't by Saturday, I will have to purchase some new gear. Either way, I have developed a plan to get a train to Talavera de la Reina on Sunday and start cycling a rail trail from there.

Even if my bag hadn't disappeared, it wouldn't have been much fun cycling this Thursday as it's consistently raining, causing light flooding in places. Rain is predicted to continue until Saturday.

Other than supermarkets being closed, it's hard to tell it's a public holiday today as nearly everything else is open. A bonus is that many museums and art galleries are free to enter, so I will take the opportunity to visit more of them. However, even when they are free, they often insist that I take a ticket. What a waste of paper and time for people handing out tickets. I'm sure they could just count visitors.

The Museum of the Americas is engaging, especially seeing the impact of Spanish colonisation on the Americas. It shows how their way of life was changed, very reminiscent of the British impact on Indigenous Australians. Many of the items are either of a human head or a whole human in various shapes, sizes, and colours. Often certain features of a person have been exaggerated. Presumably, many of the artefacts in the museum were 'borrowed/stolen' from the locals.

There are also plenty of historic propaganda paintings designed to show what the Spanish were doing in the Americas in a positive light, many with a religious influence.

During last night's bistro meal with Renata and Goncalo, Renata recommended an art gallery called Reina Sofia, opposite Atocha. In particular, she told me that the last two hours are free to enter and that the side entrance has shorter lines.

Having arrived two hours before closing time, I'm told it's been free to enter all day because it's the Thursday before Easter. It's busy, but I still get in easily, however, an hour later, the line outside is looking long, especially at the main entrance.

Inside, each of the four levels concentrates on different eras of Spanish history, allowing me to finally see some artwork relating to the Spanish Civil War, including the Picasso painting *Guernica*. I only notice it because numerous people are gathered around it.

This black-and-white painting is of a scattering of both numerous body parts and Spanish symbols. It was only painted weeks after the infamous bombing by the German air force who were on Franco's side, and was designed to show the world the impact of the bombing on civilians.

It has all the hallmarks of bombings to come in the Second World War, including the London Blitz. The Spanish Civil War sounds horrible and is the entrée to the Second World War, with both fascist and communist forces involved.

In another section, I'm finally able to see some Franco era artwork, which has a pessimistic view of Spain, while the modern section is more optimistic.

Unlike Eastern Europe, where the Second World War and the subsequent communist era are prominent in museums and artwork, there is a noticeable lack of focus on the 20th century in Spain. Instead, they tend to focus on centuries before, during royal times. Unlike Eastern Europe, where Russia is blamed for everything, it was an internal issue here in Spain, so agreeing on history is harder

Originally I had looked at using a suburban train to get out of Madrid, probably to Aranjuez and from there cycle to Toledo. However, since I'm still waiting on my bag, I will experience a high-speed train in Spain and have a full day in Toledo.

Other than China, Spain has the most extensive high-speed railway network in the world, and is still building more dedicated lines in standard gauge, which is different to the wider Iberian Gauge that the slower trains run on in Spain and Portugal. This allows fast train services between Spain and France but unlike in France, where the fast TGV trains can, if needed, run at a slower speed on the older tracks, in Spain, they cannot mix.

Estación de Madrid Atocha is one of the largest railway stations I have ever seen. It's Madrid's first railway station and clearly it has been expanded over the years because trains don't run anymore in the oldest section. Instead, it's a waiting area with many large tropical trees growing in the middle under the large glass windows. Trains now depart below on a few levels in a larger more modern but blander-looking part of the station.

The front and the older section of Estación de Madrid Atocha

Besides going through security with luggage metal detectors, it's a relaxing ride on a clean, modern train for €11 each way which takes just over half an hour without stopping to get to Toledo.

The railway station is outside the historic city of Toledo, but it's an easy short walk, which includes a crossing of the Rio Tajo, which forms a horseshoe around this city built on a hill. Thankfully, at the moment, rain is staying away as I go over a medieval stone bridge and through an old-looking, large, decorated stone gate into the centre of the old town.

Don't buy a map at the railway station, as free ones with better information are offered in visitor information centres located in a few places in Toledo.

It's quiet at 10 am, but this would change as the morning went on. With today being Good Friday, just like in Madrid, some museums are free. Most have a religious focus as Toledo was and still is the religious capital of Spain. It also used to be a political capital before the monarchy moved to Madrid nearly 500 years ago. I'm only visiting the religious places if they are free as I find that all the money they spend on their buildings is too much for so-called charities. Imagine if all the money spent on religious buildings was used to help people instead.

Still, there is some pleasant-looking architecture, plenty of religious paintings, and numerous statues of religious figures on the outside walls of the main cathedral.

Main cathedral in Toledo

Outside the central triangle-shaped plaza, numerous people with umbrellas are offering free guided tours, but nearly all are in Spanish. Thankfully, I have found an English version at 11 am, with a guide who has a yellow umbrella.

My guide explains how different religions have controlled this city at times, so some areas are still referred to by their religious history. For example, there is a Jewish area with synagogues.

Until around 500 years ago, modern-day southern Spain had been under the control of Islamic Moors for centuries, including Toledo for a few centuries.

The majority of mosques in Spain didn't face Mecca. Instead, they focused on Córdoba south of here, the spiritual centre of Islam in this region. It reminds me of how the Orthodox Church in Eastern Europe split from Rome.

Once this region was finally conquered by the Catholic royals to form the country we know as Spain today, it all changed. Many people were forced to convert to Catholicism or leave the country.

It's the opposite to what was happening around the same time in modern-day Turkey, where it went from Christian to Islamic. So, just like in Turkey, religious buildings here changed too. Many mosques were converted to churches by adding parts to the facility to change the shape so prayer could be done differently.

We are shown an example of this. At first glance from the outside, the whole church looks the same, but as the guide explains, only the right side of this bricked building was a mosque. When it was converted to a church, they added the left side. A closer look reveals some differences, including different styles around the windows and a different roof.

Visible below this building are remains of a rough Roman road built out of large stones. All of these different styles show that this place has had a varied history.

Left side was added later, while below is an even older Roman road

A symbol for finding water

Tight roads

Our guide also points out a small symbol of a human head on a few buildings. This informed people that water was available here from a well. Otherwise, the river is a fair way down below. It's always nice to learn about simple symbols I have to actively look for.

A few times when exploring on my own, I've become lost due to these narrow cobblestone streets often taking dogleg routes through built-up areas. Sometimes even the numerous tall buildings are built right across the road, making a narrow tunnel. Despite the lack of room and the number of pedestrians, cars are allowed on most roads.

All up, Toledo reminds me of Avignon in France, with a heavy tourist focus on religion and not much sign of locals living in the city centre.

On a sunny day, this would be a scenic place to go for longer walks. But since the rain is becoming heavy in the afternoon, I will return to the railway station.

Helpfully, the railway staff allow me to catch an earlier train back to Madrid without a change of train fee required.

I arrived in Madrid on Monday, it's now Saturday, and after four days of ringing Emirates twice a day, still no one knows where my bag is. Regretfully I have now finally accepted that the bag is lost forever, so I will purchase some new gear.

I also contacted my travel insurance, but they aren't much use as my bicycle specific gear isn't covered fully. I always assumed if my gear went missing, it would have been stolen along with my bicycle when left unattended while I ducked into a shop or visited a museum, which is nearly impossible to insure. I never considered my bags being lost for this long while flying. I'm not sure what else I can do to find them.

Since I took one of my pannier bags as carry-on luggage, I only need to replace one. So I'm initially searching for one Ortlieb or similar waterproof pannier bag. However, the two bicycle shops I have found which have these bags will only sell me them as a pair.

In the end, I have to buy two pannier bags. So I will leave one at Renata and Goncalo's apartment.

On the street called Calle de la Ribera are half a dozen camping stores located close to each other, which allows me to go in and out a few times to find what

I'm after. Eventually, I have a Trangia stove, sleeping bag, sleeping mat and rain jacket. All these camping shops take a siesta break between 2 pm and 5 pm, so I have purchased all my new gear by 2 pm.

So now, on my bicycle rack over my back wheel, I will have two different styles of red Ortlieb waterproof pannier bags. The new bag will carry my sleeping bag, spare clothing, ebook, electronic chargers and other items I want to keep clean and dry. The older pannier from Australia will have my new stove, food and anything else which doesn't matter if food spills on it.

My new air mattress and rain jacket will be stored in my Revelate Sweetroll bag, along with my tent, compressible pillow and inner sheet. This Sweetroll is strapped horizontally under my bicycle's butterfly handlebar.

After dropping all my new gear back at my Warmshower's home, I return to the other bicycle shop, as I need a helmet and a spare tube, as both are in with my lost bag. Before returning to the apartment, I purchase groceries because tomorrow is Easter Sunday, so I'm not sure what supermarkets will be open in this Catholic country.

Since I have been delayed in Madrid, I take the opportunity to watch a men's La Liga football match at a stadium a few metro stops from me. Rayo Vallecano is a small club with an old stadium. They are second last in the league and are playing Huesca, who are last, so it's a relegation battle, which means it's an intense, packed atmosphere. When the home team scores, the atmosphere increases, but it's then ruled out by the Video Assistant Referee.

Eventually, it finishes nil-all, so presumably, both teams will more than likely be relegated from La Liga. The only downside from this experience is how many smokers are in the stands, making it stink and distracting me from enjoying my experience.

My first La Liga match

As I pass a convenience store on my way home, I remember I need a Tupperware style container because mine is in my lost bag. I find them useful for storing food while touring, especially protecting fruit or keeping any leftover dinner.

In hindsight, staying in Madrid longer allowed me to see more of the city. Anyway, with the terrible rainy weather over the past few days, it wouldn't have been much fun cycling.

Adios Madrid

After not cycling many rail trails last year, I have managed to find a detailed website www.viasverdes.com which lists all of them in Spain. *Vias Verdes*, translates as Greenways, a common name for rail trails in many countries.

Their website is useful for finding out about each individual rail trail, especially what the surface is like, what highlights there are to see, the history of the rail line and most importantly, if it has been developed into a trail yet as there are many still being planned. Individual rail trails are grouped by region, but I'm still figuring out where each region is in Spain. Helpfully, I have found a pdf map of the whole of Spain, which has helped plan my overall route.

Since I have been delayed in Madrid, I have found a Media Distancia train to Talavera de la Reina. From there, I can start cycling a rail trail.

Media Distancia trains travel all over Spain using the older Iberian gauge railway network to fill in the gaps where the fast trains don't stop or travel yet. They are slower and make more stops, but still travel just as quickly as any train in Australia. Thankfully, unlike the fast trains, most Media Distancia routes allow fully assembled bicycles to be taken on board. I just have to book a bicycle space and pay €3 extra for journeys over 100 kilometres. However, as the fast train network expands, some cities are now unreachable by train with a bicycle, which means more planning for which routes I can take as I will probably have to take more trains during my time in Spain.

After I got back from the football, I tried to book my bicycle ticket on the Spanish train website RENFE, but it won't accept the booking despite the option being listed. Even at Estación de Madrid Atocha in the morning, the ticket machines won't let me book a bicycle ticket, so I'm concerned the bicycle spaces are booked out.

Stairs to access the bicycle area

A ticket office is nearby, so I walk my bicycle there and thankfully the man behind the counter is friendly, speaks some basic English and can sell me a bicycle ticket.

The modern white Media Distancia train is quiet as I board. Weirdly the only issue with getting my bicycle onboard is that once inside the train, I have to lift it up three steps to the bike area. There are three empty spots where I'm supposed to hang my bicycle, but since I appear to be the only cyclist, I just lay it upright against the bottom of the racks. I have a set seat, but as the train is less than half full, I sit where I can keep an eye on my bike.

During my time in Spain, each train I rode had slightly different set-ups for bicycles. Some had no specific space, while most had hooks to hang a bicycle, some with stairs to ascend first.

It's a relaxing, quiet train ride to Talavera de la Reina, on a train slower than the one to Toledo, but still reasonably fast.

It's easy getting off the train with a level platform to an unoccupied, modern looking, two storey red-bricked station that is away from the platform and without a verandah.

Estación de Talavera de la Reina

With only a few shops open this Sunday morning, it's quiet as I head into the centre of town. Other than a short decent path around the remains of a stone castle, I'm not finding much that is interesting to see.

As I meet the Rio Tajo, it's a little more engaging with a paved cycle path beside the river.

This takes me past a lovely mural showing a romanticised history of this place as a fishing village. It's on the outside of a museum, which unfortunately is closed this Easter Sunday.

A mural in Talavera de la Reina

After a kebab lunch, I leave town on a bicycle path, which soon runs out. The road is busier than expected and I'm soon lost.

Once I figure out I have taken a wrong turn at a roundabout, I'm able to find the correct road for an easy ride to Calera y Chozas.

Just before the town beside the still-active railway line is an abandoned two storey, yellow, cement railway station with a sign for the start of *Vía Verde de la Jara*, a rail trail. I think a tourist information centre is inside the station, but it isn't open today.

A path begins beside the rails and heads towards town, while the still-active rail line branches away, so I join the path.

After briefly stopping to look at an information panel informing me about the rail trail, it crosses the highway on a new steel pedestrian bridge. From here, it appears the trail properly starts as it takes me away from town.

I'm soon passing under the first of many cement bridges and cycling through a few small cuttings. Most of these bridges aren't being used because farmers are crossing this rail trail on the ground. With little traffic, it's not an issue for me.

A Via Verde sign and a bridge over the trail

Silos' cement station

With most of the trail having a narrow bituminised surface on one side of the path, which is wide enough for a bicycle, it's an easy, relaxing ride. I'm also beginning to see numerous maroon signs with gold writing, informing me how far in kilometres to the next former station site.

The first station is Silos. When I first saw a sign for this station, I thought there may be grain silos here, but there are no signs of this. So far, the farms are more orchard-based rather than cereal.

This yellow, cement station in the middle of nowhere is two storeys and is obviously abandoned. This was a common sight on the various Vias Verdes, with many stations covered in graffiti, rubble all over the floor, and holes in the roof. So they were not much use for sheltering in. Thankfully sometimes next to these abandoned stations were picnic tables and drinking water fountains but rarely a toilet.

After initially passing through farmland, soon down below in a deep canyon, the Rio Tajo appears again.

Viaduct over the Rio Tajo

Once through a tunnel without lights, a large, long, high cement rail viaduct appears with numerous arches holding this bridge over the Tajo Canyon. It looks so well built that a train could safely cross it right now. Instead, I cycle over. An information panel on the other side explains that this bridge was only built in 1962.

Even while climbing away from the viaduct, I can sometimes glimpse back at it until the trail leaves the river behind and passes through another tunnel. On the other side is another abandoned station on the edge of a small town. Beside the station, a few people are out enjoying a late Sunday picnic. Often stations are located near a rail tunnel; perhaps they were camp locations when digging the tunnel.

South of here, the rail trail feels more remote as the occasional stations are not near towns. Initially, I'm randomly encountering people out enjoying the trail, but then as I don't see a soul or roads for ten kilometres, it feels even more remote. The only signs of civilisation are the remains of a few stone houses in a dry, shrubby, hilly landscape.

Stations are often near a tunnel

I'm soon following a small river most of the time while gradually climbing through many cuttings, which are becoming deeper. I'm also still crossing on a few viaducts, but none are as spectacular or high as earlier. The occasional tunnel is always without lights, but thankfully, most are short enough to not need one because mine is in my lost bag. I still have the light on my iPhone, just in case.

There are many cutting on this half paved rail trail

Gradually, the afternoon has become more overcast and colder, so after exiting another tunnel as a large station appears, this will do for my first camping spot in Spain. This white railway station in the middle of nowhere is a larger complex than previous ones, and it appears to have been converted to a restaurant with the addition of a couple of train carriages and a tall wire fence around it. After closer inspection, it looks abandoned, possibly recently as catering items are still here, but there is also plenty of graffiti and broken windows. After jumping the fence, I see that the toilets have no water, but there is still toilet paper.

Despite being in the middle of nowhere, a few people are around and strangely, while cooking dinner at a picnic table beside the station, a man jumps the fence and starts graffitiing a train carriage. Thankfully, everyone soon leaves, allowing me to set up my tent and lay out my new sleeping bag and mattress.

This is the first chance I have had to use all my new camping gear, so as I begin cooking dinner, I realise my only utensil is a spoon leftover from my flight. I also have no washing up equipment. Just a couple of the few items I'm still missing from the lost bag that I forgot to replace.

My first night camping at a station turned into a restaurant

After a quiet night's sleep, I'm happy with my new camping equipment, and it looks like today will be sunny.

For fourteen kilometres, the Via Verde de la Jara continues gradually climbing beside a river as slowly a mountain range appears.

Just before the mountain range is the large abandoned Santa Quiteria Railway Station. Along with the familiar two storey cement station, there are more buildings and rail platforms here. Past the station, a tunnel is visible going under the mountain in front, but signs are telling me that the Via Verde stops here.

Sunny morning ride with bridges and abandoned stations

Santa Quiteria Railway Station

As I walk closer to the tunnel, it's obvious why, because it is flooded and overgrown with blackberries.

Back at the station, a fallen wooden noticeboard shows a few walking routes in the area, some of which are steep, but I can see a possible way ahead. So I will leave the rail right of way behind and join a paved road that slowly climbs to the small town of Puerto de San Vicente.

I can't find a decent grocery store but have found some passable muffins as I'm getting hungry. From here, I have no choice but to begin climbing.

Fortunately, it's a short climb before a longer descent.

A walking track is next to the road, but it has a stony surface, so it doesn't look great for obtaining any grip. It's probably safer to stay on the road as I descend quickly.

As it flattens out, a road bridge crosses over what appears to be the rail right of way. It's overgrown and not able to be cycled.

A few times the hiking trail crosses the road

From here, it's becoming even more mountainous with some climbing to do, and I have lost any sign of the former rail right of way. I consider the walking route, but it appears to be steeper as it's going up and down the hillsides instead of more around as the road does.

Just after 2 pm, I'm in the small town of Alia, but I have been caught out by siesta, as the supermarket closes just as I arrive. So I will continue to the larger town of Guadalupe to hopefully get some fresh food. Apparently, this was the only place where the rail line was designed to go through. Many other towns were bypassed if they were not at a suitable gradient.

It's off the main highway on top of a hill and to access town I follow a small river which soon goes under a high stone railway viaduct. Compared to the Tajo viaduct, this one appears narrower with skinnier support towers but broader arches. The town centre is still high above so I'm searching for a gentle route up. Eventually, I have no choice but to walk my bicycle up a steep track.

It doesn't take me long to realise this is a religious town, with numerous souvenir shops and restaurants surrounding a large cream cathedral that looks more like a castle. I still can't find a decent supermarket, but I do manage to finally obtain a dry sandwich at one of the restaurants. I'm not interested in religion, so after a brief look around town, I begin searching for a way to access the viaduct.

Once I find a way down, I can cycle across it, even if it is a little muddy. In the opposite direction is a former rail tunnel. Another abandoned, derelict, graffitied cement station is through the tunnel, while the local football pitches are further along. The rail right of way appears to continue briefly, but it soon stops from what I can tell.

Anyway, I'm supposed to be going the other way, so I will turn around and head west across the viaduct. From an info panel on the viaduct, it was built in 1959, but the rail route was abandoned in 1962 before the rail line was completed. So that is why I haven't seen many signs of the rail formation between Santa Quiteria and Guadalupe - it was never built. It's a shame because it would have been a spectacular ride, either by train or by bicycle.

Guadalupe Viaduct

While writing this book, I learned that a couple of the other Vias Verdes I cycled were never completed either, with many also abandoned in 1962. However, when I cycled them, I was unaware of this, so I will keep this narrative to what I knew at the time.

After the viaduct, the rail right of way can still be cycled, but it's less developed than earlier in the day as I begin descending towards the highway. Once there, the rail formation is not a surface I can ride on, so I will continue on the road.

As the highway begins to climb, the rail right of way becomes a vehicular track that branches away, so I follow it on what appears to be a decent well-used track.

The main track leaves the rail formation as a short tunnel appears, but a rough path continues through it. Once through, the trail deteriorates and becomes singular and muddy, with a few puddles to dodge. Soon another tunnel appears.

It's darker inside, and there is debris on the floor from the ceiling, so I carefully walk my bicycle. In one section, so much of the roof has collapsed that there is only a small gap to get through, but something must be using it as there is a worn path.

Once I'm through, another abandoned station with another tunnel is ahead, but the path is blocked by blackberries, while high above, cars are crossing over this hill. So I will leave my bicycle and try to see if I can access this tunnel.

Once I find a path around the blackberries, I enter the tunnel. It's dark, with no light visible in the distance, and there is plenty of debris.

A couple of tunnels, lead me to an abandoned station and another tunnel

Soon the bottom half of the tunnel hasn't even been dug out, and it doesn't take me long to realise that the tunnel was not completed as I literally hit a dead end.

Once I'm back at my bicycle, I have to figure out how to get back to the road. I would prefer not to have to turn around and go back through tunnels. The alternative is finding a way up to the highway visible above. After searching around, a goat track should take me up.

It's so steep that I have to push my bicycle all the way up to the pass.

At the top, an information panel informs me that the tunnel below was the reason the railway line was abandoned as it was found to be unstable. So a train never made it to Guadalupe despite the viaduct and stations being built before the tunnel.

I now have a choice between routes to descend to Logrosan. Rather than visiting a town along the way, I will take the quieter, slightly less hilly route. As I descend into an open valley, this lets me see remains of the rail formation in the distance. As I re-meet the rail right of way, the embankments, bridges and tunnels have been built, but they are not possible to cycle on until the town of Logrosan.

By now, it's 8 pm, but thankfully a convenience store is open, allowing me to get some basic pre-packaged food.

With the railway station on the edge of town, I will aim to camp down there.

Despite this section being briefly used by trains, this red-bricked station looks just as abandoned as previous stations that never saw a train.

With it looking more overcast now and the possibility of rain overnight, I try searching for a sheltered space. However, with the station roof having holes in it, my best option is a tiny verandah coming off the goods shed. It may just keep part of my tent dry.

With light overnight rain, thankfully most of my tent has stayed dry under this verandah.

Before leaving, I lock my bicycle beside the rail trail and walk up to town to get some food at a supermarket as there aren't many towns on the route today.

The railway line and station were below Logrosan

From here, the Via Verde de las Vegas del Guadiana starts, and my first impression is of a decent surfaced rail trail.

As I set off slowly descending, the weather is looking fine, but over time it deteriorates. It starts with a cold wind, but then every so often, heavy rain appears briefly. I'm glad I purchased a rain jacket in Madrid.

The trail is flat, and as I'm passing through farmland, the landscape is not particularly inspiring.

Wire gates need to be opened and closed

At one stage, I have to open wire gates because a flock of sheep and two inquisitive guard dogs are on the trail. I'm also passing a few more cement stations which are in even worse shape than the ones on the Via Verde de la Jara. Most have collapsed roofs, rubbish everywhere and no drinking water, but a few still have picnic tables. Thankfully, the trail surface has stayed decent.

The weather isn't helping, but I'm just not enjoying this flat rail trail, especially when having to divert away from the rail formation just after crossing the Rio Guadiana on a rail viaduct where the wind is at its strongest. So I'm relieved once it finishes in the city of Villanueva de la Serena.

While checking the weather online using the wi-fi at Burger King, I'm surprised to see that I have an email from Emirates saying they have finally found my bag in Dubai. It can be delivered to me anywhere in Spain. Since I want to be back in Madrid to vote in the Australian federal election sometime between May 8 and 17, I will wait until then to collect my gear. Thankfully, Renata will look after my bag until then.

Once I'm back in Madrid, I will have pairs of gear, including two sleeping bags, two stoves and four pannier bags. So I now need to work out the simplest way to get the spare gear back to Australia, or if it makes more sense to just leave them in Spain.

With the weather looking similarly cold and rainy for the next two days, instead of cycling directly to Córdoba using a route that doesn't appear that interesting, I will use the rail system to visit Seville, as otherwise, I would have missed this city. Since I have found an Airbnb in nearby Merida, I will catch an afternoon train there.

Maps at the station and on this train help me determine which rail lines Media Distancia trains travel on, which is helpful for figuring out where I can go by train in Spain with my bicycle. I have been using the Spanish rail operator RENFE's website to plan any potential train routes, but sometimes this isn't as informative as physically showing up at stations. As I make my way south to Seville, Merida will work well as a place to change trains.

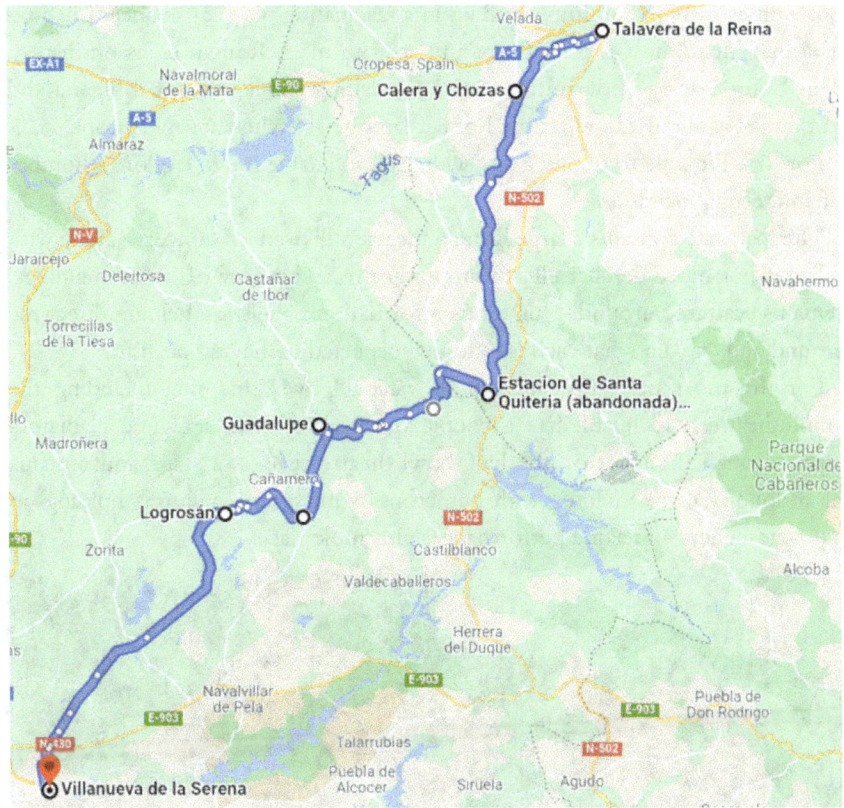
Talavera de la Reina to Villanueva de la Serena (Google Maps)

Romanos

Sometimes you just randomly end up in a fascinating place by chance. I had no idea that Merida is a former Roman town with many Roman relics on display. This brings back wonderful memories of visiting similar sites in Bulgaria and Turkey, showing just how far the Roman Empire stretched across Europe.

For €15, I'm able to obtain a city-wide pass to enable me to explore a number of interesting locations.

The main site contains a large Roman theatre still used for concerts, along with a larger but more derelict elliptic amphitheatre and plenty of other buildings' remains scattered around. Numerous information panels are helping direct me around and explain what each location is suspected of having been for.

For the most part, I'm allowed to walk all over this site, including the amphitheatre, which still has a couple of intact archways, where gladiators went through. In front of the half bowl theatre seats is a stage and remains of a double-storey building with numerous skinny white columns holding up balconies where I imagine performances also took place.

Roman theatre and amphitheatre

This Roman house had mural floors

Nearby and across the road from a bullfighting ring are more former Roman remains, including a house with low sections of walls of certain rooms still here, while on the floor of many of these rooms are murals, most have missing pieces. These murals once again remind me of my time in the Balkans.

Not far from the central plaza is Puente Romano, a Roman stone bridge which is at least 2000 years old that still crosses the wide Rio Guadiana for non-motorised traffic. With 60 arches, it's apparently the longest, still standing, Roman-era bridge in the world.

A Roman-era bridge, that allows a view of the Alcazaba

The cobblestone surface is a bumpy ride which just leads to suburbs across the river. However, it does allow a better view looking back at the city, including the high walled Alcazaba on the right side of the bridge.

It was built as a Moorish fortress, but changed hands numerous times over the centuries, from Moors to Spanish royalty to both sides during the Spanish Civil War. Each time a new force conquered it, they would change it to suit their military and cultural needs. With closer inspection, the previous owners' styles are visible.

The outer wall is in reasonable condition and allows a high view of the river. However, in the courtyard inside, most of the former buildings are just low wall remains. Thankfully, information panels help describe its history.

Through an entrance of an Islamic era building, stairs lead down to a Roman cistern. It's dark as I reach the bottom of these stairs, so I can just make out a pool of murky water. It's amazing at times what survives.

Remains inside the Alcazaba, including stairs leading to a Roman cistern

With plenty of time before my next train, I make my way north of the station, where in the middle of a park is the remains of a tall, three storey Roman aqueduct. Less than 200 metres of this aqueduct is left, with many vertical piers still standing, but most of the top horizontal part where the water would have flowed across is missing. Looking more closely, I can see how it was mostly built out of a few layers of cream stones with a couple of rows of red bricks separating a few layers.

First aqueduct

Second curvier aqueduct

At the other end of the park is a lower but longer aqueduct, in much better condition. With small regular gaps it appears to be more robust, so much so that possibly water could still go over it. I'm only guessing, but perhaps it was built more recently. There is only one small gap made for a single lane road to go through, so cars have to wait for vehicles coming in the other direction.

Beside the second aqueduct is an uphill bicycle path allowing me to see how this one isn't straight as it snakes its way across. Not sure why but aqueducts intrigue me; perhaps it comes from watching water appear in channels once a year when growing up on a farm.

Nearby is the Roman Circus, a large chariot track uncovered after being lost for centuries. Beside it is a museum with roof access, allowing an overview of this track which has stone remains on the outside right around this long ellipse. In the middle is a row of stone remains, surrounded by a grass area, it's like a long cricket pitch is in the middle.

Remains of Roman Circus

A sign explaining how the chariot races work

Turn your attention to the chariot gates located at the far right of the building.

Each one of them symbolises the twelve months of the year.

The Chariot, pulled by horses, symbolised the sun and the charioteer represented the god Apollo.

The seven laps of each race were identified with the seven days of the week, and usually 24 races were carried out, equalling one day.

Four divisions, or teams, existed. Each one was identified by a colour, which symbolised the four seasons of the year.

As I walk around the whole chariot track, various remains are left with some sections as tall as me but most are at waist height or lower. So I'm only getting an outline of what was here.

Roman infrastructure fascinates me, possibly because it has survived 2000 years after often being buried and forgotten for centuries. Perhaps it reminds me of finding old railway infrastructure.

So far in Spain, the weather has been changeable; one moment it's sunny, the next it's cold with wind and heavy rain coming from various directions. Fortunately, the forecast looks like the sun will return in a couple of days, so I will train to Seville in the meantime. But with only one train a day from Merida to Seville, I will take the opportunity to split my ride in Zafra.

Heavy rain begins just before my arrival into Zafra, but it has since stopped. Zafra is more Catholic focused with a small former walled area to explore, but with overcast weather, I'm not appreciating it.

It's a quiet three-hour ride on a less than half full train to Seville as we pass through a scenic mountain range. A couple of mountain bikers board halfway through, so next time, this may be a place to visit.

Seville's main station, Santa Justa, is busy with a dozen platforms and a few cafés. As I make my way through the station, I spot four touring cyclists. They are Polish and are my first experience with meeting fellow touring cyclists in Spain.

I could only find one night available with Airbnb for a reasonable price, so I set off to leave my bicycle there. Thankfully, Seville has a few cycle paths to follow, so I'm soon at my apartment, where I'm staying with an older lady.

Apart from Seville regularly winning football's Europa League, all I know about this city has come from friends' photos who have been here recently.

As I take a random street towards the river, I soon spot a tall scenic amber-bricked building decorated with blue astronomical colours. There are three walk-through archways, which look okay but are nothing special.

Plaza de España

As I exit a walk-through, I'm suddenly in an amazingly large and open multistorey semicircular building with numerous columns holding up a verandah that curves right around. It's also jam-packed with tourists and horse-drawn carriages. Inside the semicircle is a canal with a few small bridges surrounding a fountain.

I soon learn this is Plaza de España, and as I look closer at this building's artwork, I can see a collection of tiled murals next to each other. Each mural represents a province of Spain; usually, it's a medieval representation, while above is the province's name and then even higher is the local crest. Helpfully on the base of each mural is a map of the province so I now know roughly where each one is. They are all separated by individually decorated brickwork.

Every province is represented here

As I make my way into the city centre past some gardens, it doesn't take me long to see that this is a very touristy city, with long lines to get into places. It's a different feeling to Madrid and the rest of Spain so far. Rather than wasting my time in queues, I just spend the afternoon walking around, seeing what quiet places I can find.

Eventually, I end up near the main river, which I soon learn was once a busy port. Inside Torre de Oro, a lonesome twelve-sided, stone, single tower with a smaller tower sticking up higher from the middle, is interesting information on Seville's naval history. This city was a main departure port to the Americas.

Back at my Airbnb, I finally do some laundry and relax in the evening, planning my route once I start cycling again tomorrow.

I leave my Airbnb by 8 am using one of many cycle paths to enable me to get to the Alcazar before it opens. Hopefully, I will find a smaller line than yesterday. However, even at 8:30 am, an hour before it opens, the line is around the corner, so I find a tree near the entrance to lock my bicycle up and join the queue.

Torre de Oro

Also in the line around me are two Australian couples which helps pass the time as we chat about how each of us got here while we wait for the line to shorten. It turns out that one couple, Terry and Jan, know someone I went to school with – what a small world.

Lining up for the Alcazar

After waiting an hour and a half I'm finally through a medieval gate to an interesting royal palace and gardens, which are well worth visiting even if it's touristy. Straight away, the yellow architecture over the walls and ceilings stands out. It vaguely reminds me of Islamic artwork in Turkey. Each building has various styles of archway entrances and different reasons why it existed. My favourite room is full of large tapestries showing many historical events.

Building styles in the Alcazar

Gardens in the Alcazar

It's busy inside, so thankfully, there are a few small square-shaped gardens behind the main palace to get away from the crowds. With a range of plants to admire, including palm trees and hedgerows, along with many I'm not familiar with, there is also a dividing wall which I'm able to walk around on top of.

After a couple of hours, I have had enough. Thankfully, my bicycle was fine merely locked up to a tree outside the entrance.

My original plan had been to cycle directly from Villanueva de la Serena to Córdoba, but rainy weather changed my plans. So to get back on track, I have booked a train to Córdoba in the afternoon to get back on track.

With a little bit of time before my train, I will utilise a bicycle path that follows the old city wall. Parts of the wall and some gates are still standing in certain sections and eventually this path takes me close to the railway station.

The original dedicated high-speed line in Spain was built between Madrid and Seville via Córdoba. However, since fully assembled bicycles aren't allowed on these trains, I'm taking a slightly slower Media Distancia train. Still, it's a reasonably quick service on this packed train, but a few of the fast trains on their dedicated track next to us are quickly passing by.

Córdoba feels like a mini Seville, in that it has a main religious area with a heavy tourist focus and long lines to enter the main cathedral, which used to be a mosque. I'm feeling overwhelmed by all this tourism; I'm not sure how people do this all the time while travelling. Still, I will go for an explore.

I soon find the La Inquisition Museum, which focuses on the Spanish Inquisition. This was a period especially in the late 15th century when people were tortured if they were suspected of not being Catholic. Around this time, the Islamic part of Spain had just been conquered, so they wanted to remove all Muslims, and while they were doing this, they included the Jews. So you had the choice to either convert to Catholicism or be expelled from the country.

Inside the museum, various machines used to torture people they suspected hadn't converted are shown, including devices to squash or stretch certain body parts. Many of them have spikes. Nasty stuff, designed to make people suffer and usually die in the end. Not the most pleasant place to visit but still something we should learn about.

As I go to pay cash for something, somehow I have managed to lose €50. Presumably, I dropped it as it was briefly in my hand, but I can't find it after retracing my route. Therefore, I take it as a sign it is now time to leave Córdoba and start cycling again.

In hindsight, I should have explored inside the main cathedral as I have heard since it's fantastic to see inside. However, I was just over tourist sites and wanted to cycle.

Chastity Belt

Sierra

After crossing the Rio Guadalquivir on an old stone bridge and passing through an industrial part of Córdoba, I soon meet the start of the Via Verde de la Campina, where it splits from the still-active rail line.

This rail trail follows a route built as a shortcut between Córdoba and Cadiz, avoiding Seville, and unlike the previous Vias Verdes, was previously an active line.

When cycling through busy areas, I have been using headphones to distract from traffic noise, but once on the trail, I put them away into my small handlebar bag.

Not long after going through the only tunnel on this trail, my stringy headphones randomly fall out of my bag. Before I have a chance to stop, they have wrapped themselves around my front wheel. As I unwrap the headphones, I soon see that I have severed the end that plugs into my iPhone.

I suddenly burst into tears and cry out that everything is just going wrong - from Emirates losing my bag, to the rainy weather, to losing €50 earlier in the day and now my headphones.

After calming myself down, I continue on this slightly overgrown trail, with a two-wheel track marking my route. Despite the grassy surface, it's a scenic ride as it follows the contours at a railway grade through farmland with fenceless paddocks mostly in crop. It's quiet as I only see a couple of cyclists.

Other than this tunnel, this Via Verdi just passes through farmland

After an hour or so, I'm at a former station site a few kilometres away from a nearby town. There are a few park benches and a drinking water tap but no toilet, while with two RV's parked nearby, it feels like a comfortable place to camp. The only issue is a street light, so finding a dark enough space to sleep takes a while. Eventually, a spot beside the trail will do.

In the morning, I continue on the Via Verde de la Campina, where the surface at the start of the day is the same as yesterday evening. However, it noticeably changes after crossing out of the Córdoba region, as the Via Verde signs change, while a large map noticeboard only shows the region I'm in, rather than all of the rail trail. The map shows the potential for a well-developed rail trail. However, from here, the trail surface becomes more varied, with some sections in need of a mow, while other parts share a gravel road as I'm passing through more farmland.

Via Verde noticeboard map

A variety of surfaces this morning

In Seville, my cycle computer stopped working and looked waterlogged but now, as the sun dries it out, it has started working again.

On this Saturday morning, plenty of cyclists are out for a day ride on mountain bikes, particularly closer to Ecija which becomes scenic as the rail trail descends towards the town.

Like most towns in Spain, the railway line went around it because unlike in Australia, towns here existed for millennia before railways. Often also a cycle path will loop around the city centre following the route of the old town walls as it does here in Ecija. This is useful for finding supermarkets because with limited space in the centre, they are usually located on the edge of town. They often take a siesta break between 2 pm and 5 pm but stay open until 9 pm. The siesta time is annoying as this is the warmest part of the day when I most want a cool drink.

Finding a way into town centres has been a challenge as streets are often narrow one-way roads that take many doglegs before arriving into a town square. Because these roads are so tight, if it's a two-way street and two cars meet, one has to back out. As well, with many buildings being double-storey or higher, it's hard to tell which direction I'm travelling, so becoming disorientated is common. It doesn't help on my way into Ecija that I nearly end up in a wedding.

Ecija has a small museum next to the tourist information centre focusing on pre-Roman and Roman history as a Roman-era city was found under the main square. There is plenty of information inside the museum, as well as many mosaics and gold relics from that era, including jewellery. Some old paintings remind me of indigenous art in Australia.

Items in the museum including gold jewellery and rock paintings

Along with being a little warm in the afternoon, the rail trail is not as well looked after, particularly between Ecija and La Luisiana, where it becomes a narrow goat track next to a freeway and soon peters out. Fortunately, a secondary road beside the freeway is available to take me to La Luisiana.

Past La Luisiana, as I re-join the Via Verde, there are two similar-looking gravel tracks next to each other. I only know which one is the rail trail because of a green sign with an arrow pointing to the left for cyclists and walkers, while another indicates to the right for cars.

As I join the Via Verde, the surface has now improved, while the quiet gravel road is nearly always beside the trail. The only time it's not is at a few creek crossings when the Via Verde and the road becomes one path as they use the same old rail bridge before splitting again once over the creek. At times there is no difference between the tracks. However, in certain sections, the rail trail is overgrown with stinging thistles. My sandals and shorts don't offer any protection from these spiky plants, so it's more pleasant to join the road next door.

The only traffic is a man on foot chasing sheep, so it's an easy ride. I'm not sure this rail trail needed to be built or maintained in this section because the quiet road is adequate.

A couple of times in the middle of nowhere are rest stations with picnic tables and drinking water available. It's obviously only a recent development because all the trees planted here are tiny, so there is no shade available on this warm day.

This rail trail parallels a road, while beside the trail is a new picnic area

With the trail passing through open farmland, there is nowhere to camp out of sight before it ends at Marchena. A still-active railway line passes through here on the passenger service between Seville and Malaga, while the actual town is located on a hill.

After looking around town for a while, I can't find anywhere to stealth camp, so I will continue. Before I leave, I collect some groceries for the next two days as tomorrow is Sunday in this Catholic country, so I expect supermarkets to be closed.

With no idea where I'm sleeping, I leave town by taking a gravel road in a southerly direction, hoping to find somewhere to camp, but there aren't many options. Olive groves dominate the surrounding landscape, while any spare space is covered in thistles. Even an abandoned farmhouse has no clear space to set my tent up away from the numerous thistles.

Eventually, a small space on a quiet road beside a farming fence will do for a camping spot on some leaves. It's not the best, but it will do.

Camping beside a fence

Having read about a scenic rail trail that travels through mountains, today is a day I have been looking forward to. However, I need to get there, which will involve cycling south on roads. Despite a minor climb, it's a quick ride to the town of Moron, which has an abandoned castle on a hill. The top of the castle provides a reasonable view, enabling me to see the best option to cycle further south.

So many white houses in southern Spain

Looking back down at town reinforces how most houses in southern Spain are white, which presumably helps them stay cool in the summer heat. Perhaps the Islamic history of the region is a factor as well.

Today people are voting. I later learn there were national elections, so I'm not escaping elections while overseas.

Over this weekend, I have seen plenty of cyclists out riding, including mountain bikers and road cyclists. However, so far in Spain, I'm not seeing people using bicycles as an everyday vehicle for travelling between towns or for local travel like visiting a supermarket. This is quite different compared to my time in Eastern Europe or France. I feel like I see more cyclists in Australia. As well, other than rail trails, I'm not seeing any cycling signs in towns or out in the countryside. I do however, pass a motorbike race with children going around a track on the way to Montellano.

The longer climb to Montellano provides some views, but I can't find a water tap in town, and with it being Sunday, it is harder to find shops open. Bars appear to be open but with too much of a focus on alcohol for me.

The shortest route to the start of Via Verde de la Sierra at Puerto Serrano involves ten kilometres of highway cycling, but it has a good shoulder, with respectable traffic and soon scenic views of a mountain range appear in the distance.

Just before Puerto Serrano is a railway embankment on either side of the highway, but the rail bridge is long gone, while the western side of the rail formation isn't a rail trail.

Before joining this Via Verde, I will go for a short explore of Puerto Serrano on the other side of the Rio Guadalete.

I can't find anything special about this town, so I make my way to the start of this rail trail.

Estación de Puerto Serrano

Unlike the previous derelict Via Verde railway stations, this one at the start of the trail is busy as it has been converted to a restaurant, with plenty of people sitting down for a meal, while others are also out enjoying this rail trail.

Before leaving the station, I learn that there are people known as trail angels helping others on this Via Verde. One gives me advice on how a couple of longer tunnels have no lights and that the start of the trail has a steep section away from the rail right of way as a tunnel is abandoned.

For 36 kilometres, this Via Verde climbs 300 metres through 30 tunnels of varying lengths, some with solar-powered sensor lights and some so short they don't need lights. Helpfully these tunnels act like air conditioning, cooling me down as I pass through on this warm day. Every tunnel has signs in both Spanish and English at each end, even two bypassed tunnels. I'm not sure they need the English translations because most of what is being said, including the length of the tunnel and how far to the next one is obvious in Spanish. One sign even says sorry that a tunnel doesn't have lights.

There are four viaducts to cross, with brief information in Spanish and English, but the whole trail could do with more historical information, as there isn't a lot provided.

The many tunnels on this trail are well signed

All but one of many railway stations is being reused as a restaurant or nature information centre, so plenty of cool supplies are available along with toilets. I'm also encountering more trail angels in their four-wheel-drive cars, helping people out. This was the only Via Verde where I saw trail angels, perhaps because this was the only one which was really busy with cyclists for its whole length.

The surface is varied, in some places paved, other times gravel. It does seem in some small sections to be steeper than a train would take, but this may be because it feels like I'm climbing the whole time. The elevation map agrees with my assessment.

As for the scenery, it's spectacular, with views of various mountains on both sides as tunnels often crossed to the other side of river valleys providing differing perspectives. However, because of regular tunnels, I'm never cycling on an edge looking over a height until the rail trail leaves the river behind and begins climbing to the terminus at Olvera.

From here, the path becomes paved for the last ten kilometres and for the final five kilometres to Olvera, there are ten short tunnels. It's not hard climbing, especially with various incredible mountainous features in the distance and a valley below, motivating me up.

Climbing to the lookout at Olvera

The town of Olvera is well above the railway station, which I will explore tomorrow as it's now after 6 pm. Instead, I will spend my time relaxing at the station complex, especially as there is a caravan parking spot with a few camper vans here along with power and water, but the toilets are locked by 6 pm. The main station building is a restaurant, but it's already closed for the day, while there appears to be the option of hiring bicycles. Indoor accommodation is available in the shape of old wooden railway carriages, but no one is around tonight.

While this trail stops here, the railway line continued, but the nearby tunnel is flooded and blocked with vegetation. I have learned since that this rail line was never completed, despite the effort it must have taken to build it, so that may explain the lack of historical information.

Once it's dark enough, I find a spot under a tree near the main lookout to set up my tent while admiring a small, lit up castle at the top of Olvera. As I settle in for the night, there are a few small bugs in my tent, probably from last night's camping spot among the leaves.

Looking up to Olvera from the railway station

After packing up my tent in the morning, I leave my bicycle at the station and walk for a kilometre up a steep hill to the actual town. As I make my way to the castle at the top of a hill, I suddenly desperately need to go to the toilet for a number two. However, I can't find any toilets in town and nothing is open to ask. Eventually, I have no choice, I need to go, but there's nowhere to sneak behind. However, I do spot a rubbish bin. Apart from a plastic bag, it's empty, and no one is around, so I jump in and add my deposit. It's not my greatest moment, but that's what happens when toilets are locked.

Not sure what's going on

The view from the castle shows plenty of mountains further south of here, while there are some information panels around this castle.

I'm told the supermarket opens at nine, but there is no sign of any movement around the building, and as the time comes and goes, I soon learn of a local public holiday. The supermarket will be closed all day, but thankfully a small bakery is open. I'm not sure exactly what the holiday is for, but there are some decorated floats full of teenagers being driven around town by tractors.

Back down at the railway complex, nothing is open, despite a sign saying an information centre should be open by now. Presumably, the public holiday has something to do with this.

From here, I'm aiming to head more into the mountains to my second Warmshower experience in Spain with my host Raul, in the small town of Montecorto. The best option to get there is to redo eight kilometres of the rail trail before taking a route south into the mountains.

As I descend back through ten former rail tunnels, I can tell this rail trail would be a more relaxing ride in the other direction, something to consider next time.

At an abandoned cement station, I leave the rail trail behind and begin climbing on a quiet road that snakes its way around the side of hills. It's a relaxing ride before a steep descent to the freeway where I meet two touring cyclists heading in the opposite direction so I wish them well up this climb.

Thankfully, I only have to be on this freeway for a short time before leaving it for the town of Algodonales, where there doesn't appear to be a public holiday today. I could continue on this freeway directly to Montecorto, but there seems to be a quieter and flatter route via the other side of a large man-made reservoir.

As I cross this dam wall, I can see where I just came from while the road soon begins following this lake for a while with views of surrounding mountains. It's a quiet route, with the primary traffic being a few road cyclists out for a day ride. What is becoming standard in Spain is that another town, this time Zahara, is located high above on top of a hill, so I won't bother going there. Instead, I will continue following the reservoir of the same name.

The road takes me right around the reservoir's edge and back to the freeway, where I only have to spend two kilometres on this dual lane freeway to get to Montecorto. Traffic is light, and I'm soon off the freeway and into a small, slightly hilly town with a couple of small shops and many dogleg roads as I search for Raul's home.

Eventually, I figure out the correct house and meet Raul's brother Flo before Raul comes over. He is about the same age as me. We then share a soup meal while I talk about my tour, and he tells me about his cycling tours. Most importantly, he provides me with excellent advice on things to see in the area and offers to drive me to a semi-high point on the highway while he does some errands in nearby Ronda. This will allow me to do a no bags ride climbing up 200 metres over sixteen kilometres to the town of Grazalema before then descending 500 metres for another sixteen kilometres back to Montecorto.

After a relaxing climb using a few switchbacks with only a few cars to worry about, I find myself in an open landscape with numerous rocks scattered among grassland. Above is the town of Grazalema, located on the edge of a mountain, with a noticeable contrast between the white houses and the green landscape. As I climb up to town, a funeral is leaving, and it's being led by a man on a bicycle.

Cyclist leading a funeral, while roads snake their way over the landscape

Once in town, I try a baked chocolate item shaped in a heart which I have been seeing lately, but it's too chocolatey for me. From town, I can see how the roads snake their way over the landscape, particularly my route up and also my way out of town.

Leaving Grazalema involves backtracking for a bit before a short climb where I pass a man on his horse. From here, it's a quick descent that takes me all the way back down to near Zahara Reservoir. After shaking my hands from all the braking, I retrace the route I took into Montecorto.

After a relaxing night in Raul's place, as I begin packing my gear up, I accidentally step on something and hear a crack.

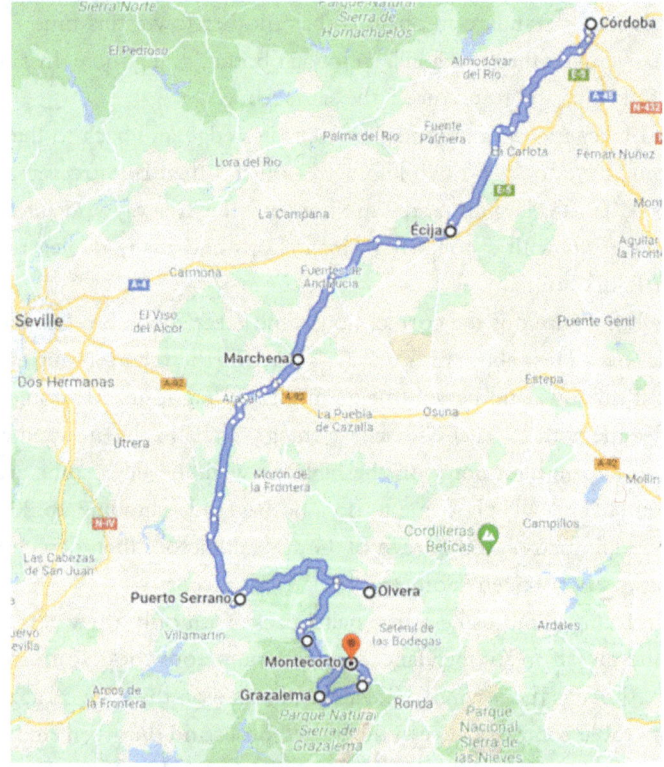

Córdoba to Montecorto (Google Maps)

Aceituna

It's my glasses which have fallen off the bedside table. Thankfully, the lenses are fine. However, as I put my glasses on, they aren't sitting right. After closer inspection, I see I have bent the frame where the hinge on one of the arms connects to the central part of the frame. They are supposed to be a rugged frame, but I must have stepped on a weak point. As I fiddle with my glasses, the hinge snaps off.

After some inner swearing by me, Raul offers some glue to help fix them. I will store them in my bag to allow the glue to hopefully stick.

I'm short-sighted, so I need my glasses to see things far away, but I should be able to manage okay today. I just won't be able to read road signs until I'm close to them.

As well, while doing some bicycle maintenance, I see that part of my handlebar water bottle holder has broken off, and is now useless, so I take it off and bin it. I have been carrying it for precisely a decade, having purchased it in Bright in Australia during my first ever bicycle tour on 30 April 2009, and now it's 30 April 2019.

Last night, I had planned a route trying to avoid climbing 350 metres up to Ronda on a highway by using a scenic train. This train travels via more of the national park south of me, so would still require some climbing to get to a railway station but not on the highway. However, with tomorrow being a Labour Day public holiday, I now need to get to Ronda before 2 pm today because siesta will probably make it harder to find an optometrist open this afternoon. So I will have to take the direct highway.

The initial climb is fine with a decent roadside shoulder, but it has plenty of traffic as I pass where Raul dropped me off yesterday. From here, it's an easy downhill ride, but as the descent finishes, ahead of me is a zigzag highway climb I would prefer not to do, especially with the number of large semi-trailers slowly climbing up. Instead, if I cycle eight kilometres away from Ronda on a flatter route following a river, I could then get the train back up.

The road isn't as flat as expected, instead it's undulating as I head south, so I'm not avoiding any climbing as I follow the Rio Guadiaro. Along the way, I stop at a local waterfall under a cave, which requires walking across the river to get to Monumento Natural Cueva del Gato. It's a nice short waterfall in an open cave but not spectacular.

Google Maps says there is a train at 1 pm from Estación de Benaojan, but when I arrive, I'm told the whole line has been replaced by buses due to track work. I will now have to retrace my route back towards Ronda and do the climb I was trying to avoid.

Once I have made my way back to where I turned off, I have found a quiet track that will hopefully get me up instead of using the zigzag highway. It turns into a goat track, so I'm soon pushing my bicycle up a steep trail to Ronda. Along the way, while resting, I'm able to look back at just how high Ronda is above the valley below.

It's 2 pm as I arrive into this busy town. Raul's glue hasn't stuck properly, so I will begin searching for an optometrist. With siesta on, the first six I find are all closed. Thankfully, near the main square, one is open.

The optometrist tries fitting the frame back in, but it just doesn't feel right. If tomorrow wasn't a public holiday, I would try to see if the glue works overnight. However, since my morning ride has been blurry, I will get a new frame now. Otherwise, I will probably have to wait a couple of days for the next opportunity to visit an optometrist. Just another item that survived Russia but couldn't survive Spain.

As for Ronda, it's very touristy with the old town part located on a high island with a deep eroded gorge separating it from the rest of the city. With only a few bridges joining this island, it reminds me of the floating city in Gulliver's Travels.

As I walk around, there are scenic views of cliff faces in the distance, and even further away, I can see down to where I have climbed from. Further around, I stumble onto remains of a medieval wall which I can walk on top of, some on developed walkways, other times just scrambling along on unguarded walls. As I make my way back across on a lower bridge, I can see just how deep this eroded gorge is with plenty of layers of erosion, while the bridge abutments go down a fair way.

Ronda is high above the landscape

Old town Ronda is separated by a deep gorge

To leave Ronda, I have a few choices with varying levels of climbing required. The most suitable route involves one long climb of 200 metres over fifteen kilometres with some traffic. Once over the hill, it's a quick descent of 600 metres for twenty kilometres, where I'm barely needing to pedal. Due to regularly needing to brake, my hands are becoming sorer than my feet.

Descending from Ronda

Once I'm down, I begin searching for a place to camp. I'm now passing through an open landscape with mountains nearby, so there isn't much cover, while the only village I pass is way up high on the side of a hill.

Eventually, on dusk, as I pass through a locality with just a few houses, I see a football pitch beside the road that could be a suitable place to camp. I can also see on top of a mountain is the town of Teba. However, judging by the zigzag road, it's just too much effort to get up to, especially now in the fading light.

As I walk onto the football pitch, I'm surprised to see that it has significant flood damage, with piles of dirt all over the pitch.

The clubhouse is in a worse state, with layers of wet mud on the floor and a few exposed electrical wires, so there is no chance of sleeping inside here tonight. Around the corner is an open sheltered area, also covered in mud. It's just dry enough for me to set up my tent on and is my best option. It's not the quietest place, due to the main road being right next door, but at least the walls keep most of the lights from the passing traffic out.

May 1st is a Labour Day public holiday in Spain, thus my morning ride is quiet as I snake my way north through small towns with nothing open. What traffic there is, includes a few cyclists out on day rides, both mountain bikers and roadies. Despite crossing an active railway line a few times, all the stations appear to have been recently closed. I'm starting to pass through olive groves, which all look the same, so at times, it's disorientating as there aren't any road signs.

Cycling through quiet towns and plenty of olive groves

While exploring the larger town of Puente Genil, I stumble on three middle-aged touring cyclists. These Englishmen are riding from Malaga on the Mediterranean to northern Spain, and they have a lot less gear than me because they are staying in motels each night. This is called credit card touring because all you carry apart from a change of clothes is your credit card, which you use frequently. We chat for a while before I bid them farewell as I make my way to the start of a rail trail five kilometres out of town.

On the way, I pass Puente Genil's Railway Station. All the signs and infrastructure is still here, so it appears that a train could arrive anytime. However, passenger trains don't go through here anymore due to a newer station ten kilometres out of town on the fast train route. With local services having ceased, many smaller towns no longer have a train service, so it's now harder using a train to get to the start of this rail trail I'm about to do.

My next Via Verde follows a former railway line known as the Olive Train. This makes sense since olive trees dominate the route's landscape as it curves its way around, following the contours at a railway gradient while still taking an undulating course. There are a few bridges and rail cuttings to go through but only one tunnel today. Compared to previous trails, it has a broader view of the surrounding landscape.

To cross the occasional highway, often a new red bridge has been built over the road. Some are a relatively steeper crossing than a train would have taken, often with a short steep rise.

Most bridges have been refurbished, others are brand new on this Via Verde

It's now above thirty degrees Celsius, so the lack of shade is making it feel warm. It doesn't help that trees are generally smaller in Spain than Australia, so there is often less shade, while the olive trees offer none. Thankfully in most towns, I'm finding drinking water fountains, so I can stay hydrated.

For the first 50 kilometres, this rail trail is paved as it passes around the edge of towns with former railway stations converted to restaurants. I'm not venturing into town centres because with today being a public holiday, I have no idea if anything will even be open, especially supermarkets. However, I am running low on food, so I plan on eating at a station restaurant.

(As I edit this book, I can't recall why in Spain, I kept not carrying enough food for a few days just in case)

While having ice cream at Lucena Station at 4:30 pm, I see that this restaurant will be open until 1 am, so I will continue to the next one. As I approach Cabra Station with a few locomotives on display, plenty of people are sitting down at restaurant tables, so presumably, I can get a meal as it's only 6 pm. However, I'm told they have stopped cooking. By the next town of Doña Mencía, the restaurant is already closed by 7 pm. Yet a bicycle shop next door is still doing business. So I will keep going.

As I begin a relaxing scenic sweeping descent to the site of Zuheros Railway Station, I can see that once again, a Spanish town is built on a hill. It's easier to leave my bicycle at this former railway station's remains at the bottom and walk up some steep steps to the town proper. Thankfully, a restaurant is open and still serving food. Dining outdoors provides a broad scenic view of the valley below, allowing me to see that the rail trail curves itself around the landscape.

Descending to Zuheros

As dusk begins, I briefly explore this town full of white buildings and a small cream castle at its highest point.

After walking back down to the former railway station, a man and his daughter who I guess is around ten, arrive by bicycle. I'm then startled to hear an Australian accent as Will explains that he and his family, are from Darwin in Australia. They are currently cycling a small section of this rail trail as part of their travels around Europe by camper van. It has been pleasant today to chat in English with a few people.

Dinning high up at Zuheros

As they leave, it's now quiet and dark enough for me to camp beside the trail, which allows me to watch an average sunset before the only light source is from cars using the road down the valley below.

Camping at the site of Zuheros Station

After leaving Zuheros, the next station Luque has toilets in former railway tanks

In the morning, the trail continues sweeping around a long bend. Behind me, Zuheros, with its white houses and the small castle, becomes more prominent until the trail goes right around that bend.

There is only one restaurant railway station today, and it is only seven kilometres into the ride at the locality of Luque. A short branch line rail trail goes from here, but I'm not planning to cycle it.

Civil War bunker

Other than a dry packet of biscuits, there isn't much food available.

Nearby, just off the trail among an olive plantation, is a Civil War-era cement bunker. The Cerro del Aceitunillo bunker is free to visit and explore underneath; just bring your torch to walk through a couple of narrow passages.

As I change municipal region, the rail trail infrastructure isn't as good. All the stations are abandoned rather than redeveloped. The surface is rougher than yesterday and it feels like this trail climbs more in this section but still at a rail grade. The landscape is also becoming drier, with just olive trees seemingly stretching to the horizon in every direction.

Earlier bridges had a smooth surface to cycle over, now I often have to negotiate rows of poorly laid horizontal railway sleepers, making a bumpy ride. Thankfully on both ends of the sleepers, right next to the protective guardrails of the bridge, there is usually a narrow smoother metal part to ride on. I just have to be careful not to bump into the railings. However, on one of the bridges, the metal part on the side still has small rivets facing up, so it's bumpy no matter the choice I make.

It's warm by lunchtime, so I'm glad to make it to the town of Martos, having spent time climbing to get there. It's my first town for 50 kilometres, so I need a cool drink.

There were a few bumpy rail bridges, which pass through numerous Olive groves

Due to the heat, I race the final 23 kilometres to Jaen while passing through a couple of tunnels. As I approach the end of the trail on the edge of Jaen, I meet an older bicycle touring couple. They are French, and as I explain I'm from Australia, they tell me their daughter lives in Swan Hill, which is close to my home. It's such a small world sometimes.

So far in Spain, it has been more challenging than I expected to find public wi-fi. I have briefly considered getting a sim card, but enjoy not having the distraction of access to the internet all the time. This allows me to be present where I am rather than focusing on my iPhone too much.

Other than fast-food chains, the most consistent wi-fi has been found at the large department store El Corte Ingles. So the one in Jaen allows me to message my host Andres. He informs me he lives five kilometres out of Jaen in the suburbs. He suggests coming straight over, so I make my way out there.

Despite the language barrier, Andres shares with me a few paper maps and provides route ideas, which vastly changes my plan towards Albacete. Rather than following a former railway line which isn't all a rail trail yet, he recommends visiting a national park called Parque Natural de la Sierra de Cazorla. He also explains how to pronounce Jaen as its pronounced "hi-aen", I have been saying it with a J sound. I have to keep reminding myself of the correct way to pronounce it.

Andres works the night shift at a hospital but has offered to drive me around Jaen tomorrow.

While going over the maps in more detail in the morning, Andres suddenly tells me he has been called back into work, so I leave his home at lunchtime, having missed seeing Jaen.

Initially, leaving involves rolling hills on quiet roads through olive plantations. As I meet a highway, I have to choose between two vastly different options– either climb 500 metres up to Baeza and onto a couple of more cities or take a lower route which doesn't go through any towns but does follow a river and a railway line. My general rule is to follow railway lines when practical because they generally follow the contours, so I will go this way.

However, soon into this route, the road becomes gravel, and I'm still doing small climbs. As I look behind me, in the distance, Baeza is looking inviting, especially as I now remember Andres recommending a visit. So I turn around and start climbing.

With a tailwind helping keep me cool, it's a reasonable climb at a consistent gradient for eight kilometres. With plenty of road shoulder, I can pace myself by stopping when I need to catch my breath, allowing me to also admire the views.

Along the way, I cross the remains of another former railway line with an abandoned tunnel and a station, both visible on the hillside. It snaked its way along, halfway down the hillside, well below Baeza. I hope to join this former line once it becomes a developed rail trail further east towards Albacete. (I now know in 2021 that this line was never completed, probably why the rail trail doesn't exist here)

Baeza is a university city with some gothic-style buildings and a free interpretive centre located in the bullring. It's interesting learning about the history of bullfighting, even if I don't understand its attraction. I'm not allowed inside the actual ring, but I can see, through a gap, a couple of men practising. One person is holding some horns rather than an actual bull and the other a red flag. As I take a photo of them, I'm told off; perhaps they think I'm a spy.

As I'm about to leave town, a sun-shower suddenly begins, so I duck into a supermarket. It soon stops, so presumably, this is the end of the rain despite some dark clouds further east.

I now need to find somewhere to camp. There is a potentially suitable place among trees on a headland on the edge of the city, so I set off.

As I reach the middle of the headland, the storm returns heavier, with only skinny trees around there is no cover from the rain. So after searching for any proper shelter right around the headland, I return to town.

It doesn't take me long to find refuge in a small wooden elevated equestrian lookout, while there is just enough dry space beside puddles underneath this shelter to store my bicycle. It's not the best spot with dripping water from the ceiling, but there is just enough room to begin cooking dinner.

Thankfully by 8 pm, the rain has stopped, but since the ground is now soaked and I have no idea if the rain will return, I begin searching for a dry place. After looking around, an undercover space near the stables should be suitable as my only neighbours are horses.

Initially, in the morning, it's a relaxing, straightforward cycle to Ubeda using a cycle path beside the freeway. Ubeda is slightly larger than Baeza and more touristy, with an old town mostly focusing on religion, so I have a brief look around.

The old part of the city sticks out on the edge of the hillside providing views of the Guadalquivir Valley below, including the former railway line visible among the trees. In the distance is a mountain range, including presumably my goal of the day of crossing a 1200 metre pass into Parque Natural de la Sierra de Cazorla. Before that, I will have to head down the valley and then climb up again.

After seeing a few churches and visiting the free but small archaeology museum, I leave town.

Before descending to the Rio Guadalquivir, I have to negotiate a small section of the freeway to the smaller town of Torreperogil, where I become lost finding my way out of town before eventually finding the correct route.

It's a quick descent as I cross the abandoned railway line again before arriving at Rio Guadalquivir. Across the river is a small café, which allows me to get some lunch.

From here, a long climb of about 800 metres over about 40 kilometres begins. However, with a couple of towns on this route allowing me to obtain some food and cool drinks, I'm able to pace myself on this warm day.

Halfway up the climb is the larger town of Cazorla. It reminds me of Grazalema in that it is on the edge of a mountainous national park and appears to be interesting.

The centre of town is busy with plenty of people out eating and drinking at the various pubs and restaurants. Despite looking around,

Cazorla

I can't find tourist information to learn of any places of interest. At least on display in the town square is a collection of large photo boards showing local history. As I sit down in the shade on a cold stone verandah floor to have a snack, I'm suddenly feeling tired from climbing, so I have a brief nap.

Twice on my way out of town, bicycle touring couples appear from the other direction as I begin climbing. I have a quick chat with one couple to understand what is ahead of me.

Initially, it is a relatively easy climb as the road follows the contours on a gentle gradient with decent views of the valley below. However, there are four switchbacks for the final five kilometres while the gradient is at times 7%.

Stopping at the end of each switchback allows me to pace myself up and look back at where I have just climbed from. At times I can see where I was half an hour ago. However, for the most part, my view is obstructed because I'm now climbing through a pine forest, but at least there is plenty of shade.

Stopping for a break on the climb

Looking back at where I was half an hour ago on this zigzagging climb

Mirador del Puerto de las Palomas

After about an hour, I have climbed the 500 metres in elevation to the pass, where from nearby Mirador del Puerto de las Palomas lookout, stretching to the horizon is the forested valley below which I will be cycling in tomorrow.

The steep descent involves a long horseshoe route, so I'm quickly into the tourist town of Arroyo Frio. It has two supermarkets and plenty of restaurants and cafés but no campgrounds, nor public toilets. However, there is a bricked water fountain spring opposite the first supermarket, which is the perfect place to cook dinner. Above this spring, there appears to be enough forest for me in the evening to sneak up and find a place to stealth camp.

Despite today being a Sunday, clearly this town is busy during weekends because both supermarkets are open. As for the cycling, it's flatter than yesterday as the road follows the Rio Guadalquivir for most of the day. With light traffic, it's a relaxing ride.

National Park Visitor Centre

My first stop is the park interpretation centre. Inside on display are various animals and plants, along with other environmental information. Sadly just like anywhere else in the world, some species are not found here anymore. Across the road is a small botanical garden, which I have a brief look through.

I don't have much of a plan for my ride because either I have misinterpreted information provided, or there isn't much to do in the national park. So I will just continue cycling. I'm appreciating the variety in trees rather than the monoculture of olive trees I have been seeing lately, as well as hearing various birds.

I'm soon passing a few campgrounds, most of which are full of caravans and RVs, but there appears to be room for tents as well. However, they are too early in the day for me to stop at. Other than here, I haven't seen many campgrounds and only near Ronda have I seen a caravan park.

Further on beside the road is a busy café. After purchasing a snack, I'm provided with the wi-fi password. Since I haven't found wi-fi since leaving Jaen, besides a brief McDonald's stop, I will spend some time checking my emails and contacting potential Warmshower hosts for next week.

With it being midday on Sunday, it's now 8 pm back in Australia, which is the perfect time for contacting home. So I end up FaceTiming with my parents while charging my iPhone. I generally try to FaceTime them once a week, I message them more often.

After the chat finishes, I see that a red motorised tourist train has pulled up. I often see them in cities, but I'm not sure why it's here. After a closer look inside the café, I realise it takes people on a zoo tour. Since I'm not allowed to visit on foot, I will go for a ride.

It's a packed train, but the conductor only speaks Spanish. By his gestures, sometimes I get the drift of what he is talking about. I'm hoping to see some exotic animals inside this reserve, but we only see domesticated deer and goats, which appear because they are being fed. Otherwise, there aren't many animals to see. So far, this tour feels like a waste of time.

Just before the end of the tour, there is an option to leave the train to go on a self-guided walking trail. This is more enjoyable as the walk provides views of a reservoir ahead of me and along this hiking path are a few sculptures of animals carved from trees. At the top of a hill is an aviary containing birds, many I have never seen before. While I had been told I may see wolves, they don't seem to be here.

Carvings

For the rest of the afternoon, it's a relaxing ride with few cars as this mostly tree-lined road winds its way along high above the reservoir. The large trees provide some shade, but there are still gaps to admire this blue reservoir and the hills behind it. I'm assuming the dam wall will be at the end, but it is halfway along as it horseshoe curves its way over the Rio Guadalquivir.

Following a reservoir

After the dam, the road is even higher away from the reservoir, so with fewer scenic views of the water, along with more climbing, it's less enjoyable. I briefly consider a track down by the lake to avoid one of the climbs, but it looks rough, and I have no idea if I can get through on this track. After the reservoir ends, I'm out of the national park, having seen nothing of interest since the café.

A roadwork sign soon appears, which will require a six-kilometre hilly detour to get around. Since it looks like no one is working today, I will risk going around the closed road sign.

Initially, the road is normal until suddenly, a range of diggers and bulldozers are around a deep-cut road. A culvert is missing, but thankfully I'm able to walk my bicycle across this deep cutting and soon re-join the road.

After making good time out of the national park, I'm aiming to join a developed rail trail and camp at a former station before riding towards Albacete tomorrow. This is the same abandoned railway line I crossed when climbing up to Baeza. By going via the national park, I avoided cycling on a highway until the developed part of this rail trail starts. Instead, I will be joining about 30 kilometres from where I believe it becomes a rail trail, so I may have missed a small part of this Via Verde.

With an abandoned cement station beside the highway, I comfortably find the Via Verde de la Sierra de Alcaraz. Thankfully, it has a decent wide surface as it climbs through a few rail cuttings and passes under some cement bridges. It's getting late now, so as soon as Genave Station appears in the middle of nowhere, I will stop here for tonight.

With town just over a kilometre away, the only rail trail infrastructure here is some picnic tables, while stored in this cement station is old farming equipment, including a green harvester. As I get closer to check it out, I can smell something familiar. Once I see the sheep poo, I realise the stench reminds me of a shearing shed. It's not the best spot to camp, but I have enough supplies, and with no one around, it should be a quiet enough space to spend the night. So I find a spot beside the remains of former railway platforms to set up my tent.

Back on a rail trail, which has farming equipment stored at Genave Railway Station

In the morning, it's still a decent wide trail with a few cuttings while passing through farmland with cereal crops still green. A couple of the derelict stations are being reused by farmers as a shelter for sheep or farming equipment. One in particular, is over packed with sheep. It smells worse than last night and with sheep sleeping in their own faeces, it looks unhygienic. Others are just abandoned as this rail trail goes around towns rather than through them. It's sad to see stations in such terrible condition.

Sheep packed into a former station

As I cross into the Albacete region, there is a slight change in the style of information boards and the kilometre markers change direction as they are now counting down, rather than up. Otherwise, the surface is the same.

I'm flying along, making good time as the scenery is keeping me engaged. After going over a bridge, suddenly a wall of red rocks is in front of me, and as the trail turns, it begins to parallel it for a little bit. After going through a tunnel, the rail trail suddenly stops near the town of Reolid. There is a large information board here, but it's not telling me why it hasn't been converted to a rail trail from here.

The railway line obviously kept going, so I will leave my bicycle and begin walking to investigate if it's only a short missing section. After walking over long stretches of railway ballast and through an overgrown cutting, it doesn't appear to be a rail trail anytime soon. So I will have to go on the highway.

A contrast between a great surface and an undeveloped section

For the next ten kilometres to Alcazar, I can occasionally see how the rail right of way still has ballast on it and in places it's overgrown with plants. A few small bridges are missing too.

The Alcazar Railway Station is fenced off and looks abandoned, while the town is high above on the opposite side of the highway. Andres recommended visiting Alcazar, and since I expect it has a supermarket, I will make my way there despite some short climbing required.

The town square looks nice, and there is an abandoned castle up a hill, but there's nothing exciting to see. So after obtaining some groceries, I'm hoping the rail trail exists near where I left the highway.

After Alcazar, there are now better bridges on this trail

Despite the Via Verde signs directing me towards a rail tunnel, the trail doesn't use it. It isn't until five kilometres after leaving Alcazar I'm finally able to re-join the rail trail. After crossing the highway on a high rail bridge, the trail turns left and goes through a tunnel to where the landscape has suddenly become dryer.

Unlike the morning, this section of the rail trail is through a hillier landscape following a river. However, instead of cruising around hills, it's going through tunnels, possibly twenty as some are numbered, but I lost count in the end. Initially, the longer tunnels have sensor lights, but they have not been installed further on, so I have to use my iPhone light.

Besides having to briefly divert away from the rail trail because of a quarry, so far, the rest has all been on the rail right of way with regular kilometre markers.

A gate across this trail

It's now flooded on the trail

Near El Jardin, there are temporary farm style gates across the trail. I'm not sure if that is to keep out motorised traffic or me, so I open the gates and keep going.

With a few small landslides on the trail and tunnels without lights, it doesn't take me long to realise that the gates were for me. In one place, a shallow ten-metre long puddle is across the trail. So I take my sandals off and enjoy a refreshing walk through water on a semi-warm day as I pass some large boulders on the trail. It's so refreshing being barefoot that I keep my sandals off for a little bit longer.

Soon after this, I'm forced off the rail right of way because of private property near Balazote. So I will take the opportunity to get some supplies for dinner in this small quiet town.

Past Balazote, a stone rail bridge stands out in the middle of a paddock. The trail goes around it, so to access this bridge requires leaving my bicycle behind. I have no idea why but a statue of a religious person has been added to the middle of this shortened bridge.

Bridge in a paddock

After the bridge, the trail changes to a flat gravel path through irrigation farmland and isn't particularly interesting. For some reason, between the 28 and 26-kilometre posts, I'm directed off the trail to ride away back towards the highway before then going straight back to the trail, seemingly not avoiding anything. I can only assume a farmer does not want people to go through.

There is enough time tonight to continue all the way to the city of Albacete. However, since I hadn't planned on making it that far, I haven't organised anywhere to stay. Instead, I will stop ten kilometres short and camp at the former San Jorge station, which has a picnic table with a shelter but no water.

In the morning, after a short cycle, the rail trail ends beside a canal. According to the app on my iPhone, Maps.me, a path beside the canal should take me into Albacete, as further on the rail right of way is now a freeway. At one point, the canal and the path beside it go under another freeway, but it's flooded. So instead, my bicycle and I have to jump over five road barriers to get to the other side.

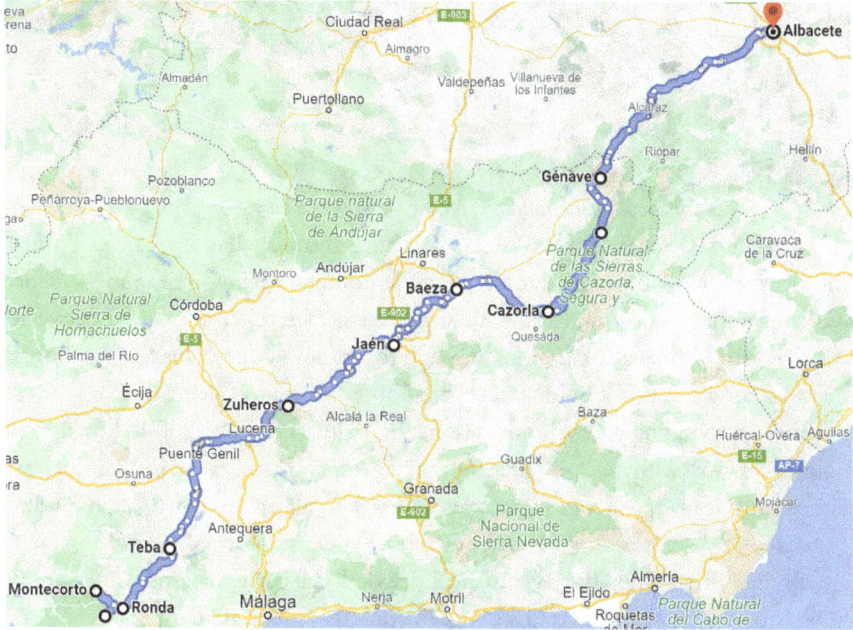

Montecorto to Albacete (Google Maps)

Moving days

Many people have recommended visiting Granada, and since the Copa de la Reina final is on in that city on 11 May, I have decided to time my arrival for then. It's now the morning of 7 May, so it isn't possible to cycle directly to Granada, instead, I have found a route using a few trains via Murcia. However, there is a 150-kilometre gap to cycle between Jaravia and Almeria.

It took a while to plan as not all train routes allow fully assembled bicycles; even then, on some, bicycles are only allowed on specific trains. There is a direct train to Murcia from Albacete, but bicycles are not allowed, so instead, I will have to go via the coastal city of Alicante and change trains there. With regular trains to Murcia, there is time for me to look around Alicante.

It's a touristy Mediterranean city with plenty of sun-bakers. However, with a few no cycling signs scattered on cement paths beside the beach, it doesn't appear to be bicycle-friendly.

Dominating the landscape is a large hill with a yellowy-creamy coloured castle at the top. However, I just can't find a way into the castle and neither can fellow tourists. There appears to be a few zigzag paths going up the hillside, but I can't find the correct route as they all end up in dead ends.

Some colourful buildings on the way up to a castle on a hill

I have booked an Airbnb in Murcia as I need a shower while I will be exploring the city tomorrow morning. However, while double-checking train times online in the evening, I see a potential issue with taking a bicycle on the train between Almeria and Granada. I can book a space for myself, but the bicycle symbol is missing, yet it exists if I book a ticket at another station on that route.

I end up spending a few hours late in the night considering if I should risk going that way with the potential of having to cycle an extra 180 kilometres directly to Granada via a mountainous route. The alternative is to use the train system to go back towards Madrid, find somewhere to store my bicycle and get a train directly to Granada. Eventually, I decide I will cycle towards Almeria and hope I'm wrong about the trains between Almeria and Granada.

In the morning, at Murcia Railway Station, no one can give me any more information than I already know so rather than explore Murcia, I will catch an earlier local train to Jaravia to save time.

Along the way, the junction point of the former railway route between Murcia and Guadix is visible, which would have saved me considerable time if it still operated today. From what I understand, only a few small sections have been converted to rail trails, and one particular gap between them involves cycling on a freeway. It's also a mountainous route as the railway line curved around a lot, so I'm presuming it would be a slower ride than the coastal route I'm taking. Hopefully one day it's made into a rail trail all the way.

After departing the train at an unmanned station, a quick descent brings me to a quiet coastal resort town with a small supermarket. It's unremarkable cycling past the resort as this quiet undulating road has views of the sea.

After about twenty kilometres, suddenly a coastal strip appears out of nowhere, so the traffic increases tenfold. Occasionally there are bicycle lanes, but the rest of my time is cautious cycling on busy roads through a monotonous populated area.

The only thing that breaks up this boring ride is hearing a few people speaking English with a British accent. Presumably, since it's common for the British to move to Spanish coastal towns, I'm hearing a few who have done so.

Continuous strips of towns is a reason I dislike coastal cycling. Another is because often roads are roller coaster in style and today is no exception. As soon as the populated area dissipates, the road begins to climb steeply before going straight down again. A third reason is the wind, which is becoming stronger throughout the day and is mainly a headwind.

I briefly consider turning around and making my way to where I had organised a Warmshower stay before cancelling it this morning. However, I need to get further tonight, and it's too early to stop now, so I will continue.

Fortunately as soon as I turn, the wind changes direction and helps push me up the hill. This curvy climb lasts for a while before it's a quick descent, with a few switchbacks right on the edge of the hillside.

Zigzagging down a hill

After negotiating another small climb, I'm in the town of Carboneras. It's a much quieter place than earlier in the day, while apparently, parts of *Laurence of Arabia* were filmed here.

After battling the wind, I consider stopping in the small beachside town of Agua Amarga. But there is nowhere decent to stay. The open stony surfaced campground is set up more for RVs, as there doesn't appear to be any facilities to use. While all the hotels are too fancy for my budget, reluctantly, I will continue cycling.

The constant wind is so strong that it's exhausting trying to cycle, so I'm often stopping just to get a break. I would love to stop for the day, but I'm in an open ugly rocky landscape with not much cover to set my tent up out of the wind, so I will keep slowly cycling.

As dusk begins randomly off to the side of the road, I just happen to spot a small cement hut. It's covered in graffiti and is obviously abandoned. As I force open one half of a double door, I'm able to enter a small room which has enough clear space for my tent. It's not the cleanest place, but all that matters is it's out of the wind.

I'm so exhausted from a day of headwinds that I'm asleep within half an hour. Hopefully, tomorrow is a better day, as I hated today because all my focus was on just getting as far as I could. Even then I didn't get as far as I hoped.

Camping inside an abandoned building

Fortunately, I awake to much less wind, and soon the dry landscape changes as numerous white greenhouses appear. Some quiet roads snake their way around these greenhouses like it's a maze. Earlier, looking on Google Maps, I had wondered what the white shapes were. I'm reminded of fruit irrigation areas in Australia, in both the climate and produce, as the local markets have delicious apricots.

It's a busy area with many people having African heritage, which I haven't noticed before in Spain. Perhaps this is because in nearby Almeria, there are ferries to Morocco across the Mediterranean, so people may have settled here.

For a while, I considered starting this tour in Morocco in March before crossing the Mediterranean to Spain after a few weeks. However, I soon realised that in the time I had available, I would have to rush through mountainous Morocco to enable enough time to rush through Spain to get to France in time for the start of the French Open Tennis in late May. I have learned my lesson from last year's trip, where at times I felt I was rushing through countries, so this year I'm trying to slow down.

Anyway, Outdoor Education work opportunities in Australia came up in late March, so I will save Morocco for another time. From what I have read, there is some challenging cycling, so it would make more sense to be cycling fit.

Roads sneak around numerous greenhouses

After passing more greenhouses and some eucalyptus trees, which remind me of Australia, I'm back near the coastline. As I pass Almeria Airport, a few cyclists are out for a day ride and soon after crossing a few creeks, a red cycle path begins beside the sea. Palm trees mainly line the path which takes me all the way into Almeria, as a long beach appears.

As I make my way to the railway station, a high, curvy abandoned rail viaduct appears. It connected the railway station to the sea, but is no longer used, despite there being a large wharf. As it's still intact all the way into the sea, it would make an interesting elevated rail trail.

Inside the station, I confirm that usually bicycles are allowed on trains between Almeria and Granada. However, trains are not currently running into Almeria because it's closed for track work, so trains are leaving at a suburban station eight kilometres north of here.

Rail viaduct in Almería, leads to the sea

However, staff at Almeria station can't sell me a bicycle ticket as the computer won't let them. It assumes everyone is catching a bus from here to the suburban station, and since bicycles aren't allowed on the bus, it won't sell me a ticket. I plan on cycling north, hoping I can buy a ticket at the temporary station.

In the meantime, I will explore Almeria. It feels bicycle-friendly with numerous bicycle lanes, including one that heads north from the sea as part of the wide median strip of the main street.

There are many signs for a tourist information centre, but it feels like they are just making me go around in circles.

Eventually, I figure out it's located inside a town square, but they are on their siesta. Thankfully, a police officer is kind enough to go inside and bring out a tourist map with English information both for me and an elderly couple. So far, the majority of cities have supplied similar maps with English information.

One of a few helpful English brochures

The main point of interest is the Alcazaba, a Moorish cream castle built on a hill. I'm expecting to pay to enter, but it's free. Inside is plenty of historical information and many places to explore, including the well looked after Moorish-era bricked waterworks. Water is still flowing through the middle of staircases in a green garden, which stands out compared to the surrounding duller cream castle. Also a few cats appear to live here.

Other parts of the castle are in more of a state of ruin, with low walls showing where structures were. There are still a few preserved towers to explore inside, with staircases leading to different levels of the castle. Inside some rooms are paintings showing how people lived in Moorish times, including sleeping on a rudimentary thin mattress.

Since it's so high up, there are scenic views of the sea and the surrounding dry hilly landscape, including an inaccessible wall of this castle which stretches across a deep valley and up the next hill.

Some parts of the Alcazaba are well maintained, other are in ruin

It's the largest castle visited so far on this trip, so I recommend a visit as it's quiet and not full of tourists. My bicycle was fine left locked outside to an actual bike rack down below.

I'm unsure if I should stay the night in Almeria as I can catch a train tonight or in the morning. After a good look around, there isn't any more I need to see, so I will cycle north to Huercal de Almeria to hopefully catch a train tonight.

After using a cycle path, climbing a bit and going past a hospital, I descend to a smaller railway station. The staff here are helpful and allow me to board this train, which is almost empty with only a handful of people on board.

Bike parking outside the Alcazaba

I'm glad I went on this train, as it's scenic as we climb a mountain range through numerous tunnels. I'm not taking any photos, instead, I'm just soaking it in.

This train goes to Granada, but I will stop halfway along in the town of Guadix before catching another train tomorrow to Granada.

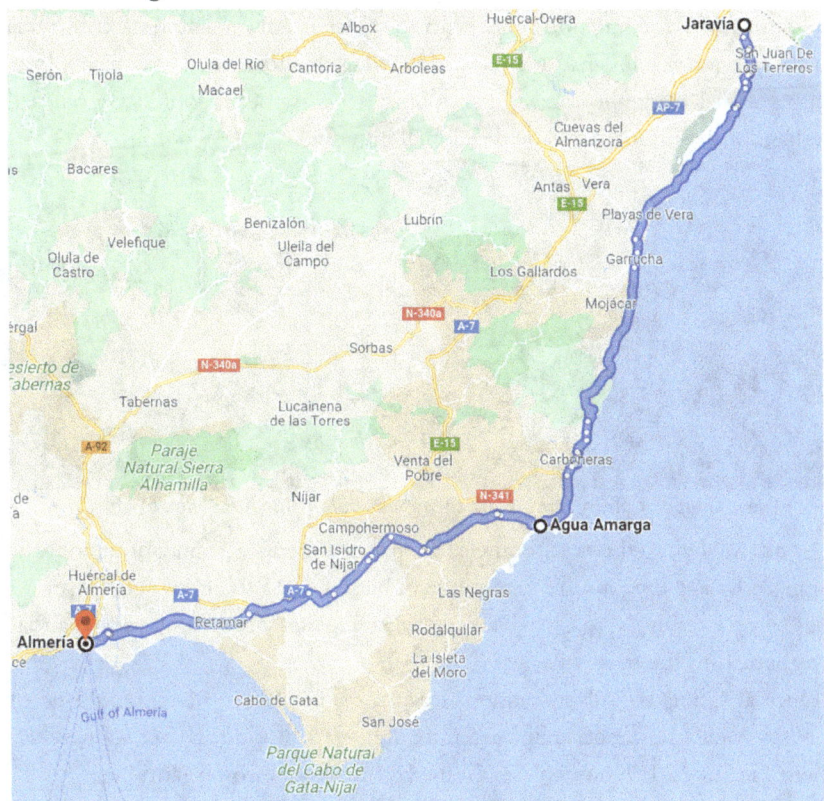

Jaravia to Almeria (Google Maps)

My first view of Guadix

The railway station is two kilometres from town, which allows me on the way into Guadix to admire the striking view of snow-capped mountains behind town. It's busy in the evening but not touristy as it appears locals are enjoying themselves.

It's now late in the evening, so I begin searching for a place to sleep. It doesn't take me long to find a spot in the forest near the athletics track.

There are four trains a day between Almeria and Granada. I'm hoping to catch the second one of the day just before 10 am. So in the morning, I have a quick explore around town before anything of interest is open.

There is a small historical area in the centre of town but the old castle has no access. While there appears to be some outdoor activities in the surrounding region, including caving and hiking, unfortunately I don't have enough time to explore before my morning train.

As I return up the hill to the railway station, there is just enough time to see the remains of the junction point with the former railway line back to Murcia, further up a dry hill. I had looked at following this former railway route, but I can see that I made the correct decision not to as it doesn't look like a rail trail. Perhaps in the future, it will be developed into one.

Near Guadix Railway Station are the remains of the junction back to Murcia

Unlike yesterday the train route is flatter as it takes a roundabout route to Granada by avoiding a mountain range in between. As the train gets closer, we pass by a route I hope to cycle back out in a couple of days. At one stage, a road is right next to the train.

Once at Granada Railway Station, I can see a fast line is being built west of here, so Media Distancia trains are not running. I'm told this fast route which opened in June 2019, now makes Granada three hours from Madrid.

While walking my bicycle out of the station, a police officer asks me for identification, so I show him. After a chat, I'm free to go. This was the only time on this trip I was asked for identification by police in Spain or anywhere else.

With views of the scenic snow-capped Sierra Nevada mountain range visible from Granada, it's an interesting city to visit with plenty of history.

Snowy mountains behind the Alhambra

In particular, there is a focus on when the Islamic kingdom was conquered by Catholic Spain in 1492, ending the dominant Islamic presence in southern Spain. Many older buildings still have examples of Moorish architecture, some prominent, others I need to look closely to find. A typical spot is under a verandah or above the arch of a window, with a style that reminds me of Turkey. It's always nice when the past is preserved.

A couple of enjoyable walking tours help illustrate how Granada changed from Islamic to Christian, with many not having a choice in the matter. Along with our guides pointing out evidence of Moorish architecture, they also show us much younger red graffiti on the cathedral's outside walls. It was put there by university students centuries ago and is now regarded as historic.

You have to look closely to find evidence of Moorish times

Seemingly half the people doing these tours were from Australia, including two elderly couples who did both as well. For such a small population, it's common to encounter fellow Australians. We do like to travel.

At Plaza Nueva, the meeting point for both tours, plenty of African-looking men are on the street selling stuff like handbags, sunglasses and shoes. These items are laid out on white sheets, so when they go to leave, they just tie

Street sellers

the sheet up and carry it over their shoulder like it's a sack. It reminds me of similar street sellers I have seen in touristy places like the Eiffel Tower.

In the city centre, the large hemmed-in gothic cathedral has a few entrances to pay to visit different sections. I will go with the one which has the crypts of Queen Isabella and King Ferdinand, who conquered Granada in 1492. It's a busy visit which reminds me of Westminster Abbey in London, with historical information but still a strong religious influence.

I prefer not to give money to religious buildings except for a particular historical context, so I won't pay to enter the main cathedral. I find that after a while all cathedrals look the same and because I'm travelling for weeks in a country, there is often an opportunity to visit free ones, usually in less touristy places.

The main attraction is the Alhambra, a large castle complex. It's an uphill walk to get to the high outside walls, and I'm unsure where the entrance is. After walking south along the wall for a while, a long line of people eventually tells me I'm near the entrance. I'm soon told there aren't any tickets available for today. So I begin walking around the outside walls, hoping to get a glimpse inside.

I soon spot people coming down some stairs, so I will walk up them. They lead me through a medieval gate and into the Alhambra. There are numerous buildings here, so presumably the Alhambra was its own town back in the day, with each building having a purpose.

Outside certain buildings, people are lining up. This is when I realise tickets are for specific buildings, rather than the whole complex. One palace is booked out for months, while other buildings are free to walk up and visit straight away.

The Charles V Palace is free to enter. Since it wasn't completed until the 20th century, 400 years after that King's death, its architecture differs from the older Moorish buildings around here. It has a circular courtyard in the middle, with rooms containing many fascinating Islamic archaeological items.

After a tip that they often release extra tickets overnight, at 5 am the following day, I book tickets for the Alcazaba and Generalife sections of the Alhambra.

The Alcazaba isn't that interesting, as it is a bare castle with just a few walls to walk on, and there is no decent information provided nor displays to look at. The Alcazaba in Almeria was much more interesting and didn't have crowds.

The Generalife, which was the royal botanical gardens, is attractive and separate from the rest of the Alhambra complex. It's narrow with two parts, a more extended outside garden and a smaller garden inside an enclosed open-sky courtyard. This building has an Islamic architecture style, in particular the archways under the verandahs. It reminds me of the Alcazar gardens at Seville, but it's not as interesting overall.

Of the three main Moorish castles I visited in Spain, Almeria was my highlight. So by all means, visit Granada, but it's not my favourite as it's just too busy. Still, it's spectacular and has lots to see.

A plainer Alcazaba

The Generalife, has more Moorish architecture among the gardens

The Copa de la Reina is a knockout cup for the top women's football clubs in Spain. *Copa de la Reina* translates to Queen's Cup, so the Queen of Spain will attend tonight's final. It's the equivalent of the Copa del Rey (King's Cup) for Spanish men's clubs or the FA Cup in England. Alex Chidiac, an Australian playing for Atletico Madrid, is the only player I know who could be involved.

During the day, there were many blue and white vertically striped shirted Real Sociedad supporters walking around Granada. However, late in the afternoon, as I make my way to the football stadium wearing my yellow Australian football top, there are more red and white vertically striped shirted Atletico Madrid supporters in the surrounding restaurants. Despite this, the Real Sociedad supporters are making themselves known by chanting loudly outside the stadium as the team bus decorated in their blue and white colours goes past.

Half and half scarves   *Welcoming Real Sociedad's bus*

There is more security to get inside the stadium than what I'm used to in Australia. I'm told I can't bring my water bottle inside. I have carried it for the past few trips, so I can't just leave it behind. After thinking for a bit, I find a quiet spot outside the stadium and gently throw it over a wire fence. As I try to enter again, I'm told I can't bring my apple inside. Instead of hurriedly eating the apple as I had to do in Russia, a security guard suggests if I break it in half, it can come inside. Thankfully, my bottle is still beside the fence.

My seat is on a sideline near the end full of Real Sociedad supporters. This club is from the Basque country in northern Spain, one of a few regions, that many locals wish were their own country. I'm assuming that the many flags made up of a red background with a combination of a white cross and green X is the Basque Flag. Additionally, before the start of the match, when the Spanish national anthem is being played, most of them turned their back to the singer. These are all signs that the separatist movement is still alive there. I'm planning on being there next week.

Over time the stadium becomes full, with the twenty thousand-odd people making a noisy, colourful atmosphere. Disappointingly, just like in Madrid, smoking is still allowed, yet I wasn't allowed to take water or even a whole apple into the stadium.

Unfortunately, as the teams are announced, Alex Chidiac isn't in the playing squad. So since Real Sociedad are clearly outnumbered in the crowd and are underdogs, I will barrack for them.

Initially, Atletico Madrid is on top, and they soon score. However, a goalkeeping error allows Real Sociedad to equalise. For some unknown reason, the large screen which was showing video before the game isn't showing replays of the action on the pitch. I'm not sure if this is a Spanish rule because there wasn't a replay screen at the football match in Madrid.

After half-time, Real Sociedad score with half an hour to go. From here, Atletico Madrid is besieging the goal, but just can't score despite some close calls. As the final whistle is blown, the Real Sociedad players and supporters are firstly relieved before the celebrations take over.

Real Sociedad footballers and fans celebrating

It's their first-ever trophy for their women's team, and it's a long time for the club as a whole. Their men's last trophy was the Copa del Rey in 1987, the year I was born, coincidently also against Atletico Madrid. Once the players receive the trophy from the Queen, they all make their way to celebrate with their supporters, and many take a Basque flag.

Picking up my bag

Because I don't have to leave my Airbnb until midday, I take my time in the morning doing some planning for my final week in Spain. I need to get back to Madrid to vote in the Australian federal election at the Australian Embassy in a few days. Having spent time in countries where people couldn't vote when I was born, I take this privilege as something I should do. Considering Spain was under a brutal Franco dictatorship for 40 years, I would like to vote here.

There isn't enough time to cycle all the way, so I need to find a train. With the route west currently closed due to the fast rail line being built to Granada, there are no trains that way. I have looked at cycling to Moreda 60 kilometres away, following the railway line back towards Guadix and getting a train from there. However, this won't work as trains on that route won't allow fully assembled bicycles.

The closest train that can take a bicycle is at Jaen. Since I have already been there, I was able to confirm this. However, I'm hesitant about cycling between Granada and Jaen because this involves climbing over the same mountain range I did last week to get to the national park. The direct route involves being next to a freeway for the majority of the time, using a secondary road. Not the type of cycling I like because presumably it will be noisy, and there will still be a section of freeway cycling required. Anyway, I have been told cyclists aren't allowed on freeways.

I even look at taking a bus by visiting the bus station in Granada, but they want my bicycle disassembled and wrapped in plastic, so I don't fancy that.

Fortunately, I have found a route following a railway line and a river initially before climbing through small towns. I won't have to be constantly near the freeway until descending on a secondary road just before Jaen, where I can catch one of four daily trains to Madrid.

From Madrid, I will get a train north to Burgos. This will allow me to then spend some time cycling through the Basque region, including some Vias Verdes around Vitoria-Gasteiz, Pamplona and San Sebastián before crossing into France.

When I do set off, my gradual climbing route is busy with numerous road cyclists riding towards me on this otherwise quiet Sunday as I follow a tram line north out of Granada.

Granada to Jaen

Sheep by a lake

Once out of the city, as I approach a lake, the road is rough with potholes but it's still a scenic ride through pine trees as I pass sheep seemingly grazing by themselves, while across the water are luxury homes. Further on, I'm briefly riding on the road I viewed from my train into Granada a few days ago.

After a brief stint on a quiet highway next to the freeway, I'm able to leave it behind. From here, the quiet road follows a river and railway line in a wide river valley. The elevation gain isn't noticeable until a short steep climb to the town of Iznalloz.

With it being a Sunday, it's quiet with nothing open except a small café where I meet two touring cyclists. They are also heading to Jaen, but they are taking a slightly more easterly route because they have a larger town they are aiming for tonight. After looking up their route on Maps.me, I see it is a longer route and has a similar amount of climbing, so I won't go that way. For the initial ride out of Iznalloz, I thought I may see them on the road, but since I take a wrong turn leaving town, presumably I'm now too far behind them.

The downside of delaying my departure from Granada is that by the time I'm leaving the railway line behind to begin some climbing, it's the hottest part of the day. It doesn't help that there isn't a lot of shade in this open farmland. The climbing involves some short steep sections of a kilometre, followed mainly by gradual climbs then a few brief downhill sections. Every ten kilometres or so is a town, allowing me to pace my way up. Fortunately, there is no real traffic to worry about.

After a couple of hours, I'm at the high point of the day, which allows me, for the most part, to relax as I'm now gradually descending on similar gradient roads. Of course, it's now much quicker, but there is still the occasional short climb to do, usually just before a town.

Today's scenery, including the high point of the day

Since today is Sunday, I assumed supermarkets would be closed, and since I finished my stove fuel in Guadix, I decided not to carry a new fuel bottle or dinner supplies. It saves me more than a kilo of weight while climbing. Instead, I have found a restaurant in the town of Cambil, allowing me to enjoy their weekend special of a three-course evening meal.

After the meal, my legs suddenly feel tired, so instead of exploring this scenic town surrounded by mountains, I just lie down on a park bench for a while.

Once it's dark enough, it's a struggle to find a quiet place to camp. My best option is to follow a path beside a canal towards the fenced-off football stadium on the edge of town. There is an open grassed space nearby, but it's near a road, and many street lights are around. It will do as a plan B, but I will keep looking.

Eventually, I see a tiny space up a goat track beside the walls of the football stadium. There are some rocks and rubbish around, but there should be enough space for my tent. So I drag my bicycle up and set my tent up in the dark.

With only 30 kilometres of mostly downhill cycling to Jaen, I can take my time this Monday morning. So while waiting for a supermarket in Cambil to open, I will climb a lookout near the school. Initially, it's not promising as the stone stairs are falling apart and are littered with rubbish.

Thankfully, I'm rewarded with decent views of this mountainous landscape at the top of this small climb, which allows me to see where I cycled from yesterday and where I am heading today. It's also noticeable just how much this town with mostly white buildings and brown tiled roofs is hemmed in by hills. I can even make out last night's restaurant near the local pool.

Cambil is surrounded by hills

It's a climb to get out of town before a longer descent to the freeway. Fortunately, I'm able to gradually descend on the quiet highway next to the freeway nearly all the way into Jaen, with a few road cyclists also out this morning. Five kilometres from Jaen, suddenly the road becomes terribly busy. After negotiating through suburbia, I'm in Jaen before midday.

A popular route for cyclists

With my train leaving later in the day, I will explore Jaen, having missed out previously while passing through ten days ago.

Other than a cathedral and some nice gardens, I haven't found much of interest. It doesn't help that I can't find the information centre despite signs saying it is nearby, while no one I ask in my broken Spanish can tell me where it is.

Since I have plenty of time until my train leaves, I will have a burger at a restaurant. However, it's served barely cooked and is raw inside. Even when I ask to have it cooked further, it is still raw. I'm not sure if I'm simply confused about what sort of burger I have ordered. It reminds me of Mr Bean's experience with a raw burger.

The train ride from Jaen is okay and becomes flatter as we make our way north through a few towns which used to be railway junctions, and according to Maps. me they now have short rail trails. If I had more time, some of these places might have been interesting to explore.

Renata, my Warmshower host in Madrid, can't host me again, so I will stop my train ride short of Madrid, in Aranjuez. Since it's at the end of the local train service from Madrid, I can catch one of many numerous trains in the morning.

After exiting the station and cycling on a tree-lined road, I find myself in the open courtyard of the Palace of Aranjuez. Since today is a Monday, it's closed.

Former royal gardens

However, the former royal gardens are open. There are lots of small human themed water fountains, sculptured hedges and plenty of trees. However, security guards won't let me even walk my bicycle through these gardens, so since it is now 8 pm and I'm hungry, I only have a quick look around.

I could camp just over the Rio Tajo, but after a Google Map satellite look, it probably isn't suitable. Instead, I will head south as I have found a lagoon on the edge of the city.

The lagoon is surrounded by thick tall grass, so only a narrow mowed path is available to get around this lagoon. Therefore, there is no clear space to camp until eventually an open spot beside a large birdwatching tower appears. I'm now near a railway line, but it's quiet during the night.

After a windy night, I know if I get an early train to Madrid, I may have enough time to collect my delayed gear, post some items home, vote at the Australian Embassy and then get a 12:20 pm train to Burgos. Otherwise, I will have to wait until 5 pm to leave Madrid, which will mean getting into Burgos at 10 pm.

The local train from Aranjuez is clean, has plenty of room for my bicycle and allows me to be in Madrid before 9 am.

Back at Renata's apartment in Madrid, her friend Maria lets me back in, allowing me to finally see my spotted black soft canvas bag. Everything I thought I had lost forever is thankfully in the bag.

I quickly sort through all my combined gear, deciding what to post home.

Picking up my bag

From the equipment I purchased in Madrid, I will keep the rain jacket and the Trangia. I will just add my cutting board from the old one. I will send home the new sleeping bag, mat, helmet and Ortlieb pannier bags along with some old gear I don't need anymore. This all fits in a large cardboard box.

Postage isn't cheap to Australia as I'm told it has to fly rather than go by ship, which is usually cheaper. My travel insurance covers the postage cost, while Emirate is giving me some money after I hounded them for a while. But it's not enough to cover the cost of purchasing all the items in Madrid when I assumed my bag was lost.

I also leave a paper map I purchased of southern Spain in the apartment, which I won't need anymore. I haven't used it as Maps.me on my iPhone is easier to use as I can zoom in, allowing me to see where old railway lines went.

Before my 2018 cycling trip in Russia, I was mainly using paper maps for navigation. However, after not finding maps in Russia, I became used to using Maps.me, along with Google Maps on my iPhone. So now I rarely use paper maps, although they are helpful for navigating in cities. For the rest of this trip, I just used apps on my iPhone and the occasional free tourist map.

Once everything is posted, I cycle back to Estación de Madrid Atocha to catch a train to Chamartín Station, the main one in Madrid for northern bound trains.

Helpfully, the Australian Embassy is located nearby on a floor of a high rise tower alongside a few other embassies. After leaving my bicycle locked up outside, I have to go through security to get in, and I'm given a key card to get to a room set up for Australians to vote. Other than having to leave my iPhone with security, it's straightforward voting with a handful of other Australians inside.

With the train to Burgos leaving soon, I race back to Chamartín just in time to catch the train. I'm supposed to buy a bicycle ticket, but the ticket machine won't let me while there are long lines for purchasing tickets from a person. With the next train to Burgos not for another five hours, I will take the chance there will be bicycle space available on this train leaving in two minutes. So I buy a ticket for myself and make my way to the platform.

Thankfully, there is space for my bicycle, with another touring bicycle already vertically hooked up. While making a sandwich for lunch, I offer to pay the conductor the correct fare of three euros for a bicycle ticket. By his reaction, I don't think he was going to bother to charge me.

The other bicycle belongs to a French cyclist. We chat for a while as he explained how he has cycled from Pau in southern France to Madrid and is training back the whole way via Irun on the French border.

For nearly five hours, it's a scenic rail route as we firstly climb our way out of Madrid, with some picturesque mountain ranges and valleys below before the landscape flattens out. I wouldn't mind coming back here one day for a proper explore.

Camino accidental

I'm starting the northern part of my Spanish ride in Burgos because a few Vias Verdes begin on the city's edge. Some are still being developed, so I have to choose the most developed one.

The current modern Burgos Railway Station is located in the north-eastern outskirts of the city as a bypass railway line has been built around Burgos. Helpfully a few riverside cycle paths allow me an easy ride into the city centre. Compared to southern Spain, there aren't just white buildings, and it feels like a more open city which reminds me of France. I feel like I'm in a different country.

Unbeknown to me, Burgos is located on the main religious walking route in Spain called the Camino de Santiago. Therefore, religion is a significant focus for the town as brochures in both tourist offices focus on religion, while neither has any information on any of the Vias Verdes in the region.

Artwork inside the cathedral

It's noticeably quiet here, while randomly on Tuesday afternoons, the cathedral is free to visit, so I head inside. It's busy, so this is where everyone is. Among a large area are many different statues, artwork, crypts and a model of the cathedral. In particular, there are numerous religious statues connected by tree roots and branches. It's nice to see, but all cathedrals look the same to me after a while.

A rare Franco reference

Nearby is a free army museum that focuses on equipment rather than any critical information on Spanish history, including a room full of military miniature soldiers dressed in specific periods of Spanish military history. I finally see a painting of Franco, which is a rare reference to him. The lack of his presence in Spain reminds me of rarely seeing references to Stalin in Russia.

With most things closing at 7 pm, it's the perfect time to leave and find a place to camp outside of the city. Before leaving, I cross to the southern side of Rio Arlanzon, the main river in Burgos, to visit the old railway station. It's in excellent condition and is being reused by the community, while there is a public park where the tracks were.

Helpfully a bicycle path that could be an old rail line takes me out of town before it unceremoniously ends in an industrial estate near the bypass railway line. After negotiating my way through, I'm soon able to find a gravel track that leads over a freeway bypass where the formation of a former railway line becomes visible. It's a rough track through farmland that is just able to be cycled.

Soon beside the trail in the middle of green grassy paddocks is a small cement block building. Presumably, it's the former station for the small town of Villarmero, which is not far away across a paddock.

This rundown building is missing its roof, but there is enough space inside to leave my bicycle out of sight. However, with a cement floor, I will sleep outside on the softer grass.

Among the rubble inside are two lounge chairs, so I will relax here while cooking dinner. As I settle in, a farmer is driving his tractor with a small plough around a few small paddocks. On second thought, I am a little concerned there may be bugs in the lounge chairs.

After dinner, I will go for a short walk into Villarmero. It's a small town with little to see, so I soon return to the station to set up my tent.

It's a slightly different feeling sleeping back on my old Thermarest mattress. As I drift off to sleep, a few cyclists and walkers pass me in my tent, but no one appears to care I'm camping here.

Cooking and camping at the remains of Villarmero Station

Overnight, the big difference from the previous night's camping in the south is that being in the north, my tent is covered in dew in the morning. Luckily, it's a not a cloud in the sky day, so my tent dries quickly.

I'm not sure if I can continue on this rough former rail right of way as Maps. me suggests the rail trail doesn't start until four kilometres away. However, after a kilometre of rough track, a decent surface rail trail suddenly starts in the middle of nowhere. There is even a wooden information board informing me of a planned longer route using a few rail trails to cross Spain by connecting Valencia on the Mediterranean to Santander on the northern coastline.

However, most of the route hasn't been developed yet. I had considered some other parts of this route for this trip, but I have read mixed reviews of their current development. I will keep this in mind for next time.

Just as I make the proper start of the rail trail, I see that my orange water bottle is missing. It must have fallen out of a holder on the front fork of my bicycle. So I retrace my route all the way back to last night's camp, but I can't find it. Fortunately soon after turning around, I spot the bottle on the side of the trail.

For ten kilometres, this flat Via Verde passes through farmland and a couple of small towns. So far, with a slight headwind, today doesn't feel special.

Ahead is a range of hills spread out in both directions. Luckily, the railway went through two tunnels to the high point of this rail trail.

Crossing a range

As the descending begins, the landscape suddenly changes to vibrant red soil with contrasting colourful flowering plants.

I'm enjoying the scenery while barely peddling and only noticing the kilometres passing by because the trail has kilometre markers. I'm not sure why but the rail trail is split in half with kilometre markers counting down from 21 to zero before starting to count down from 21 again.

Occasionally I'm passing through small farming towns, with missing rail bridges and the rail formation being reused by the community as a playground or by farmers. While on the trail, I'm passing farmers ploughing paddocks, reminding me of home, just with smaller farming equipment.

The second half is even more scenic, especially if you're into geology, as the rail trail passes through a landscape with numerous colourful layers. This Via Verde is now following a river, which presumably shaped the valley over millennia, leaving the landscape the way it is.

A relaxing railway grade descent

Because I'm descending, I can relax while admiring the contrasting colours between the creamy gravel trail surface, the yellow flowers and the different shades of red soil covered in green plants. In particular, the different coloured levels of the sides of the valley have so many shaped vertical grooves and horizontal lines separating the layers.

This via verde travels through a colourful landscape with so many layers

The Via Verde suddenly ends randomly in the middle of nowhere with only a noticeboard here while the continuing rail right of way has temporary orange plastic mesh fencing strung across it. The section ahead is clearly not a rail trail yet with rough stony ballast. However, with it looking freshly graded, maybe they are preparing to make it into a rail trail soon.

As I join a paved road, the rail formation is visible on my right most of the time, tempting me to return to it. Approaching a highway, the rail formation crosses the road. Despite evidence of a vehicle driving on the rail formation, it still looks like a bumpy, rocky ride. However, there is a gravel road next to it, which allows me to continue following the rail right of way most of the time.

End of the rail trail but a cleared rail formation continues

Eventually, the well looked after blue railway station complex on the edge of the town of Ona appears. With an undercover tennis court and a few other facilities, it looks well used by the community. The nearby town centre is okay but nothing memorable.

Ona Station is a community asset

I should return to the highway but with a rail tunnel just around the corner, why not look at it. There isn't a track anymore, so my only choice is the rough rail formation covered in numerous large stones. It's easier to just walk my bicycle all the way, including through the tunnel.

Just after the tunnel is a narrow walkway beside the rail formation, so I join it because the former rail route is just too rough. Even when walking, my hands are worn out from all the jolting every time I hit a rock.

After some stairs, this walkway leads to an old road that bypasses the newer highway tunnels but ends with a concrete barrier in the way.

A walkway beside this rail formation

In the meantime, I can see how the railway right of way went through numerous tunnels and has now disappeared from view.

After climbing over the barrier, on this quiet highway, I just have to be aware of semi-trailers on the route; otherwise, it's quiet. After a short climb and a right turn, the road travels through a deep tree-lined gorge for six kilometres to the town of Trespaderne. Halfway along, there are some natural tunnels to look at, while I lost where the railway line went until going under a bridge.

Once in this quiet town, I can't find any open supermarkets, but a local café has free wi-fi, so I stop here for a while for ice cream and to go online.

Hopefully, one day when the rail trail is fully built, I can cycle towards Santander. However, needing to head towards France, I will begin heading east following the Rio Ebro.

Initially, it's okay scenery with open rolling hills, as I follow the river on my right and for a short section a canal. It suddenly becomes scenic and narrow as I pass through a gorge with a few man-made tunnels while the water is at my level. Sadly, the gorge part only lasts five kilometres as once past the dam wall, the landscape becomes more open again.

Beside the River Ebro

My future Warmshower host, Alfredo, in Vitoria-Gasteiz messaged me an alternative route to my plan of continuing to follow the Ebro via the city of Miranda. He points out that there aren't many quiet road options that way. Instead, his alternative route will involve a climb, but it will be quieter. So literally, at a t-intersection, I have to make a choice.

I go with the quieter option, but will finish today's excellent ride before the climb in the small town of Espejo. Looking at my cycle computer at the end of the day, I'm surprised that I have done 111 kilometres. The scenery has been so distracting that I haven't been worrying about the kilometres at all.

In Espejo, the main community facility is for a type of racquet sport I haven't seen before. It appears to be a combination of squash and tennis, with competitors hitting a ball against two cement sides of this large one open-ended building. While in Spain, I have seen a few slightly different versions of sports.

My dinner is cooked in a small park beside a church because there is water and a picnic table here. I end up camping near the football pitch, setting up in the dark.

With a Warmshower organised in Vitoria-Gasteiz, I know today will be a shorter day, so I can relax for my ride. After a brief retrace on the main road out of town, I begin a steep ride.

Thankfully halfway along is the scenic town of Salinas de Anana, allowing me to break my ride, but still, this town is on a slope.

As I travel through town, on my right next to the road is a substantial cleared terraced area with many wooden walkways, structures and numerous rectangle wooden pans full of some sort of fine particle, with some of these pans covered in a murky liquid. It reminds me of visiting replicas of the goldfields, like at Sovereign Hill in Ballarat.

On the edge of town is a visitor centre, where I'm informed that this is a former salt mine and guided tours are available. However, there aren't any English tours today, so I will just have a quick look from a lookout. It appears to be a well-thought-out system, with water directed by small wooden aqueducts and a terracing system used to extract salt by gravity.

Former salt mine at Salinas de Anana

After a steeper climb to a pine-covered pass, the descent is even steeper to the small town of Pobes. After crossing a railway line and going under a freeway, another short climb and descent takes me to another valley. The railway line to Irun passes through here, so I will follow this to Vitoria-Gasteiz.

Along the way, I stop at a Roman ruin for a short explore. There isn't much to see other than remains of a couple of low floor buildings, especially compared to previous Roman ruins.

The rest of the ride into Vitoria-Gasteiz is through an industrial area before a bicycle path takes me into the city centre. Vitoria is the Spanish name for this city, while Gasteiz is the Basque name. With two names for the same place being common in the Basque region, I have tried to use what was most commonly known to me.

While checking online, I learn that Bob Hawke, Australia's Prime Minister when I was born, died today. Perhaps this could influence the federal election on Saturday as he was a former leader of the current opposition party.

Unlike southern Spain, many people here are actually riding bicycles for transport. Presumably, the cooler climate and broader streets makes cycling more enticing. While the buildings have a different style and are more colourful than the all-white buildings in southern Spain, it feels like I'm actually back in the Europe I know.

Vitoria-Gasteiz is hosting the men's European club basketball final four tournament this weekend so the busy city squares are full of temporary buildings for promoting the tournament, so there isn't much room to move around.

Flat escalator

Above the main square is the hilly, old town part of the city. Helpfully to access it, there is a glass-windowed covered one-way escalator on one steep street that leads up to the main church. Since it's a flat ride, I can take my bicycle on it.

It feels different up here to the rest of the city as it has hilly narrow streets and it's quieter. After briefly exploring, it's a steep descent back down to where I will have more of a look around the city.

On display in front of the Plaza de la Provincia are a few large temporary information panels highlighting Vitoria-Gasteiz and the surrounding Basque region, including many natural features to visit and also some informative historical information. I wish I had time to see more of these places.

Later in the afternoon, I stumble on an informative army museum that focuses on the Battle of Vitoria, which was in 1813 when Napoleonic forces lost this battle and fled from Spain. On display are many uniforms and weapons from the period, along with plenty of information.

Around 5 pm suddenly the temperature drops and clouds appear which was predicted along with rain all day tomorrow. So I will now make my way to my Warmshower host Alfredo's home. He lives on the edge of the city, so initially, my route involves using wide cycle paths with plenty of fellow cyclists as I pass the football stadium. The further out I get, the more it feels like a modern ugly city with numerous tall apartment blocks that all look the same.

More open spaces in the north of Spain

Alfredo is friendly as I spend the evening learning about his cycling travels, particular in South America. He suggests that as a native Spanish speaker, it was much easier for him to travel through there. I haven't been to South America yet because something gets in the way every time I plan to. With the weather looking terrible tomorrow, Alfredo offers for me to stay another night, so I will see what the weather is like in the morning.

Woke to a cold day with heavy rain, so I won't be doing much today, other than catching up on some journalling, planning my route to Bordeaux and doing some repairs. Whenever I look out a window, it isn't actually raining that much. It just appears it could fall at any moment while it's still bitterly cold.

Things wear out when you travel for months at a time, so today I'm assessing all my gear. Some of my clothing has minor rips in them. So for my afternoon ride to a supermarket, after searching around, I have finally found some needle and thread to fix some of my clothing.

From Vitoria-Gasteiz, there is the option of cycling two different Vias Verdes, one that heads directly north and one that goes south-east to Estella. I originally favoured the northern route because it would allow me more time in the Basque region, but Alfredo suggests it is less developed than the one towards Estella.

As I retrace my route back into town, it's similar weather as yesterday. On the south-eastern side of the railway station, I can just make out where a former railway line left the current line. A road and cycle path now follow this former rail route with a couple of roundabouts to negotiate before the developed Via Verde del Vasco Navarro begins heading towards Estella.

Initially, the rail trail is fine, with some sections paved and others gravel. Despite yesterday's rain, it's not too wet, just a damp surface. On a warm day, the forested sections would be an enjoyable ride. However, I'm not really stopping because it's cold, and there is the threat of rain returning. Despite the weather, I am seeing a few hikers and day cyclists on the trail.

A new bridge for this via verde, while information is now mostly in Basque and Spanish

A couple of new red rail trail bridges built across roads remind me of similar bridges in southern Spain, while I'm also passing a few former stations and tunnels with information boards explaining the history of this railway line. In the south, often, these types of information panels had both Spanish and some English information. However, now that I'm in the Basque region, a lot of information is only in Basque and Spanish. I understand a few Spanish words, but not enough to work out what is written.

From the Via Verde map I have, I know that I will have to leave the rail right of way to bypass a two-kilometre long rail tunnel. The bypass starts before the tunnel, but the path continues. Once I see the river of water flowing out of the tunnel entrance, it's obvious why I have to bypass.

As this tunnel went through a mountain range, all the cyclists are turning around here. Since I want to continue, I will have to go on an eight-kilometre climb over this range to re-join the rail trail.

Initially, this bypass involves a steep gravel path for two kilometres. It's too steep for my fully loaded bicycle, so I end up pushing it up this path. I understand

A rocky path over this hill

why all the other cyclists turned around because there is no point continuing unless you're doing a through ride.

I can cycle once I'm up, but it's a lot of undulating cycling for three kilometres on the edge of a hillside. It would be scenic if rain wasn't imminent, especially when passing through a few gaps in between rocks. As I begin descending, light rain begins, and as I re-join the rail trail, it becomes heavy.

I dislike cycling in the rain because I feel like I'm cycling with blinkers on, only looking at the path ahead, while all my focus is on the next time I can get shelter, rather than the landscape I'm passing through.

Fortunately, the town of Maestu is not far away, so I can shelter in the former railway station, which is now a community centre. However, with a railway-themed interpretive centre in the next town of Antoñana presumably closing soon for siesta, I will continue on.

After going through a couple of shorter tunnels, I'm forced off the rail right of way and onto a highway, because a couple of abandoned rail bridges are inaccessible. Thankfully, the highway is quiet.

The interpretive centre in Antoñana is closing at 2:30 pm, so I have half an hour to look around this stationary railway carriage. Inside, a man is offering assistance, while there are maps of the area and information on things to see off the trail, but with rain around, it isn't the day to go exploring.

The majority of information is on the railway line's history. This line was built in stages between the 1890s and 1930s and closed in 1967. It used a one-metre wide rail gauge, which is narrower than the Iberian Gauge of 1.668 metres.

Interpretive centre in carriages

The rain looks like continuing all afternoon, so finding somewhere dry to stay tonight is my priority. If I do another sixteen kilometres, I should make a caravan park.

Soon after leaving Antoñana, the rain eases and basically stops for the rest of the day. As well, with a slight tailwind and gradual descending route, I feel like I'm flying along, so instead of visiting the caravan park, I will just keep going. It's become more of an open farmland rail trail, which is rough in places.

As the landscape becomes hillier again, a large rail viaduct appears, and on the other side is a tunnel. Fortunately this one and half kilometre long tunnel is open and has lights, so it's a relaxing ride. Once I'm through, it's more undulating than before but still an open farmland with hills in the distance. Unfortunately, from here I have to occasionally leave the rail right of way with some short hilly detours required.

After one final tunnel, a paved road on the former rail right of way takes me into the city of Estella, where the former station is now the bus station.

An old station in a park

The trail is more open now, but I'm still in the mountains

I haven't found wi-fi today, so when I find some outside a Santander Bank, my priority is to find out the result of the Australian election. Going by the pre-election news I have been hearing, I'm assuming a change of government. However, I'm shocked to read that it hasn't gone as predicted and the current conservative government has survived.

After visiting a tourist information centre, I learn that Estella is on the same religious Camino Santiago trail as Burgos, so it has many religious sites and tourists. I'm not meaning to be on this route; the various Vias Verdes have just taken me this way.

Thankfully, most museums are open later in the evening here, perhaps to attract pilgrims after their day's walk. Now that Spanish is a second language here, it's less common for museums to have English information. I recognise some Spanish words but not enough to understand them all, so I'm relying on pictures.

A bonus of being on the Camino Santiago trail is that many basic but cheap pilgrim indoor accommodations are available. My simple room allows me to dry off, but there isn't a kitchen, so I will cook my dinner on my Trangia stove in their courtyard.

The cold rainy weather continues in the morning, so my rugged-up ride to Pamplona is about getting there rather than enjoying the scenery. Except for one four-kilometre long climb before a descent, most of the ride is on undulating secondary roads beside a freeway.

A few of the Camino hikers

Mostly, I'm near the busy Camino de Santiago walking route. The sheer number of people hiking in the opposite direction is extraordinary. In the town of Puente la Reina, I'm guessing I saw more than 100 hikers while negotiating my way through town. I have heard of this trail but had no idea just how popular it is. I'm also seeing plenty of luggage being transferred from accommodation to accommodation.

It's not just hikers; I'm also seeing a few touring cyclists, including an older couple from New Caledonia. Many people assume I'm cycling the Camino de Santiago. Before today I have barely seen any touring cyclists in Spain.

Unfortunately, I have made Pamplona just after 2 pm, so I have missed the tourist information centre being open this Sunday. Museums are also closed, and it appears they will be closed on Monday as well. So instead, I will just cycle around, seeing what I can find. I have heard of Pamplona because of the running of the bulls, but the only bulls I see are statues in the mall.

The open free citadel is of most interest to me. It is a low walled stone citadel with moats and a few walkways to wheel my bicycle over. It reminds me of the Belgrade Fortress I saw last year, but it's flatter and much quieter here. On display around the citadel is environmental artwork, including a piece showing plastic surrounding Africa.

The open free citadel with environmental artwork

By late afternoon, the weather has partly cleared with the sun occasionally appearing, but spits of rain are still randomly occurring. I could head out of town and find somewhere to camp but I'm still feeling cold from getting wet on the ride here. I can't change into warm clothing because I have been wearing all of them. If I do camp, trying to dry my clothes while staying warm will be a challenge.

Fortunately, because I'm on the Camino route, plenty of reasonably priced indoor accommodation is available. Mine has a few rooms on the same floor with a shared kitchen, just what I need.

Thankfully, the sun is out in the morning, so I'm looking forward to staying dry today. The plan is to cycle the Via Verde del Plazaola on a former metre gauge railway line from Pamplona to Andoain near San Sebastian, which closed in 1958.

When I see some rails still in the ground near a road crossing, this confirms I'm on this former railway route near the current active rail line. Since the first section leaving Pamplona is not an official rail trail, there aren't any signs, while it's just a gravel track with a few walkers on it. Soon the rail right of way goes through an army base, so I will have to divert away.

It takes a while to find the right of way again. Eventually, I figure out that the railway line used to go through a tunnel, which isn't visible anymore. Instead, it's marked with a stone archway above it.

Once I'm back on the rail formation, it's a much rougher surface as it climbs to a pass shared with the highway, and the path is lost again. As I join the highway, I realise my camera is missing from its usual location in a bag on the top post of my bicycle.

Thankfully after retracing my route on the rail formation, straight away I find my camera. As I pick it up, a couple of mountain bikers appear on the trail. During morning tea in nearby Sarasa, I chat with one of them.

From Sarasa, the rail trail starts with a decent surface, and for the next ten kilometres, most of the route is on the rail right of way with a couple of decently refurbished rail bridges. However, some sections require diverting away, usually meaning some short steep sections.

The further I go, the more scenic it's becoming as a large mountain range appears on my left, while houses have an alpine appearance with pointy roofs.

Looking more mountainous now on this via verde

In the town of Irurtzun, my cyclist friend is here again. He explains that I have to get around a closed tunnel and suggests a route. However, I have found another way on Maps.me, which looks like it connects to where the rail trail restarts on the other side of a river.

After crossing under a freeway, I join a track which leads to a skinny pedestrian bridge over the fast-flowing Rio Larruan. Once over the bridge, I soon discover this track is a goat track, so I begin dragging my bicycle up it.

I soon leave my bicycle to walk on a bit further to see if it improves, but the track is becoming muddier. I could keep walking further, but will be dragging my bicycle for a while on a slippery path from what I have seen so far. I also have no idea if it actually connects to the rail trail. So I will turn around and return to my bicycle.

Looking across this fast-flowing river and above the freeway, I can see a secondary highway, which seems to be the most sensible route, so I will backtrack to join it.

Once I find my way up, the road goes through two tunnels which I suspect were railway tunnels, as it looks like the railway line came in from the eastern side of this road. Below the freeway is going through a significant natural gap beside the river.

As the road ducks under the freeway, I'm now next to the river, while somehow, the rail trail is on the opposite side, despite no obvious evidence where it exactly crossed the river. I can't see a way to get there, so I will continue on the highway.

After going around a bend and back under the freeway, the road crosses the river, and then the rail trail crosses the highway. I will re-join it as it follows the highway for about five kilometres before diverting away. From here, for the most part, the trail is consistently staying on the former rail route. It's still going around some former rail tunnels, but a flat track usually curves around them.

From Mugiro, I'm starting to enjoy the ride more as I don't have to worry about diverting away from the rail right of way.

As I approach the high point of the day, I am concerned about a 2.7-kilometre long tunnel that may be closed, just like the tunnel on the way to Estella. Thankfully, it is open with passable lighting, but since the tunnel is straight, daylight is visible at both ends. The more significant challenge is that the majority of the floor is covered in flowing water, and in some places, I can feel the water on my feet as I pedal. Still, it's an enjoyable ride and better than any alternative, which presumably would involve climbing.

Lekunberri station is now a visitor centre

Ankle-high water in the tunnel

Once out of the tunnel, it's more remote, and for the most part, this railway line went around the edge of towns, generally high above, so I'm not going into towns. Instead, I'm enjoying the views while descending at a railway grade for 30 kilometres. Along the way, I'm passing a few colourful woolly sheep.

Descending now

Water falling from the ceiling of the tunnel

Unlike the uphill route, which only had a few tunnels, I'm now going through numerous tunnels, which are often short but sometimes up to 600 metres long. Since there was rain over the past three days, most have puddles inside, with some having water falling from the roof. One tunnel has water falling for ten metres. Initially, these showers are fun, but as the day becomes cooler, I put my rain jacket on to prevent myself from becoming soaked. Fortunately not a drop of water has fallen from the sky today. By the end of the trail, I'm sick of these rainy tunnels as I'm getting cold.

When I cross from the Navarre region to the Basque region, the kilometre markers reset and change type, while suddenly all the tunnels don't have lights, no matter the length, but thankfully, all have cement floors. Unfortunately, the rest of the trail has become a rougher surface because the ballast has just been flattened, and I suspect vehicles use this part of the trail. This is confirmed near the end when I pass logging trucks on the rail right of way.

Thankfully, it's downhill all the way beside a fast-flowing river. In reverse, it wouldn't be much fun climbing on this rough surface, especially as there is often water flowing across the trail, creating dips. In contrast, most of the Navarre section had a graded surface with sandy gravel added, and cars appeared to be banned, so it was a more relaxing ride.

In the afternoon, I have seen a few hikers every so often but no cyclists. This suddenly changes for the final five kilometres to Andoain when the number of people increases, creating peak hour conditions. This must be why for the last three kilometres, the trail is paved.

After a relaxing day with little traffic, cycling through built-up Andoain feels busy. Once out of town, there are some short steep sections to end this long day.

I have organised a Warmshower with Aritz to camp on his family farm near the town of Hernani. He told me he wouldn't be home, but his parents would be. It takes a while to find the exact location as there are a few small farming blocks around.

Eventually, when I think I'm at the correct place, I can see an older couple, so I open a gate and ask in my rudimentary Spanish if they know Aritz. They do, so they let me into a small block with a few fruit trees and veggie gardens, while in the middle is a small building which I'm not allowed in. There is an outside shower out the back and some seats to sit on while cooking dinner, so I have all I need.

In the morning, I make my way to San Sebastián, using some bicycle paths and a short steep descent near the Real Sociedad football stadium. At one stage, I have to lift my bicycle down a flight of stairs to get to the stadium, which is being rebuilt, so I don't have an opportunity to see if there has been any commemoration of their Copa de la Reina win.

From the stadium, I join a bicycle path that follows the scenic river, which looks more like a canal, into the centre of San Sebastián.

Near the tourist office, a free walking tour starts at 10:30 am and 4 pm each day. Having arrived just after 10 am, I enjoy a two-hour guided tour of the old city and the magnificent crescent sandy beach. On this beautiful sunny day, I can see why many people, including royalty, visit this city.

Market in San Sebastián

Helpfully, I learn about the Basque's culture and language, including that San Sebastián is known as Donostia in the Basque language. Our guide shows us a local snack *pintxo* (pincho in Spanish) which isn't an actual specific food; instead, plates full of various snack-sized foods are placed at the front of counters of many cafés and bars. The majority are bread-based with toothpicks to pick them up, but there are also cakes and desserts, while some can be heated. Because I can see them, I mostly know what is in each one. To purchase a pintxo, you select and pay for what you want.

After the tour finishes, based on my guide's recommendation, I make my way to the STM museum in a former church. It focuses on Basque history, so I'm learning a different perspective from elsewhere in Spain. Other than a few large seafaring paintings in the main hall, I wish I could remember more about this museum.

Inside STM museum

I could spend longer here, but a sunny day is tempting me outside. So I will leave to walk up the hill above the museum.

It's a popular walk with plenty of hikers around a large spread out highpoint that provides reasonable views in between trees as various trails

The bay from the headland

zigzag all over this hill. Still, I can once again see the large crescent bay, while around this headland are plenty of cannons that once defended the city. There are remains of a stone fort, but the museum up here is closed today.

The twenty kilometres between Donostia and Irun is basically all suburban cycling; the alternative is a longer hilly route. With it now nearly 4 pm I will take a train to Irun. With plenty of room for my bicycle, it's a cheap, quick way to get there.

The tourist office doesn't inform me of anything of interest I need to see, so I won't spend much time in Irun. I at least try some snacks in a Pintxo bar. They are not that special as they are just mini sandwich-style meals which are available in a pub.

I could cross the Rio Bidasoa into France here, but I have found a Via Verde which follows the Bidasoa south for a while. Once the rail trail finishes, I will cycle a low pass over the Pyrenees into France.

Initially, while I'm on a cycle path, France is visible across the Bidasoa before the river isn't the border anymore and so France disappears from view.

Across the Rio Bidasoa is France

Once on the rail trail, it's an easy ride, but since it's following a river and highway, it's noisy and unlike previous Vias Verdes, there aren't any tunnels or major bridges, so it's boring. The only variable is the surface which sometimes is paved, other times rough gravel, with cars allowed on most sections. A few cyclists are using the rail trail, but even more roadies are on the busy main road next to it.

Eventually, on dusk, as the rail trail briefly goes away from the highway, there appears to be a quiet enough space to camp beside the trail. However, as I settle in, a couple of cars go past on the trail.

After a dewy night, I finish the Via Verde as it becomes paved just before it finishes in Legasa. From looking at maps, it appears the railway line continued further on, but it is not a trail. So I'm back on the road, which for the most part are secondary roads except for three kilometres.

Occasionally, I'm finally seeing some EuroVelo cycling signs. Apart from when on the various Vias Verdes, I haven't seen many bicycle direction signs in Spain. They were more common in Eastern Europe last year.

After lunch in Erratzu, I begin making my way towards France, which will require a 400-metre climb with at least half a dozen switchbacks. It's a gradual climb towards these switchbacks in a green valley with little traffic. Once I'm on them, it feels like a gentler gradient compared to before the switchbacks began. Being a relaxing climb, I'm able to constantly look back at the valley below as I pace myself up in about an hour, with only a few cars to worry about.

Zigzagging up to France

The actual pass isn't that high but still has a decent green view, while beside the pass is a small restaurant with a few patrons around. With open European borders, I'm free to cross here, so only a blue sign informs me I'm entering France.

About to enter France

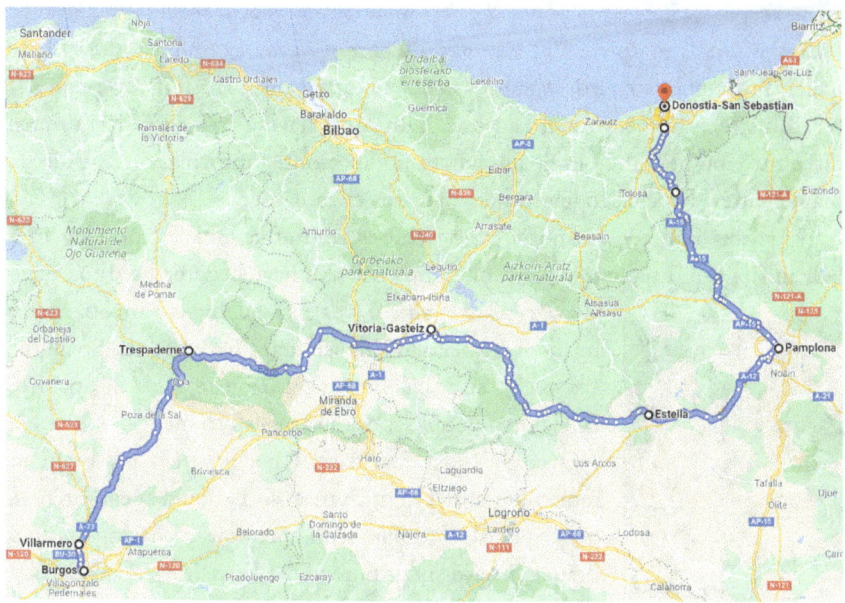
Burgos to Don Donostia (Google Maps)

Bienvenue en France

From the pass, the road snakes its way down on the edge of a mountain, while the hills in the distance have a blue haze.

For eight kilometres, it's a quick relaxing descent, with just a small stone barrier separating me from a drop. It reminds me of the Going to the Sun road in Glacier National Park in the USA, except there is less traffic. Still, some motorbikes are racing past me at a respectable speed.

My hands are becoming numb from the need to constantly pull on my brake levers, so every so often, I need to stop to give them a rest, otherwise, it feels like eventually I won't be able to hold onto my handlebars. A bonus with needing to stop is this allows me to admire the amazing green views.

Stopping to admire the view, while looking back at Spain

By the time I'm down, I'm in a town where it's easy to find a tourist office which in French is called *Office de Tourisme*. During my 2013 tour of France, I recall that nearly every town had one, with most having free wi-fi. It's a much different vibe here than in Spain, where finding tourist information outside of main centres was challenging, while wi-fi was even harder.

Inside this one are a handful of brochures, and after initially speaking to a lady in English, I reply to a question in Spanish as I have become used to saying *Gracias* (thanks) and *Si* (yes), so she thinks I am Spanish. I hurriedly explain in English that I have been in Spain for six weeks, so it has become a habit to reply in Spanish, even when people speak in English to me.

Sometimes French is just bad spelling

Over the next few days, I had to train my brain to remember that I'm in France, so I should speak French, not Spanish. Along with previously having visited France, I have spent time in the French parts of Canada and briefly did French at school, so while it's better than my Spanish, it's still rudimentary.

Outside of language and a slight change in diet, not much else has changed; I'm still using the same currency, time zone, and supermarkets.

After passing through a few quiet towns, suddenly, as I arrive in St-Jean-Pied-de-Port, it has become jam-packed with pedestrians, many wearing hiking backpacks. A narrow river which looks more like a canal splits the town in half and is postcard-worthy with multistorey red-tiled white houses on both sides.

A stone pedestrian bridge layered in cobblestones takes me through a fancy medieval gate to a busy tourist pedestrian mall. Religious souvenir shops are everywhere, and many businesses sell stuff specifically for hikers, including accommodation and luggage transfers. It doesn't take me long to realise once again I have accidentally ended up on the Camino de Santiago.

Main river and gate in St-Jean-Pied-de-Port

Apparently, a few pilgrim routes from all over France meet here before everyone goes the same way across the Pyrenees. I'm told it's common for more than a thousand Camino hikers to pass by here every day during the hiking season.

In the busy Office de Tourisme, I'm given a map showing cycling routes in southwest France. There is at least one small section that I could use, but with most routes travelling in an east-west direction, they are not much use to me as I'm aiming to travel in a northerly direction. I won't be spending much time in this region of France as I have a train to catch from Bordeaux in five days to enable me to get to Paris for the tennis.

Behind the pedestrian mall on a small hill is an old citadel with plenty of paths and steps to explore, along with multiple grass areas with sheep grazing. The main set of buildings in the middle is used by a school, with a basketball court reminding me of a similar court in Belgrade's Fortress.

I'm in St-Jean-Pied-de-Port because I have organised a Warmshower with Dennis and Claire. They make me feel welcome as I'm given some helpful ideas on my route to Bordeaux, and Dennis cooks us a delicious meal. We also talk generally about the region, especially the impact Camino tourism has because while it brings money, the number of tourists is overwhelming. Before this trip, I had heard about religious routes, but I didn't know where they went or how popular they were. I just happened to keep finding myself near this route.

The direct flat road from St Jean to Saint-Palais looks busy, so Dennis recommends not going that way. Instead, in the morning I take a slightly longer, hillier route which should have little traffic. Initially, there is some climbing before eventually, I'm descending beside a river to Saint-Palais. The first fifteen kilometres of climbing took longer than the last 22 kilometres of descending. Along the way, I briefly chat with a man in his seventies cycle touring.

Saint-Palais is a small town with an Office de Tourisme where a map mentions a street called Gare, the French word for a railway station. After a combination of asking at the Office de Tourisme and looking at Maps.me, I see that a railway line used to go north from here, and it could be a rail trail. So I make my way to Avenue de la Gare, where a few factories remain but no railway station.

Just north of the factories is a gravel rail trail with a few people walking. However, soon after crossing on a former rail bridge, the trail slowly becomes overgrown with grass. With vehicles clearly using this trail, it's still okay to cycle with just a bit of mud to avoid. Further on, in a few places, diagonal planks of timber have been placed across the trail, presumably to try to keep out motorised vehicles. I just have to lift my bicycle over them.

After detouring around a factory that still operates the rail right of way's surface becomes worse as it's now mowed grass. I'm still able to cycle, but it's slow.

Saint-Palais rail trail surface starts with gravel but turns to grass

Just before the town of Arbouet, on the other side of a road crossing, the rail formation is overgrown with blackberries, so I have no choice but to return to a road. It's about a ten-kilometre gap before another rail trail is available.

A rail trails starts before the town of Escos. Dennis recommended visiting here, but I can't recall why, so I will go for a look. It's a small town, and I can't find anything interesting other than a small private castle. As I begin leaving town, two adult touring cyclists appear. They are an English father and son following the Camino Route, in the opposite direction to me. So after a minute or two of chatting while cycling together, I turn around and join the rail trail.

This trail has a decent paved surface and soon crosses the River Gave d'Oloron on a rusty steel rail bridge. Temporary orange barriers are in the middle, presumably to stop cars from crossing.

Shortly after another rail bridge, this trail unceremoniously ends in a random part of the town of Salies-de-Bearn. I'm a little confused about exactly where I am, so it takes a while to find my way around.

While discovering that the Office de Tourisme is now permanently closed, I see a young man with a small homemade touring bicycle setup. As I

Rail trail bridge

begin wheeling my bicycle around to chat with him, my bicycle suddenly loses balance, causing me to embarrassingly fall over as well. He helps me up, and after a brief chat, I realise he isn't a touring cyclist.

I'm not sure if the rail trail continues north from here. From what I can find, the former route is overgrown, and I think it went through a tunnel. So I will return to a road.

After crossing the active railway line at Puyoo, I begin making my way north using a few dogleg roads to avoid the busy road towards Dax. Just before the town of Hinx is a rail trail, so I join it as it begins heading east on a reasonable gravel surface.

As I approach the town of Montfort-de-Chalosse, I pass a large abandoned railway station complex with an open park which should be fine to wild camp at. After taking a ramp up to the town proper, I see a large open shelter with multiple brick columns holding up the roof. There is a sink with water, and plenty of power points, so it's a perfect spot to cook dinner as light rain begins.

As night falls, with rain looking like continuing tonight and tomorrow, finding a dry spot to camp is my priority. My two best options are either stealth camp at the former railway station or at the more visible in town rugby ground. With nowhere to shelter my bicycle down beside the rail trail, I will camp at the rugby ground because there is a clean toilet block to store my bicycle out of the weather.

This shelter is just what I need

My bicycle stayed dry in a toilet block

By 8 am the rain has eased, so I begin packing up my wet tent inside the toilet block. However, by the time I'm ready to leave town, the rain returns. So after visiting a bakery, I make my way to the shelter again and wait for the Office de Tourisme to open at 10 am.

There isn't much information there but the rain has eased, so I can finally leave town by making my way back down to the rail trail. It's now muddy with puddles but is still ride-able on a pair of tracks among the grass. Since it's cold and wet, I go to plug in some podcasts, but my headphones are missing. I was using them earlier in the day around the shelter, so I will go back to see if I dropped them there.

After looking around, I can't find them. It's my second pair lost or damaged on this trip.

After the town of Mugron, heavy rain begins, so a farm shed will have to do for shelter during lunch. Once the rain eases, the rail trail soon ends at a former rail junction, as the other line still has rails here, but is clearly abandoned and overgrown. So I'm back on the road to the small town of Saint-Sever.

Rainy day on a rail trail bridge

After more heavy rain for fifteen minutes, I begin heading north to the city of Mont-de-Marsan, using a quiet route that crosses a closed railway line a couple of times.

Mont-de-Marsan still has a passenger train service, but it only heads west, while I want to head east. I have considered using the train to get out of this weather, but with a rail trail east of town, I will keep cycling.

Before leaving town, the Office de Tourisme provides me with a map of a few sites, including a war memorial and a few references to the Second World War. There is even a walkway dedicated to when the city was liberated on the 20th of August 1944.

In Spain, I rarely saw a war memorial to any battles in history and had to search for references to the Spanish Civil War.

It takes a while for me to find the start of the rail trail as I'm becoming disorientated while trying to find the right road to take.

East of Mont-de-Marsan, three rail lines used to split here, but they all look abandoned, with the middle one now a paved signed fifteen-kilometre long rail trail. It's suddenly sunny as I begin this trail, so it is an enjoyable ride.

This doesn't last long as the heavy rain returns for a few minutes before easing to light showers as the rail trail ends on the edge of the town of Villeneuve-de-Marsan.

So many bicycle signs in France

This cold weather is the perfect opportunity to make my way to a library to sort out compensation for my lost bag with Emirates because I need a computer to fill in a few forms. It takes a little longer than I hope because French keyboards are different, with some letters in a different place to the Qwerty keyboard I'm used to.

From Villeneuve-de-Marsan, I'm trying to re-find the rail trail on the other side of town. Eventually, I discover an overgrown path on a highway curve, so it makes more sense to stay on the road. After finding the right road to leave town, I follow bicycle signs as light rain is returning. Soon the signs direct me back to the rail trail, but it is not developed, just another path through grass, but since it has taken two kilometres to get here, I will cycle on it.

Unfortunately, the rain becomes heavy again, and soon the trail is covered in muddy puddles, so it's a struggle to ride while it feels like water is soaking me in every direction. Fortunately, a cement road overpass appears, allowing me just enough room to shelter under it as the rain continues. I'm still nearly ten kilometres from the next town, and not near a road, so I will have to wait out the rain.

The rain eases after 30 minutes so I will continue on this now muddy rail trail covered in puddles. As soon as I cross a road, it makes sense to cycle on the presumably quicker road, especially as I have no idea if more rain is imminent.

This quiet paved road is undulating, but allows me to go much quicker to the town of Labastide-d'Armagnac. This small authentic town has an unbeautified old town square with the facades of the many double-storey buildings having various styles of architecture. Most importantly, on three sides, all the second storeys have extensions out over the street, providing a verandah space for me to shelter under. The most dominant building is a church on the fourth side, which looks like a castle.

On this Friday evening, only a pizza restaurant is open, it's tempting, but I have enough food to make a pasta dinner. Wi-fi is available outside the Office de Tourisme in the town square, and since I'm sheltered, it's the perfect spot to cook dinner while checking the weather online.

Town square in Labastide-d'Armagnac

After dinner, thankfully the heavy rain has disappeared, so I begin searching for a quiet place to camp.

Across the main road is an open rugby ground with the former railway station located further behind. In this part of France, I have seen many rugby union fields rather than football fields, reinforcing what I have heard about this part of France being strong for rugby. Unlike last night, tonight I will camp on the rail trail as it is more hidden than the rugby ground.

Today was a challenging day; I'm hoping tomorrow will be better.

As I pack my tent up in the morning, there is still light rain around, so maybe I should return to Mont-de-Marsan and get a train to Bordeaux if the weather continues to be just like yesterday.

Fortunately by the time I check the weather at the Office de Tourisme, the rain and the clouds have disappeared, so it looks like it will be a better day to continue cycling towards the Canal de Garonne. However, I have to choose between following the rail trail to Gabarret or using the road. Since the trail is still wet and wasn't particularly engaging yesterday, I will go by road to save time as it's shorter.

Just before Gabarret, the rail trail crosses the road again, so I ride the last two kilometres of this trail into town on an average surface to an abandoned cement station. The rail line continued further on but is not a rail trail.

The next 30 kilometres involves a direct undulating road, but it's never gaining any elevation, rather, I'm slowly descending to the Canal de Garonne. I pass through a few towns, with nothing memorable until the town of Vianne, which still has its medieval walls and gates to admire. From the centre of town, I can nearly see all four gates at once.

One of the gates in Vianne

Soon afterwards, green cycling signs appear, and they begin directing me to the Canal de Garonne, where I cross it on a narrow lock. This canal connects Bordeaux and Toulouse and is a well-known cycling route, with signs telling me that Toulouse is 133 kilometres away, while Bordeaux is 168.

Compared to recent rail trails, this flat path beside a surprisingly wide canal is paved the whole way. I was expecting it to be skinny like the canals in England. The various boats are narrow like those in England, so it's easy for them to pass each other.

Signs on the Canal de Garonne

A few touring cyclists pass me in the opposite direction throughout the afternoon, along with day riders. The few going my way are not travelling at the same pace as me, so I only get to briefly chat to a few, including a slower elderly couple on touring bicycles.

Often beside the river are fishermen with long poles and camping set-ups, including chairs, umbrellas, and eskies. Perhaps a fishing competition is on.

I had been expecting the path beside the canal to be a towpath like the UK, but clearly it isn't because there are often rows of tall trees between the water and the path. This is reassuring as other times when there aren't trees, it feels like I could accidentally ride into the water if I daydream too much.

I'm going under numerous bridges which cross this canal, including an abandoned rail bridge. Occasionally, there are a few remnants of former industries which once utilised this canal to transport their produce, including an auger spout to presumably load a boat.

Every so often, there are information panels, but only a welcome message is in English. My French is okay with reading a few words, but these panels have too much writing, so I'm not understanding a lot of what is being said other than from photographs.

Sometimes trees are between the canal and the path, sometimes not

Evidence of former industry on the canal, while narrowboats still use it

The downside of this path is that I'm mainly on the northern side, while nearly all the small towns beside the canal are on the southern side. Usually, a bridge is available, but even so, I have to be selective about when to visit a village. Anyway, with it being Saturday afternoon, I'm unsure what will be open, especially after the only town I deliberately visit is deserted. The larger towns are all beside the curvy River Garonne, which at times is close to the straighter canal, but other times it's well away to the north.

After a relaxing afternoon, late in the day, just off the canal, is the small, probably man-made Fontet Lake. Around this lake are public toilets, drinking water fountains and a car camping area but nothing for tents. So once it's dark enough, I find a spot to camp behind an unoccupied cabin, out of sight, out of mind.

This canal ends well before Bordeaux as boats can navigate the River Garonne downstream from here, and as far as I'm aware, the cycle path runs out too. However, a rail trail starts just over fifteen kilometres north of here, so I will make my way there.

It's quiet crossing the River Garonne on a large cable bridge to the town of La Reole. Not much is open this Sunday morning, but I'm still able to obtain some fresh pastries before starting a slow, gentle climb to meet the rail trail.

On the rail trail

Thankfully, this trail is paved and takes me nearly all the way into Bordeaux. It's popular with many families, along with numerous road cyclists who actually use it. While the canal was flat and became monotonous, there is some variation here as it passes through a green landscape with some nice small railway grade climbs. There is only one tunnel, but there are a few scenic rail cuttings.

However, just like in Spain, the rail route went around towns rather than through them. Thankfully, it appears most of the stations are being reused by the local community, including Creon's station, which is now a busy bicycle hire depot.

In the suburbs of Bordeaux, the trail ends, but I'm soon back at the now wide River Garonne with a cycle path leading me into the eastern side of Bordeaux. The city centre and the main Saint-Jean Railway Station are on the western side, so I make my way there over a long stone bridge with seventeen arches to confirm train times for tomorrow. I'm also aiming to obtain information on Bordeaux as I will be spending Monday exploring this city before taking a train to Paris to watch the tennis on Tuesday.

Through the city are plenty of cycle paths, while many roads which are one way for cars, allow cyclists to go both ways. This can be hazardous sometimes as drivers don't always look both ways because they aren't expecting traffic from the wrong way.

Cycle paths take me along the area beside the river allowing me to admire many scenic buildings. A reflective water pool provides a different view of a square reminding me of one in St Petersburg surrounded by a semicircle of large creamy-yellow scenic buildings.

Reflective pool

In the morning, after a relaxing Warmshower last night, I begin exploring Bordeaux with a free informative walking tour. It's just a shame that the overcast day and the occasional rain shower means it isn't a photographic day. Still, the tour allows us to see a few different styles of castle gates around the old part of the city, with many having different symbols and crests on them. One in particular, with tall purple cone towers, could belong in Disneyland.

We are also given a small sweet called canelé to try. It's a mixture between jelly, custard and pastry, made in a thumb-sized canister shaped like the head of an Allen Key. It's okay to eat, but has too much of an alcoholic taste for my liking.

After the tour, I still have plenty of time before my train, so I begin following the river north for

A gate in Bordeaux

a while before looping back on the other side. It appears that away from the city centre Bordeaux is allowed to look more modern, especially on the eastern side.

The market end

Whereas the city centre is clean, at the other end of a long pedestrian mall which goes for more than a kilometre, it feels dodgier, louder and just busier. The sheer number of people around a tall market gate with a giant skinny monolith in front of it is overwhelming for someone like me who prefers quiet places. It reminds me of how busy Istanbul was. After finding a quiet spot to catch my breath, I end up visiting a barber, who gives me my first shave of this trip.

So far, being back in France after nearly six years has brought back a few memories, in particular, how much cycling is appreciated and thought of. A simple example is a dedicated undercover bicycle parking space next to the shopping trolleys at supermarkets.

Sheltered bicycle parking at a Lidl

In France, there are so many bicycle signs directing me, including routes that are just a quiet road option without any dedicated cycling infrastructure. I'm also seeing regional cycling maps, which I didn't see in Spain.

A downside from leaving Spain is that I'm missing Spanish supermarkets and bakeries as pastry selections in France so far are either plain, chocolate or sugar-based. I'm missing the pizza buns and cheese rolls I was enjoying.

When you tour a country for a while you get to know which supermarkets have the best selections for specific cravings. I particularly enjoy visiting Lidl because they have a sizeable self-service fresh bakery, where I can use my own bread bags to collect what I want from the numerous items on display. So each time I shop, which can be a few times a day, I'm not creating any plastic waste.

A wide selection is available at most bakeries and supermarkets in Spain including at Lidl

I prefer a mixture of cheese or chocolate-based snacks like cheese and chocolate twists, pain au chocolat, apple turnovers and brownies. My favourite is a small focaccia which is covered in pesto and topped with goat cheese and tomato.

Lidl was the only regular franchise of supermarkets I saw in Spain, France and the UK, while I also visited them in Eastern Europe last year. Bakery items changed slightly depending on the country, while French stores often never had fresh milk.

Paris is more than 500 kilometres from Bordeaux, but with a dedicated TGV express railway line to Paris, a non-stop train takes only two hours. It's a busy service with express trains departing every half-hour. If you book ahead as I did, it's a reasonable price, unlike expensive same-day tickets. This is one of only a few TGV lines that allow fully assembled bicycles on board, unlike the TGV route through Lyon.

It's relatively simple to get on this modern, clean train where I find a dedicated bicycle space. There are plenty of spare seats as we travel at 300 kilometres an hour, with a lounge car allowing views of the landscape flying past.

TGV lounge car

Irun to Bordeaux (Google Maps)

Roland-Garros

Since the train arrives in the evening, my priority is making my way to my Warmshower host, Anny's apartment nearby. An elderly lady opens the door. She only speaks French, so Google Translate is helpful. Still, she is kind enough to take me out to experience a crêpes meal.

A tip for attending the French Open tennis at Roland-Garros is to book tickets early, like the hour they come out, as I was an hour late and missed the day I wanted. From what I understand, there are fewer tickets available than at the Australian Open. I also tried going in the raffle for a ticket to Wimbledon, but wasn't successful, and anyway, I will still be in France for most of it.

Also, check you have the correct name on your tickets as I have to show my passport to get in and be body searched on the way in. I wasn't sure about the water situation, so I brought plenty of water and food, but thankfully, drinking fountains are available along with free wi-fi.

It's packed inside, and it appears that the whole Roland-Garros complex is in a much smaller area than the Australian Open, so there is less seating available on outside courts. I presume this is why general tickets sell fast.

However, from a few big video screens, the centre court looks half-empty for Australia's John Millman's match against Alexander Zverev. It looks like that match will be going to five sets, so I try to sneak inside, but with every entrance having two guards, there is no way to get inside to watch. I'm not sure if I can buy tickets today to get inside or how expensive they are, so instead, I will find an outside court.

Australian fans at the tennis

A few Australian fans are here, including a group of middle-aged women dressed up in singlets and cork string hats. We firstly watch Australia's Bernard Tomic not appearing to be trying in his straight-set loss. Later in the day, it's a more enjoyable atmosphere when Matthew Ebden from Australia is playing the Frenchmen Grégoire Barrère, so naturally, most of the crowd is against the Australian. Despite Ebden losing in four sets, he is appreciated by the crowd.

The strangest thing about the day is that when the score is 40-all, the umpire isn't saying *Deuce*, which I always thought was a French word; instead, they say *egalite*, meaning equal.

The Palace of Versailles is closed on Mondays, so in 2013 when I flew into Paris on a Sunday and left on a Tuesday, I didn't have enough time to visit. Since I have a free day in Paris before needing to leave towards Reims, I will take the opportunity to visit. I'm particularly interested in seeing if it's different from a couple of the palaces and gardens I visited last year near St Petersburg, which were modelled on Versailles.

Versailles is in the western suburbs of Paris, about twenty kilometres from Anny's home. So instead of spending an hour or two cycling through the suburbs of Paris having to constantly check for directions, it will be easier to get the direct train. Along with allowing more time to explore Versailles, this will allow me to briefly explore around Paris while making my way to a railway station.

From Anny's home to the River Seine, I'm following hundreds of locals cycling to work, so I'm feeling respected and safe cycling on Paris streets. Cycling east along the southern bank of the Seine towards Gare d'Austerlitz, from a distance the fire damage to blocked off Notre Dame is obvious, with parts of the roof missing. Below me, I can hear trains under the street, while the occasional open gap below the road allows me to see them.

In order to purchase some groceries, I depart a station earlier than the Versailles Station. Unplanned, this has the added bonus of allowing me to cycle the last part to Versailles, rather than suddenly being overwhelmed. Instead, it slowly appears with a brief glimpse before the whole large magnificent palace appears with its large golden gates, allowing me to appreciate it before the tourists start to appear.

Initially, I lock my bicycle outside the main golden gate beside other bikes and walk inside the front gate, where a visitor information centre is off to the side. After waiting my turn in a queue, I'm told most of the gardens are free to visit, while cycling is allowed in some of them. So I return to my bicycle and cycle around to the back of the palace using side roads.

Lines to enter Versailles

Once in the gardens, I can cycle around an enormous man-made canal shaped like a cross; it's so large that it stretches to the horizon. I'm not the only cyclist inside the gardens, and there is even the option of a guided bicycle tour. All this makes me feel comfortable with leaving my bicycle locked in the gardens while exploring areas I'm not allowed to take it.

Cycling around Versailles

Fountains and sculptured gardens in the backyard of Versailles

Initially, having seen the lines out the front of the palace, I thought it would be busy everywhere. While it's reasonably busy in the gardens directly around the palace, once away from there, I'm able to find quieter spots.

Compared to the former royal gardens at Peterhof in Russia, Versailles doesn't have as many spectacular water fountains and garden features. It doesn't help my impression that none of the fountains are on today. I'm told because of the age of the pipes, the water is turned on only on certain days. Still, each fountain has its own style of sculpture, with many having animals like dozens of turtles or horses or a mythological person. Many of the well maintained gardens are set out in labyrinths. There are plenty of hedgerows to walk through, with smaller statues and fountains scattered around.

One of the many fountain

My highlight is a separate garden called Trianon. Inside this tucked-away garden is an old farm site with a few uneven multistorey buildings with thatched-roofs built around 1780. They are all closed but still a delight to see.

Farming buildings in Trianon

When I return to the palace, the line is smaller but it's still about 200 metres long. There isn't a bicycle rack nearby, so I just leave my bicycle locked up to a metal post. Presumably, I will have to line up for a while, but the line moves quickly, so I'm inside within ten minutes. This is a lot quicker than in Russia.

There are two lines, one for individual visitors and one for groups. The individual line takes me to a temporary exhibit where I'm soon confused about which direction I'm supposed to be walking because not long after entering the palace, I find myself back outside in the courtyard. After walking around for a while, I figure out that I should go into the group entrance for it to make more sense, otherwise, I would have missed seeing certain parts of the main palace.

I found Peter the Great's Palace at Peterhof so packed we were shuttled through like sheep in less than an hour. There are times when it's packed here, especially when in narrow rooms or if a tour group is around. At other times, there is plenty of space, particularly when I leave the main route to visit the crusade room, which has numerous joyous paintings of the crusaders in the Middle East centuries ago.

Colourful rooms

Louis XIV was the first royal to live here, while each subsequent king added buildings before the French Revolution changed Versailles's relevance. With many objects sold off, it was left derelict for a while. Today, many rooms have been restored to when royalty lived here with many fancy items on display such

One of many Crusade paintings

as furniture, chandeliers, and curtained beds. Many are still covered in various paintings, symbols and crests, including the ceiling.

So many rooms full of furniture like this, while another has numerous chandeliers

Other rooms have post-French Revolution editions, principally a remarkable long corridor of numerous large paintings depicting different French historical battles over the centuries. The majority focus on Napoleon's battles because all these paintings were added not long after the Napoleonic Wars.

A long corridor with numerous paintings of French battles, particularly Napoleon

It took me nearly three hours to get through the palace, and I was at Versailles for almost seven, so if planning to come, you need a full day. I would recommend a visit because there is so much detail in each room, while the gardens are enjoyable to walk around. It wasn't until I left that I realised there was no mention of the treaty of Versailles, which ended the First World War.

With it now late in the afternoon, I will return to Paris by train as I hope to be well east of Paris tonight. As this train gradually fills up closer to Paris, I probably should have departed earlier due to now just being in the peak hour times when bicycles aren't supposed to be on the train. Anyway, I'm off near the Eiffel Tower.

Having been up this French landmark in 2013, today I just briefly see it again from the road. The main difference now is a transparent security glass wall separating the base of the tower from the road. There are still plenty of street vendors selling tourist junk, including miniature Eiffel Towers.

It's now late in the day, so I won't spend much time in Paris. As I make my way to Gare de l'est, I'm cycling along the northern side of the Seine through a few landmarks I recalled from 2013, including the glass pyramid above the Louvre.

A suburban train takes me east out of Paris, and because it's after 6 pm, the train is half empty, with the main passengers being teenagers, some of whom are smoking. I'm departing at Triliport because nearby, there appears to be a couple of wild camping options, including an open space beside the River Marne.

Camping by the River Marne

Once off the train, a path beside the River Marne takes me under the railway line and into a green cropped paddock. There is enough space to set my tent up on the riverbank, while across the water are some fishermen.

Le front occidental

After a relaxing night, as I unzip my tent, it's looking like it will be a cold overcast day with rain threatening. Thankfully, a decent bakery in Trilport with some delicious pizza buns encourages me to start cycling.

Today I'm planning to follow the River Marne and a railway line east, but initially, I will have to do a short climb on a busy road. It's a relaxing two-lane road as I climb pass a forest on the north side of the road where a few people are out exercising. It's a quick descent to the next town, where I cross the river and begin following a quieter route.

Near the town of La-Ferte-Sous-Jouarre, as I again cross the river to continue my journey, I suddenly need to go to the toilet, so I make my way to McDonald's. Since the sun still hasn't come out yet and I only need to do a short day today, I will stay here for a bit to do some planning. With the FIFA Women's World Cup starting in about ten days, I have some planning to do on my route after Reims. I also book some trains in the UK, as the sooner you book, the cheaper the tickets.

Today is the opening match of the Men's Cricket World Cup, so throughout the day, whenever I find wi-fi, I'm checking the score between England and South Africa while occasionally catching some radio commentary.

If the FIFA Women's World Cup was not on simultaneously, I would be now in the UK for the cricket. Despite the Cricket World Cup only having ten teams competing, it goes longer than the 24 nations FIFA World Cup. With the cricket finals on after the football finishes, I will be in England when they are on. However, I don't have any tickets for the cricket due to the small English grounds which sell out fast. Anyway, I would prefer to attend Ashes test matches, which I do have tickets for.

While visiting a nearby supermarket for lunch supplies, I'm hurriedly told to leave because today is a religious public holiday and they are closing at 1 pm. For the rest of the day, other than some shops being closed and seeing children out of school, I wouldn't have known it was a public holiday.

For the rest of the day, I'm passing through small towns where often I'm leaving one while being able to see the next, and sometimes there is no gap at all between towns. I'm clearly in a river valley because away from the Marne, small hills are visible all day, while whenever I drift away from the river, there is some minor climbing.

By the time I arrive in Chateau-Thierry, the largest town of the day, it's late in the afternoon, but there is still enough time to explore a castle on a hill behind the main square. It's free to visit with many stairs to climb to a garden at the base of a castle wall. To go higher, I have to duck inside a tower to get to the inside of a well maintained outer wall.

The front side of Chateau-Thierry Castle

A ten-minute video in a visitor centre shows how the castle developed over the centuries, while informative panels are scattered around this large site. Further around are more, mostly intact layers of castle walls to admire, along with a moat surrounded by stick fences. Through gaps in a fence, I can hear children laughing and playing in the inner part of the castle. A few children's activities are on, with staff dressed up in medieval attire, while there is also a raptor show. Since it's not designed for me, I begin making my way back down to my bicycle while admiring the high view this castle provides of Chateau-Thierry.

A few American flags are on display around town, including at the Office de Tourisme because during the last German advance of the First World War in 1918, the Americans helped stop the Germans from advancing past Chateau-Thierry and onto Paris. They would retake this town seven weeks later, so America's sacrifice is remembered here. Soon I will be crossing where the front line was for most of the war.

I wish I had arrived earlier into Chateau-Thierry to have a more extended look, but I need to push on to get to Dormans before the supermarket there closes at 7 pm. I'm heading there because on Maps.me, there appears to be a few options to stealth camp beside the river.

Thankfully, it's flat as I race along for the next 24 kilometres, following the river on quiet roads. I have comfortably made it in time to visit the supermarket in this nice-sized town with most of the village on one side of the river. The other side is quieter with the local sports ground, a public park with picnic tables and a caravan park. The caravan park's free wi-fi is accessible from the picnic tables, so it's a perfect spot to cook dinner while listening to highlights of England's comfortable win over South Africa in the cricket.

Throughout the day, I didn't see many trains despite mostly being near a railway line, but since being in Dormans, I'm seeing a lot of trains passing by on the opposite side of the river directly in front of the layers of the town. It's a mixture of passenger and freight trains carrying numerous automobiles.

The caravan park is busy with families, and a number of lights come on at night, so the more sensible decision is to follow a paved cycle path beside the river to search for a quiet, dark place to wild camp. It doesn't take me long before a spot among trees will do for the night.

Opposite Dormans is a nice park, while I camped nearby among trees

In the morning, while waiting for the supermarket to open, I take the opportunity to visit a nearby small chateau with gardens. Behind the chateau is a large cream First World War memorial building with a few small cone towers. Surrounding this building is a memorial garden with a couple of remembrance symbols made out of bunches of flowers.

First World War memorial at Dormans

There is also a noticeboard with a map showing where the front moved in this region. In 2013 I saw many Australian Western Front sites further northwest in France and also in Belgium. Since Australian forces were not involved in this region, I don't know much about what happened here. So I wonder what I will see.

Once back across the river, I join the paved cycle path which follows the river past where I camped last night. It's a pleasure to cycle as I pass through a couple of small towns with the cycle path usually always beside the river. Navigation is easy with the green cycling signs found all over France. The river has been straightened in places and has a few locks along the way, so it feels more like a canal. Eventually, a canal comes off the river and takes a more direct route than the windier River Marne.

I could leave the canal near the town of Epernay and take a direct hilly route to tonight's final destination, Reims. However, since I still have enough spare time this afternoon, I will continue cycling east on this canal before going around the hill. I'm now passing former industrial sites, including silos, so presumably, it was once a busy freight route.

In Conde-sue-Marne, another canal branches off here to the north, which will connect me with another canal that will take me into Reims. It isn't a signed

Industry on the canal

bicycle route; however, Maps.me suggests that a path follows this canal. Since it's a paved trail as I begin heading north, presumably, I will get through, even if there are 'no trespassing' signs.

Unfortunately, the path soon becomes gravel and then grass, so it makes more sense to return to road cycling as soon as a road crosses the canal.

I'm now on the side of a hill, negotiating a few undulating dogleg roads while passing numerous wineries. As I briefly stop in at a First World War cemetery full of white crosses, visible in the distance on a flatter route to the north of me, is a busy freeway and an equally busy TGV train route.

While cycling through Champagne region, I pass the first of many WW1 cemeteries

Thankfully after finding a way over both the TGV line and the freeway, the final section into Reims is on another canal path, making it an easy ride to the city. As I approach the city centre, the canal path is on the wrong side, and while many bridges are crossing high over it, they don't have a connecting path to the canal. So while I can see across the water to where I want to go, I can't get across. I'm soon past where I wanted to turn off, and still, there is no way off this canal.

Eventually, some stairs appear to a road above, and as I slow down, I spot a lift next to them.

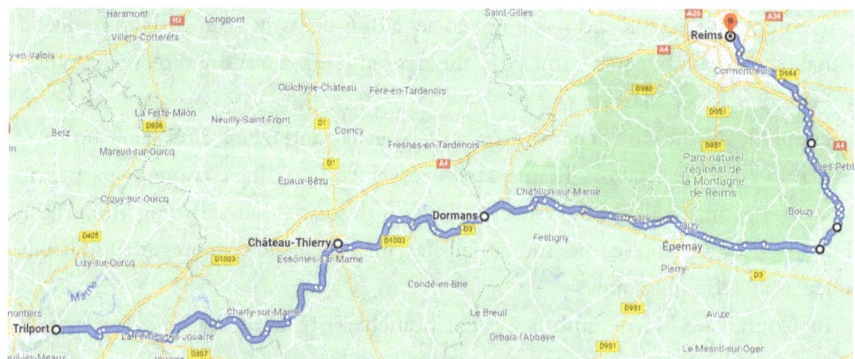
Triliport to Reims (Google Maps)

A sizeable Gothic Cathedral dominates the town centre, with a busy Office de Tourisme nearby. It's bustling because the annual Joan of Arc festival is this weekend which I have timed my arrival to attend.

This gold-tinged cathedral has numerous human statues on the outside, large archway entrances, some large round windows and a couple of tall towers. It's free to look inside.

Numerous statues on the cathedral

It's a different style from Spanish churches with fewer religious statues and artwork inside. Instead, it's plain, except for the many colourful glass religious windows. I'm told they are only a 21stcentury addition, having been added for the 800th anniversary of the cathedral in 2011.

Dinner with Laurence, Dominique & friends

After cycling back over the canal and out into the suburbs, I meet first-time Warmshower hosts Laurence and Dominique. They are friendly, as they share meals with me, including a cheeseboard with a wide variety of cheeses and a delicious rhubarb pie. In the evening, they offer to drive me around to show me highlights of the city and for us to watch a light display on the cathedral. For fifteen incredible minutes, various symbols and colours are projected on different features of the cathedral to a large observant crowd.

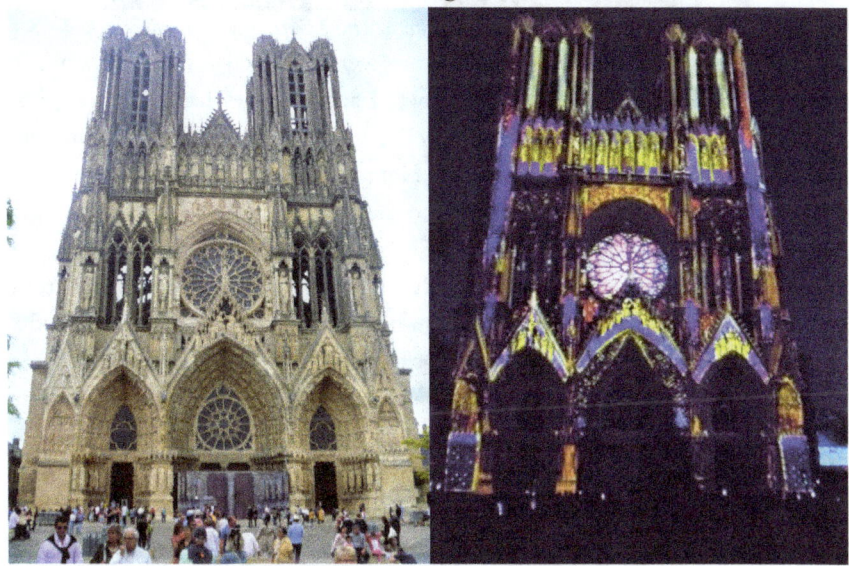
Reims Cathedral had a light show projected on it

A lot of cities have a tourist card you can purchase, which allows access to specific sites. Often it ends up forcing me to visit certain places while ignoring others not on the list, so I always try to work out if it's worth it. Reims has a card, but it will be a similar price for the few museums I want to visit to not purchase it, especially as the card only lasts 24 hours.

I enjoyed visiting the Museum of the Surrender, where in an unremarkable room in a nondescript red-bricked building, Germans signed their surrender to end the Second World War in Europe. It's fascinating to see a place that ended so much suffering. There is plenty of information and a few items on the whole war, including a room with Second World War maps covering all the walls. Nearby, a local market is on, selling a range of things, including a delicious baked pastry pork pie, along with plenty of fruit.

A room full of WW2 maps, in a building where Germany surrendered

Reims was the place where French kings were crowned for centuries in the cathedral, so that is the focus for the town. Each year they have a Joan of Arc festival because she helped get Charles VII crowned here. Yesterday around the cathedral was an open space, however as I return in the morning, high temporary fences are blocking off most entrances to the area around the cathedral. To get inside requires going through security to enter a now busy square.

The Palace of Tau behind the cathedral is engaging, with a few relics from the cathedral on display, including a room full of remains of stone statues and a tapestry showing various battles and kings being crowned. No idea why but there is a room with a display on a 19th century Romanian Queen, who doesn't appear to have a connection with Reims.

I wasn't sure what to expect from the Joan of Arc festival as I have been given mixed reviews from a few Warmshower hosts around Reims. Around the cathedral, numerous people are dressed up in medieval or fantasy attire, with many performing or operating various medieval games, which the crowd can participate in. Weapons, suits of armour, food, bags and other items are on display, along with a range of souvenirs.

However, with so many people, it's hard to walk around. While there are some reasonable performances, overall, it isn't that interesting, especially because I'm not learning any historical information, which I had hoped to.

Plenty of people are dressed up

Busy Joan of Arc festival

With the next day being the first Sunday of June, many museums are free to visit, so I saved money not purchasing the Reims City Pass. After retracing my route out of Reims on the canal, a track through farm paddocks leads me to the back of Fort de la Pompelle. However, the entrance is only accessible from the two-lane freeway in front of me. I should cross the freeway, cycle a hundred metres and then cross the freeway again, but instead, with a wide road shoulder, it will be quicker and probably safer to cycle against the traffic for 100 metres.

Fort de la Pompelle was a decommissioned fort that just happened to be near the front line during the First World War, so it was used in the war effort. The nearby canals were also used by the French Navy, with large naval guns firing on the Germans.

Most of the fort is in ruin, so there are only a few sections to walk around outside, but there is a decent museum inside a preserved part. Numerous war artefacts are on display, including an extensive collection of German helmets, each with different styles and symbols. Most have a distinctive point at the top of the helmet, with some having long hair attached to the end of the point. There are also artillery guns and plenty of other smaller items on display.

Of course, there is plenty of written information about the First World War. My biggest takeaway is that groups of Russians were sent around the world to fight here, which was impressive in itself as they had to use the Tran-Siberian railway to take them to the Pacific before ships took them halfway around the world. This explains why there is a Russian flag beside a memorial outside.

Most of Fort de la Pompelle is a ruin

Plenty of war equipment is on display, including numerous German helmets

After a short section on the freeway, I will be on quiet roads for the rest of the day. I'm now passing through towns which were near the western front line for most of the war because after the French pushed the Germans back in 1914, the line barely moved from here until mid-1918, hence why I'm passing numerous war cemeteries with the number of dead hard to imagine; one small cemetery has 20,000 graves.

Stones marking where the Germans got to in 1918

The Marne 14-18 museum at Suippes also has free entry on this first Sunday of the month. It starts with a video focusing on letters between four siblings during the war, adding a personal touch, especially when one dies. However, this video ends before the war did, so I don't know what happened to the rest of the family. The rest of the museum shows how the front line moved occasionally and tells stories of the impact on everyone from both sides to civilians in the area.

Out the front of the museum is a stone marker, one of many located where the Germans got to during their big push in 1918. It looks like a man crouching with his helmet on top of a decorated pyramid.

Most of the front line followed ridgelines, so to access them requires some small climbs, including near the end of the day, where on the edge of the town of Massiges, I make my way up a hill to a site that still has First World War trenches.

I'm able to walk around this site seeing numerous aspects of trench life, with plenty of barbed wire, wooden posts, sheets of tin, sandbags and a few underground shelters. Shockingly, signs are saying that bodies are still being found here, including some only in the last decade. Because we are so high up, this view allows me to see where the main front was, not far away in the middle of paddocks. Nearby are remains of a small tramway used to transport supplies, while there is also a display of wooden barrels explaining how vital water was during the war.

Trenches at Massiges

I have been struggling since leaving Paris with finding water fountains, as they are not so obvious to find as in Spain. Fortunately in the town of Vienne Le Chateau, there is a cold one beside a small park, so it's a perfect spot to cook dinner before camping on the edge of the football pitch behind pine trees.

However, the next day, it's a struggle to find water again, so I have to buy some. Earlier in the day, a bus driver directed me to a water fountain around the back of a building to a park, so maybe I'm just missing them. There have also been fewer public recycling bins; instead, I have been forced to sneakily use private bins.

Some days I just feel rushed and today was like that. Initially, I felt okay while finding some interesting First World War remains and memorials in pine forests. Most of the infrastructure is still here more than 100 years later. Some sites are being looked after, while others have been left to slowly be reclaimed by nature.

A few fenced-off tunnels are still here, which were dug to allow explosives to be placed under the enemies location. The effect of this is the most striking sight, with a still deep cone-shaped crater now covered in vegetation.

Trench and mine crater remains are slowly being reclaimed by nature

Bunker remains

Another site has a couple levels of roads on a hillside with numerous small bunkers to look inside, between, above and below these roads, along with the remains of a tramway.

I'm in Verdun before 1 pm, but I make the mistake of visiting the citadel tourist attraction, which involves a half an hour automated train ride with videos and displays showing how the citadel was used during the war. This modest ride just took too long to wait for it to start, so I don't have much time to spend in Verdun because I want to get up a hill to visit more First World War sites.

The Office de Tourisme isn't informative on what to see around town, so I'm ready to leave after briefly visiting the scenic river and a stair-based war memorial. It's a busy main road leaving town before a quieter climb begins. It takes a while to get up, so much so, I'm not entirely up until 4 pm.

Halfway up are a few small memorials among a few grass-covered bunkers, while a noticeboard informs me about cycle routes that connect the various cemeteries around here. Eventually, I'm at the top of the hill at the sizeable main cemetery with a large pointy memorial surrounded by thousands of white crosses. There are a few museums around here, but I won't visit them as I'm feeling war fatigued and still rushed.

In the evening, as I arrive in Longuyun, I'm now close to Luxembourg. It's too late in the day to visit the Office de Tourisme located in a rail car. However, I do catch a lucky break with a power-point and free wi-fi, both available in the town square, allowing me to do some planning while cooking dinner. After looking around for a while, the best place to wild camp is a spot among trees behind the fenced-off football stadium on the edge of town.

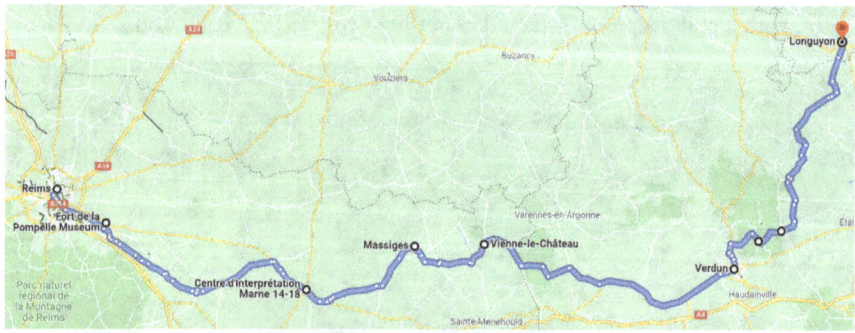
Reims to Longuyun (Google Maps)

Lëtzebuerg

I don't know much about Luxembourg, so I'm entering this Tuesday with an open mind. Initially, getting there involves negotiating busy suburbia in a river valley, with barely a mention of a border crossing and only a few service stations show the border. Otherwise, the built-up area continues uninterrupted into Petange.

Fortunately, a rail trail heads north and is well signed with information on how far the next few towns are. This signed bicycle route takes a longer meandering route to Luxembourg City, so I soon leave for a shortcut on quiet roads through small villages. As I re-join the bicycle route, a paved path takes me past dairy farms, and eventually, green bicycle signs direct me all the way into Luxembourg City by 1:30 pm.

Bicycle signs

After finding some water in a dedicated blue drinking fountain in the middle of this semi-busy city, I make my way to an open square where organised children's games are on. Also here is the tourist information centre, with the staff speaking perfect English, one of them sounding Irish by his accent, but apparently, he is a local. I'm soon informed of a two-hour guided walk for €14 starting at 2 pm. This is perfect for the time I have available to look around.

With only a handful of people on this tour, it's a friendly size group to learn about this city. The initial focus is on the recently deceased Grand Duke Jean of Luxembourg, who died this year aged 98. Around the square are photos of his life, including his time in the army during the Second World War as he played a part in removing the German occupiers in 1944. He abdicated nearly twenty years ago but was still clearly respected and admired by the locals. Outside the small royal creamy-yellow palace, they have a changing of the guard just like at Buckingham Palace.

Near the palace, is a display on the life of the recently departed Grand Duke

The highlight for me is that Luxembourg City is high above the curvy River Alzette, so this provides some decent views of a deep valley below. We are taken onto a bridge in the inner curve of one horseshoe part of the Alzette, where fortress remains are right next to the bridge. Our guide explains that part of this fortress was built in the rock outcrop directly below us, creating a few tunnels.

As we walk off the side of the bridge and onto a part of the fortress, more remains are visible, while below are some well-kept gardens, including what looks like veggie patches among more fortress remains. Distracting me in the distance is a busy stone rail viaduct that crosses high over this horseshoe valley.

Below the fortress remains are vegetable gardens

Tunnel underneath the fortress

After the tour, I return to the fortress to explore the tunnels. There are a few passages to walk through in low light leading to a few different levels, so it feels like a maze. The occasional open side gaps in the rock allow differing views of both sides of the valley below.

I could spend longer exploring the city, but I need to keep going if I want to get back into France in time for the first match of the Women's World Cup in a few days. Once I make my way down to the river, I begin following it by initially using busy cycle paths, but other times, I'm on the main road.

Strangely the main supermarket in Luxembourg is called Cactus, with its logo a green cactus. The food appears to be more expensive than in France; so was any accommodation I found online. Instead, I have managed to find a cricket ground located four kilometres north of the city. A few men of subcontinental origin are batting in the cricket nets, while on a field across from the oval, rugby training is on. I can't hear any English being spoken as I cook dinner, so presumably, locals are playing traditional English sports.

Once everyone leaves and dusk begins, I'm about to assemble my tent when a thunderstorm suddenly develops.

Luckily next to the rugby clubhouse is a former green army box trailer, which I can open. It's large enough for me to set up my tent inside. It's a little humid inside and slightly dirty, but my tent, bicycle, and I should all stay dry. I'm also out of sight and I don't have to worry about street lights keeping me awake.

I slept inside an army box trailer

Fortunately, the storm never arrived, but still, it was a quiet out of sight place to sleep.

While still overcast in the morning, it's easy cycling north on perfect surface cycle paths beside the busy railway line or the River Alzette. Along the way is some thoughtful artwork of people with disabilities, and some self-service bicycle tube vending machines, which is a brilliant idea. Helpfully every so often is a decent bicycle map of Luxembourg, so it's easy to navigate, but it's enticing me to spend longer here than I can.

Self-service bike tubes

Late in the morning, the cement path beside the railway line is undulating at times, but without traffic to worry about, it's a relaxing ride as the sun appears.

Ettelbruck, along with the rest of Luxembourg, was occupied by the Germans during the Second World War until September 1944. This freedom didn't last long as the northern part of Luxembourg, including Ettelbruck, was re-occupied at the end of 1944, during the Battle of the Bulge. A museum focuses on this, named after General George Patton, who led the Allied retaking of northern Luxembourg. Inside are rooms full of items from the war, mainly weapons, while there is information on the various battles.

After the stories of the horrors of war, as I fill my water bottles at a fountain in the centre of town, the Lion King song *Can You Feel the Love Tonight* is loudly being played, which lifts my mood as I leave Ettelbruck past the Patton statue of him holding binoculars.

The cycle paths have run out from here, so I'm back on the road, which initially continues following a river. I'm assuming this road will be busy, but thankfully, it's quiet as the houses disappear, allowing a relaxing, sunny forested gorge ride.

Eventually, I have to leave the river behind because while the railway line goes through tunnels, I have to do some

Quiet afternoon cycling

climbing. Once over the climb, a scenic zigzag returns me down to the railway line and a different smaller river. At times, a cycle path follows the Wiltz River before a road takes me into the town of Wiltz, where the railway line now terminates.

After Wiltz, a rail trail begins. It's a relaxing climb with four tunnels and I only realise I'm in Belgium when the trail surface changes from bitumen to cement. Along the trail is a sign saying this is a way of peace from Paris to Moscow via Bastogne.

Rail trail leaving Luxembourg

Longuyun to Bastonge (Google Maps)

Belgique

As I approach Bastogne from the east, another rail trail comes in on my right from the north-east. Since no trains go through Bastogne anymore, as the trails merge, I'm able to ride right through town. I'm not sure if it continues southwest of Bastogne as I have conflicting information from maps.

Once the trail ends at the well looked after former double-storey Bastogne South Station, it's clear by the fenced-off grass-covered former rail formation in front of me, that the rail trail hasn't been developed further.

Once again, I'm having trouble finding indoor accommodation, so I will stay at my first official campground of this trip. While it is only €10, there are no facilities for campers like picnic tables or a camp kitchen, which you get in Australia. There is just grass for my tent and a couple of bathrooms with showers and washing machines, surrounded by permanent caravan park homes. It does have wi-fi, so I can listen to the radio coverage of the Cricket World Cup. The nearby supermarkets are closing at 7 pm so once I realise this, I race to get there in time.

I take the opportunity to do some laundry, so of course, at 9 pm, suddenly heavy thunderstorms begin. I seek shelter in a bathroom as there is nowhere else except my tent. Since I'm the only camper, I will leave my bicycle, bags and wet laundry inside the bathroom all night while I return to my tent and try to sleep as the thunder and rain continues.

I have heard of Bastogne from the Band of Brothers mini-series as my favourite episode, the one with the medic focus, was here. So when I realised I could visit I took the chance.

In December 1944, when the Germans looked defeated, they surprised everyone by attacking in this region, creating the Battle of the Bulge as they retook areas freed the previous September. The town of Bastogne was surrounded for a week, while it took a month for the Germans to be totally forced back.

Thankfully, there is no rain in the morning, but it's still overcast as I make my way back through town on the rail trail. On the edge of town beside the trail is a memorial to nurses who played a vital role during the siege of Bastogne.

Nurse war memorial

Main American war memorial

The prominent American memorial is located on the edge of town in the V between two rail trails, one of which I arrived in on yesterday. On this sizeable star-shaped cement memorial with an inner circle, along with the names of various military companies, each American state is written, while nearby is the main museum.

It's just as large and takes me two and a half hours to get through as I spend time with an automated audio guide with four points of view from the following: a German soldier, an American soldier, a 13-year-old boy and a 25-year-old female teacher. The only issue is that if I move too quickly, the audio guide changes to another recording, so I have to restart individual stories all over again.

Along with a mixture of traditional photos and information boards, spread throughout the museum are four sound and light shows which each go for about twenty minutes. Each is based at a different location during the battle, including one where we are in a foxhole in the forest, reminding me of the Band of Brothers.

Sound and light show in a café

The final sound and light show is in a café in the middle of Bastogne during a bombing raid where we learn that all four people who have been guiding us by audio guide ended up sheltering together and all survived the war. The 13-year-old boy is still alive, and he lives in Bastogne, but sadly, his parents died during the battle, with his dad executed by Germans. After the war, he developed a bicycle race in the region.

There is a brochure for a cycling route around some battlefields at the museum entrance, so I will follow this instead of returning to Bastogne. It's still an overcast day, but it's a quiet route on narrow roads through farmland.

The first site is Bois de la Paix which is a large cleared circle surrounded by pine trees. It's a peace park with a few sites dedicated to infamous worldwide massacres. A few obvious ones like the Holocaust and Rwanda are here but so are ones

Peace park

I didn't know about, like the Boves massacre, where in 1943, as the Italians surrendered, the SS murdered civilians in the town of Boves. Each site has a few planted trees and an information board explaining the massacre. It's eerily quiet with no one else around as the only noise is from a few birds tweeting away.

Besides my large scale paper map, this cycle route isn't well signed, so I'm soon lost after taking a wrong turn.

Once I figure out where I am, I'm further away from Bastogne, but this does allow me to cycle on the other leg of the rail trail back towards town through a pine forest. Along the way, beside the trail is a memorial to the 101st Airborne Division Easy Company. This company was the focus of the Band of Brothers mini-series, so I'm recognising some names who made the ultimate sacrifice.

Easy Company memorial

I'm now near where the front line was, so I will leave the rail trail to explore. It doesn't take me long before I'm coming across actual battle sites. There are a few memorials here, while some foxholes are still visible under tall skinny pine trees. Left among these fox holes are numerous mini American flags and wooden religious crosses.

Crosses near Fox holes

Among the forest are shallow remains of fox holes

After visiting a German cemetery near the small town of Foy, I have finished seeing all the war sites on the map. However, I'm now well north of Bastogne, and since it's after lunchtime, I need to keep going. I have missed exploring Bastogne, but from what I saw, it didn't look that attractive. I did miss another museum on the Battle of the Bulge, which looked interesting, but it may just be a repetition of what I have already learned.

I have found a route with rail trails that will hopefully allow me to cycle back into France in time to arrive in Valenciennes by Saturday evening. However, getting to the cycle route requires passing through numerous small towns, which on this overcast day involves multiple small up and down climbs, so it isn't much fun of an afternoon, but it's better conditions than the snow in Christmas 1944.

Suddenly around 5 pm, after a long descent, I'm into the industrial town of Jemelle as the sun makes an appearance. From here, a rail trail branches off an active rail line. I'm aiming to stop beside this trail once I find a nice place to camp.

With the sun out, I'm enjoying the trail so much I end up cycling all the way to the end, twenty kilometres away at Houyet, where an active railway station is unoccupied but has brochures and maps inside. There appears to be some interesting sites in this region, but I don't have enough time to have a proper look around.

In the evening, I travel back on the rail trail until a grassy spot beside a bridge is suitable for setting up my tent in the dark.

Camping and cycling on this short rail trail

Bastonge to Houyet (Google Maps)

From Houyet, I can't find a sensible cycling route, so instead, if I catch a train north for fifteen minutes to Dinant, I can join a canal and cycle west from there. The ticket is cheap using a ticket machine.

As the train crosses the canal on this sunny day, the conductor tells me I need a bicycle ticket. Since I didn't know I needed one, he lets me off with a warning. I soon learn that a bicycle ticket would have cost more than the train ticket. However, that bicycle ticket covers every rail trip you do in a day, no matter how far you travel all over Belgium, or how often you change trains.

The canal is actually the wide River Meuse located in a scenic valley, while a large castle is prominently on the other side of the river on a high rocky outcrop. As I cross the river, there are a few large decorated saxophones and various countries' flags on the bridge because an annual jazz festival is held here. Beside the river, a farmers market is on, with some delicious mini baked potatoes and some fruit available.

Unlike in Russia during the men's FIFA World Cup, I can print this year's World Cup tickets myself, while I don't need a Fan ID to enter a stadium. So before leaving town, I make my way to a library to print my tickets for Australia's first three matches.

Jazz festival in Dinant

A signed cycle route follows the Meuse for a while as I pass some tall rock formations. Along the way, a sign informs me that Dinant is the furthest point west the Battle of the Bulge got to.

Dinant

After crossing back on the other side of the Meuse using narrow paths across a lock, I continue following the river using a road. I'm soon beside a closed railway line with rails still here as I pass a closed cement station. Soon I'm at a former rail junction with one undeveloped railway branch heading south back into France beside the Meuse while the other heads west as a rail trail. I'm aiming to head west, so I will take the developed rail trail as it slowly drifts away from the French border. I'm soon coming across evidence of the storm two nights ago with trees fallen across the trail, so I help a group of elderly cyclists clear some branches away.

Storm damage on the rail trail

On the edge of the town of Mariembourg, this rail trail finishes as I find another recently closed railway line coming from the south. A railway museum is also here, but it's closed today, while an active passenger railway heads north.

There is a dotted line on Maps.me, showing where a former rail line went west of here that eventually connects with more pink coloured rail trails. I'm assuming I can cycle on this dotted line route as I have been elsewhere. It appears to start behind a supermarket on the edge of town, however, it's overgrown with vegetation, so it's not able to be cycled. I will just have to use back roads for now.

As light rain begins, using wi-fi outside a car yard, I have found an Airbnb apartment in Hautmont in France, 60 kilometres away. This will allow me to watch the opening match of the World Cup starting tonight. As I begin to leave town, the rain becomes heavy and looks like continuing for a while.

What's the point of cycling in the rain when I can catch a train. So I purchase a bicycle ticket this time, but of course, no one asks if I have it. This modern train north to Charleio is full of school children and the rain eases as we travel further north. I have to change trains in Charleio, and the second train is much older and uglier. When the train terminates at the border town of Erquelinnes, the railway station is in terrible condition, presumably abandoned. The rails continue into France, but most passenger trains don't cross into France here.

In the end, taking a couple of trains took just as long as it may have been if I cycled directly to France, but I had no idea how long the rain was going to last. Having a few set destinations to get to on this trip means I sometimes need to use a train instead of just waiting out the rain. However, there are plenty of times when I have no choice but to cycle in the rain.

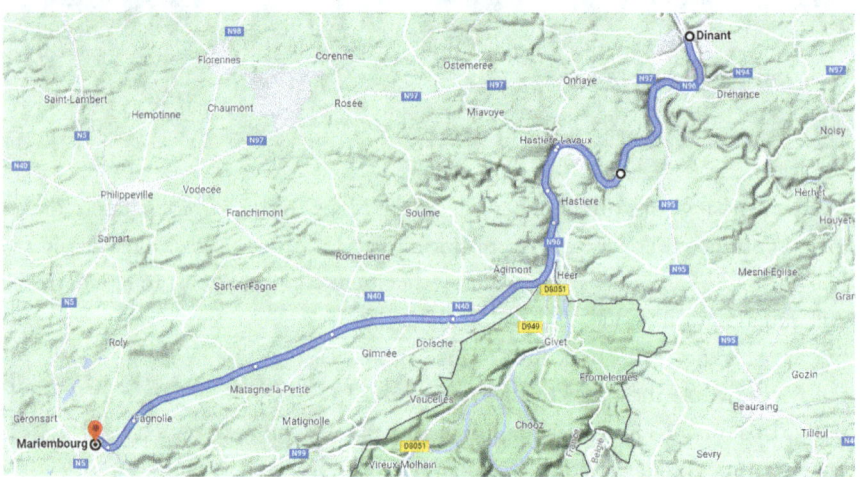

Dinant to Mariembourg (Google Maps)

Coupe du monde

It's a simple ride into France before I find a path beside a canal that will take me to Hautmont, a suburb on the other side of the city of Maubeuge. As the sun is now out, other than having to occasionally cross to the other side of the canal, it's a relaxing late afternoon ride, where I'm passing under a few bridges while avoiding continuous built-up suburbia.

I'm sharing my Airbnb apartment with a man from Strasbourg who is also going cycling soon, but currently has a car. He soon leaves the apartment to go for what I thought was an errand, but I never see him again. I'm happy with having the apartment to myself as this allows me to watch the opening match of the FIFA Women's World Cup on television as France comfortably beats South Korea 4-nil.

After visiting some food street markets and briefly exploring the remains of the grass-covered dirt mound castle in Maubeuge, I begin using secondary roads to make my way to Valenciennes. Initially, it's fine with a few doglegs required to avoid the main roads, however, it's becoming more overcast, and eventually, a few passing showers appear. As I join a cycle path on the edge of Valenciennes, the heaviest storm of the day appears. So I'm soaked as I arrive at my Warmshowers host home, just after lunchtime.

Julien had initially planned for us to visit the city of Lille by car, but he has hurt his back, so instead, we play a few board games and just chat as he speaks English well. It's nice to just relax for the rest of the afternoon, especially as I have a few busy days coming up. I'm so distracted that I miss seeing Australia's Ash Barty win the French Open women's singles title.

Australia's first World Cup match is at 1 pm, so I don't really have any time to explore Valenciennes beforehand. Not far away from Julien's home is a tram line, so I will leave my bicycle in his storage shed. After a couple of stops, it's a short walk to the stadium. Along the way, at a few pubs and cafés, are numerous Australians dressed in a range of yellow football shirts, along with just as many Italians dressed in blue, while I soon recognise a few Australian journalists.

It's a modern stadium, so I will go for a walk around it since I'm early. This being France, there is a couple of long dedicated bicycle parking shelter sheds around the stadium. Each has some artwork on the wall behind the bicycle racks, including some local landmarks and a few different Valenciennes Football Club crests over the years.

Bicycle parking is part of this stadium

From last year's men's World Cup experience, I know that FIFA has some strict rules about what you can take inside stadiums, including banning all food and liquids, while the weirdest thing they do is take the lid off bottles they are selling inside.

This year signs are saying no bottles allowed, but I'm soon relieved to learn I can take food inside so I don't have to scoff down all my food, but I do take on as much water as I can. There are also signs inside saying no smoking, but security isn't enforcing this as they are more focused on stopping water from getting inside.

Australia's national women's football team is nicknamed the Matildas from the song *Waltzing Matilda,* and we are one of the top six seeded teams at this tournament. However, we are not playing like it against the lesser ranked Italians. Fortunately, the video assistant referee saves us a couple of times with the Italians caught just offside after putting the ball in the net. Halfway through the first half, we are awarded a penalty which Sam Kerr misses but scores on the rebound.

Australia versus Italy

We are lucky to be 1-nil up at half-time, and this doesn't last long as Italy scores early in the second half, so it's now a nervy situation. As the 90 minutes are up, we are holding on at 1-1, but there are five minutes of injury time to go, and the Italians are still creating chances.

So when they score a scrappy defended goal just before the final whistle, it feels like a fair result, as the Matildas played terribly.

Since it's only 3 pm, I will visit the city centre by using a tram full of sombre Australians. Still, it's nice to chat to a few people from home and learn about how other people are travelling around France, with many catching a train back to Paris tonight.

As I walk around the city, there are numerous mini flags of each nation playing a match in Valenciennes.

The main city square just off from a tram stop has been overtaken by a FIFA Fan Fest zone which is smaller than what was in Russia and has less security. It's set up for children to play a few games, rather than having large screens or selling sponsored food as it was in Russia.

Surrounding this square are a few restaurants with outdoor seating showing the other two World Cup games today, including the other match in our group as Brazil comfortably beats Jamaica 3-nil. So most of my afternoon is spent chatting to fellow World Cup tourists while watching the football on a giant television. Strangely two men dressed in Wellington Phoenix A-league shirts are here, despite New Zealand playing in other cities. Apart from the result against Italy, I enjoyed being back among Australians.

During half-time between a game, I search for an Office de Tourisme to learn what there is to see tomorrow in this city. I can only find a small one and the staff aren't particularly helpful as they don't have many suggestions on things to see in Valenciennes, especially as tomorrow is Monday when most things are closed.

Being Sunday, the last tram of the night isn't that late and it's still daylight as I make my way to a tram stop. Also waiting here is an Australian man of similar age to me wearing a Catley number 7 Matilda's shirt. So we chat about how disappointing the Matildas were, while hoping for an improved performance against Brazil.

Australia's next match is in Montpellier in the south of France in a few days, so that is way too far to cycle. The easiest way to get there with a bicycle is to catch an overnight train from Paris to Toulouse and then another to Mazamet. From there, I will cycle mostly on a rail trail to Montpellier in time for the Matilda's second match on Thursday. Since the train is leaving Paris after 10 pm, I haven't booked my train from Valenciennes until late in the afternoon, which means I have all Monday to explore.

It's reasonably easy cycling into the city centre from Julien's home, especially as a cycle path is beside the tram tracks. In the city, I can cycle around a long public garden with a cement path in the middle, which presumably was where the old city walls were. Beside a pond in a park, the same man I saw at the tram stop last night is here, so we briefly chat again.

Remains of the wall around the city

It doesn't take long to cycle around Valenciennes as it's such a small city, with not much to see. If it wasn't expensive to change my TGV time, I would leave earlier, which would allow more time in Paris.

Erquelinnes to Valenciennes (Google Maps)

Miracle à Montpellier

There are regular TGV's to Paris, so it's an easy ride to Gare du Nord with dedicated space on the train for my bicycle. After the reasonably quiet Valenciennes, the number of people in Paris is overwhelming. Otherwise, it's an easy ride retracing a route I cycled in 2013 along a canal path to Gare Austerlitz.

Compared to the modern looking TGV train, my overnight train to Toulouse is much older as I line up to board this long train. With numerous teenagers waiting with hiking backpacks, presumably, I will have to share a sleeping compartment.

However, I'm surprised that I have an antiquated one all to myself.

I have slept fine on trains before, but this one is bumpy all night, so as the train pulls into Toulouse at 6 am, I'm tired. The TGV from Valenciennes to Paris had been a smoother ride; this could be because the sleeping train is much older, while presumably, the track is in worse condition. There aren't many night trains anymore in France, and I wouldn't recommend taking one if they are all this bumpy.

I have about five hours before my train to Mazamet, so I will begin exploring on an overcast day. Initially, the streets are quiet with barely anyone around, so I feel like an intruder to the peace. Slowly over time, people begin to arrive, and at different times, shops begin to open. It's always interesting seeing how a city slowly wakes up.

What strikes me the most about Toulouse is that nearly every scenic multistorey building is made out of red bricks. With most high above the River Garonne, I presume flooding is common, so that is why there are many high walls beside the river. On top of one of these walls is a walkway with plenty of information panels on both the river and Toulouse's history, including the red-bricked Point Neuf bridge, the oldest in Toulouse, which has half a dozen arches for the water to flow under.

On top of a wall beside the River Garonne, which Point Neuf crosses

This bridge is similar to the main one in Bordeaux, which makes sense as both cities are on the River Garonne. Many people cycle between the two using the Canal de Garonne, which starts here, while another canal continues east to the Mediterranean. I had considered cycling that way, but I don't have enough time to do that and get to Montpellier for Australia's next match.

Inside a square castle tower in the centre of town is the Office de Tourisme, where a brochure informs me that you can go inside the nearby town hall to see some artwork, so I will. It's well worth the visit with artwork all over the walls and ceiling, mostly showing historical paintings of life in Toulouse. I imagine the large square out the front hosts many local events.

Whereas I had too much time to explore Valenciennes, I feel like I could spend longer in Toulouse, but with my train leaving soon, I just have enough time to cycle around the old wall to see a few other sites, including the war memorial before returning to the railway station. Maybe I will cycle through here following the canal one day, or perhaps this will be my only visit.

The local train to Mazamet is brand new and has a decent space for bicycles. When booking this train, I managed to find a ticket for €1, as prices can fluctuate. Another train taking a similar amount of time on another local route will cost me €36. During the journey, I chat to a few locals using a mixture of French and English.

There isn't much to see in Mazamet, so I soon join the rail trail with a decent gravel surface. There is some climbing required to get up to a tunnel, but since it's a railway grade, it's an easy climb as I cross a range before descending over a few refurbished rail bridges and through a few more tunnels and rail cuttings. Over time the landscape is becoming more mountainous, but the rail trail is a leisurely cycle. Since it's still a cold day, I feel like I'm focusing too much on getting somewhere rather than enjoying the scenery.

Office de Tourisme in a castle

Artwork inside Town Hall

A few rail cuttings on this trail

I'm passing through numerous small scenic hilly towns, where the rail trail is often high above or below, presumably because the towns existed long before the railway came. In Olargues, the former railway station is down below and being reused by the community, so I take some time to walk up to see some interesting buildings. However, there isn't really anywhere sensible to camp here, so I will keep going.

Artwork beside this rail trail which goes around towns like Olargues

As dusk approaches, just after a bridge, beside the trail among trees, is a picnic table with enough space for my tent.

With the sun out in the morning, it's a much more enjoyable cycle. However, after going over a few rail bridges, this rail trail regrettably ends after only a couple hours of cycling due to another railway line still existing at Bedarieux.

After camping beside the rail trail, I travel over a refurbished rail bridge

Landscape leaving Bedarieux

I'm in a mountainous landscape, so initially, as I make my way towards Montpellier, there is a lot of up and down cycling as I'm trying to avoid busy roads. As it flattens out later in the day, I'm now passing through numerous towns, while a few abandoned railway lines are along the way, including a large viaduct as I leave Bedarieux, but none of them are a rail trail.

Overall my afternoon focus is on getting to Montpellier rather than visiting anywhere in particular. As I enter the north-western suburbs of Montpellier, I pass the football stadium before I follow tram tracks to my Warmshower host Joel's apartment nearby, for a relaxing night.

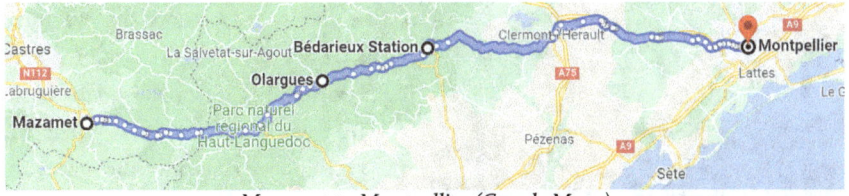

Mazamet to Montpellier (Google Maps)

With the match against Brazil not until 6 pm, I have all day to explore by using a tram to get into the city. As I exit the main tram station, I'm in a quiet, beautiful pedestrian plaza which is both long and wide, and surrounded by large creamy – yellow scenic multistorey buildings, so I spend some time just admiring the architecture. While it's currently empty, by lunchtime it becomes jam-packed.

My first impression of Montpellier

After walking through a tree-lined park on the eastern side of the city centre, I make my way into the old town. It's easy walking around the many curvy, narrow streets with a range of buildings to see. I'm regularly meeting numerous Australians dressed in yellow, including randomly near a large creamy coloured church, the man I met twice in Valenciennes. While exploring, I'm briefly interviewed by Michelle from Optus Sport about my predictions for today's match; I'm hoping we will win 2-1.

Somehow I end up stumbling onto an artwork treasure hunt where more than a dozen temporary three-dimensional artworks have been set up around the city in many buildings' courtyards. It's probably more suitable for children, but it's a fun way to see the city and admire a wide variety of pieces of art.

The artwork treasure hunt, includes an archway made out of clothes pegs

My favourite pieces are the more reflective ones with a nature theme where at different angles, the sunlight provides different reflections of transparent insect wings or colourful lily pads. There are also simpler pieces like an archway made out of clothes pegs.

Aqueduct stretching out into suburbs

Sticking out high on the western edge of the city behind a skinny Arc de Triomphe is an open square with a statue of Louis XIV on a horse. In the gardens surrounding the statue, a few journalists are broadcasting back to Australia.

While on the far end of this square, stretching out into the suburbs, is a long aqueduct.

Later into the day, as the city becomes busier and warmer, it's becoming overwhelming, so I follow the aqueduct to see where it goes. Eventually, it just randomly ends, so I catch a tram to the football stadium.

As I approach the stadium, there is a noticeably louder vibe than Valenciennes due mostly to the Brazilian supporters singing and wearing a range of colourful outfits. Australians are still making noise but the Brazilians have their own style.

At times it's hard to tell who is Australian and who is Brazilian as it's mostly a sea of yellow as we both usually wear yellow, but today Brazil will be playing in blue. It's friendly banter between everyone as we are all here to enjoy ourselves.

I'm sitting with a few Australian supporters inside the stadium, one of whom has a blown-up kangaroo toy.

Our terrible form from the first match continues in the first half here as we go 2-nil down. If it stays the same, we are probably out of the World Cup.

Thankfully just before half-time, Caitlin Foord scores, while in the second

Harrison and Kennedy signing items

half, we rally and overrun the Brazilians as Australia is now playing well. So naturally, the Australian supporters lift and are now loudly making themselves known. As the match finishes 3-2 to us, we are all celebrating and staying after the game to applaud the Matildas. A few are kind enough to jump the low-security fence to sign autographs even if security doesn't want them to.

On a packed tram ride back to my Warmshower host's home, I get talking with a few Australians. Many are planning to be in Grenoble in five days for Australia's last group stage match against Jamaica.

Jamaïque

On social media, a few fellow Australians have been visiting nearby Nîmes and Point Du Gard aqueduct, so I will go for a look myself.

After a sunny day in Montpellier, the weather has returned to overcast as I leave this beautiful city which had more places of interest than Valenciennes. Initially, cycle paths beside the road take me out of the city.

After a few back roads, I find myself in the town of Sommieres, where after crossing a small scenic river, a paved rail trail winds its way nearly all the way to Nîmes. Along the way, I'm going under a few cement road bridges, through a few rail cuttings and passing some former large double-storey cement railway stations which remind me of similar ones in Spain.

Rail trail to Nîmes

Nîmes has a few Roman-era buildings and feels very touristy with a sculptured park containing numerous Roman statues surrounded by a canal. Nearby is a large former Roman temple with columns out the front.

Roman gardens and a temple in Nîmes

The dominating feature is the most preserved Roman arena in the world. It's a large unroofed sports stadium with a small oval playing area suitable for tennis or basketball. It's still used for concerts and other events: Elton John is playing here in a few weeks.

Outside and inside an ellipse Roman arena in Nîmes

Roman arena in Nîmes

It's a reasonable visit using an informative audio guide, but often, the audio just goes for too long, so I feel I have to wait for the audio to finish before continuing. I'm allowed to walk around most of the arena, including a few levels of the enclosed passageways of the outer part, along with the outdoor seats that go right around this bowl arena. I'm even allowed to walk up to a high point to view the surrounding sprawling city.

I could spend longer in Nîmes, but I want to make Port du Gard tonight before it closes at 7 pm, so I will continue. It's always hard to judge how long to spend in any one place.

Leaving Nîmes isn't much fun as I have to take a busy road. At least there are some fruit sellers with delicious apricots.

Thankfully eventually I'm able to join a quiet road, then a short rail trail before a bicycle path takes me all the way to Port du Gard.

Port du Gard

It's quieter than expected, so while admiring this double-storey aqueduct from a distance, I can hear Australian accents from a family. They are travelling with three kids under ten for the World Cup. Otherwise, outside of World Cup cities and Roland-Garros, I haven't seen many Australians in France.

I'm able to cycle straight over on a low bridge right next to the aqueduct, while cars have to detour a fair way to get to the other side of the River Gardon. I can walk up to an end of the aqueduct, but I'm not allowed to walk across the top, so I just admire it. It's no more impressive than the ones in Merida or Montpellier.

On this side of the low flowing river is an informative museum on the history of the aqueduct. It was built to transport water to Nîmes from near the town of Uzes. A lot of skill went into deciding a route that allowed water to flow in a gravity-fed channel for about 50 kilometres. Despite taking fifteen years to build, it was disused within 200 years as maintaining it was too hard. There were other bridges along the route, but the stone from these bridges has been reused for other buildings.

After initially taking secondary roads through farmland, I find myself on the main road to Uzes, where a large shopping complex is on the edge of town. A railway line used to go past here and a paved rail trail begins here, so after collecting dinner supplies, I join it. It looks brand new, and presumably, this may lead me into town, or at least there will be a suitable place to camp beside the trail.

However, after only 500 metres, the rail trail randomly stops at a road crossing despite the continuing rail formation. There's nowhere suitable to camp, so I will keep cycling using roads which are occasionally near the rail formation. I'm aiming to make my way towards where presumably the railway station was, below town.

The station site is overgrown with weeds but further below, across a paddock away from town, is a sizeable circus tent among a cleared space. It may be a possibility of a camping spot, so I will make my way there.

It's an equestrian centre, with no people or horses around. As thunder suddenly begins, I duck into the large tent. Inside is a range of equipment for horses, clean rubbish bins and hay bales, but still, there is plenty of room for my tent and bicycle for me to stay as light rain begins.

After a quiet, unobserved night, I make my way up to Uzes, where many Saturday market stalls take up most of the ring road right around the city centre. Plenty of delicious fruit is available along with many other items I don't need, like clothing.

Camping in an equestrian tent, while a Saturday market is on in Uzes

A church tower

An old church with a tall multi-windowed round stone tower is on the town's eastern side. Behind it, a forest stretches out across a river valley. There are walking tracks down to the River L'alzon, but I soon discover they are overgrown, so it takes a while to find my way down.

Once I find myself in a more open space near the river, I soon spot the remains of an aqueduct. Presumably, it's the same one that went over Port du Gard. It's hard to spot in places as nature is slowly reclaiming the route it took, with trees growing between stone remains.

After briefly becoming lost while finding my way back to my bicycle near the church, I visit the Office de Tourisme to find ideas on things to see in the region. The prominent place to visit appears to be Gorge de L'Ardeche. This will get me to the River Rhone, where I can join a cycle route, which will take me all the way to Grenoble.

After leaving town on this overcast day, it's a quiet morning with some minor climbing on peaceful roads. Around lunchtime, on top of a hill, there appears to be a small town surrounding this relatively flat landscape.

Remains of aqueduct near Uzes

There is only one road to access Lussan, so I'm into this small town after a short sharp climb. It's a quiet spot for lunch, and after a quick ride around town and a brief look inside the town hall, I soon leave.

After a longer, more gradual climb on the edge of a mountain range with scenic views of a valley below, I'm soon descending to Saint Ambroix.

My afternoon has easily been decided because Maps.me shows a rail trail starting further along the River Ceze. Getting there is a little dicey as the road beside the river is a little busy.

I'm not sure where the start of the rail trail is, but a few coal carriages are on display, while some former rail bridges and parts of the rail right of way are visible but not the trail. In the meantime, some loud thunderstorms are beginning in the distance.

Rail trail through Gagnieres

When I eventually find the unsigned rail trail, it starts reasonable as it goes through the centre of a couple of towns as a short shower of rain briefly appears.

However, past the second town, it soon becomes rough, and neither of the two tunnels, one being over a kilometre long, have lights, while large rocks have been placed to prevent cars from going through them.

After the second tunnel, the track becomes even worse with ballast still here, so it's a bumpy ride. There are signs of improvement as a newly refurbished bridge with cement surface is temporarily fenced off, so it should be a better trail in the future. For now, I will leave it. I just need to figure out how to get off this embankment and onto a nearby road.

Abandoned rail tunnel

Thankfully not far along, a track is available to take me to a road, which conveys me north as the sun finally appears. Briefly beside the road is a decent paved rail trail that takes me over the River L'Ardeche on a refurbished stone rail bridge.

From here, I have to leave the rail trail to head east to Vallon Pont d-Arc. Anyway, I'm not sure if the developed rail trail continues further north for much longer. I'm soon briefly beside the wide open scenic L'Ardeche, with a few campgrounds across the water.

After crossing River L'Ardeche on a rail trail bridge, I begin following the river by road

With plenty of people around, it's easy to tell that Vallon Pont d-Arc is a tourist town, especially with all the souvenir shops, restaurants and advertisements for canoe trips in the Gorge de L'Ardeche. A cycling couple recommends Camping Le Torrent, as there are numerous campgrounds in this area. With so many people around, stealth camping doesn't look that inviting, so I will check it out.

It's quiet, with a few campers around, including some cyclists. There are even fewer features here than in Bastogne; at least this time there is a picnic table. The strangest thing is that the toilets don't have a seat or toilet paper. I have come across this in public toilets but not at paid accommodation before. I'm carrying some toilet paper, but it's still weird compared to Australian campgrounds, which have a lot more features.

Two of the cyclists here, Matt and John, are from the southwest of England, where I will start the English part of this tour in about four weeks, so they can offer me some advice. They have cycled from Saint-Malo on the northern coastline of France and are planning on heading to Nice, having followed a cycling route I haven't heard of before.

After a hard night sleep, I realise my sleeping mattress probably has a leak. By placing my mat in a sink full of water, I can see air bubbles coming out of three separate locations. I have a few patches, so I should be able to seal them up.

Even with this delay, I'm still ready to leave town in reasonable time. On this Sunday morning, the road is busy with numerous road cyclists, and many buses with empty canoe trailers are also passing me.

Initially, the road follows the river at the same level as it takes me past a natural arc that crosses the L'Ardeche. This was the only way to cross this river for centuries, as bridges hadn't been built. With plenty of space above, it looks like you could still safely cross today, but it doesn't appear to have a track over the top.

However, plenty of canoeists are going under it. Which looks like a spectacular way to see the gorge, especially as the road will soon begin climbing.

Reasonable flat cycle on the way to Le Pont d-Arc

By pacing myself up this 10% gradient road which switchbacks once, it is a reasonable three-kilometre long climb as a few roadies pass me.

Once up this 300-metre high climb, there is a spectacular lookout where many road cyclists are turning around and heading straight back down. Others appear to be getting lifts up and will be starting their cycle from here, having avoided the major climb of Gorge de L'Ardeche. Presumably, they are part of an organised cycle tour as a few vans with bicycle trailers are passing me.

As for the view, rows of mountains are stretching out in every direction. There are many sheer vertical clear cliff faces, while where it slopes more, the landscape is generally covered in trees. Way below, the river snakes its way through, having carved out the side of mountains with plenty of eroded white rocks to admire. Clearly, the river has changed its course over the centuries because in places, it has nearly cut back on itself.

View from the top of the Gorge de L'Ardeche

From here, the road stays high above the river, with numerous lookouts on this semi-warm day. The road isn't flat; it follows the contours causing me to constantly be going up or down, about a maximum of a 100 metres at a time. The road mostly stays near the edge, which doesn't have safety barriers, while way down below in the river, the canoeists are now only tiny dots. There are a few access points to the river in this section, which I'm assuming are steep, so I won't head down.

After lunch, while randomly looking at my bicycle, I'm shocked to see that near where the wire cable for my front brake connects with the braking mechanism, the wire has split apart. Only a few wire threads are still connected, so my front brake still works, but I'm concerned it may fail at any time.

This has never happened to this bicycle, nor can I recall any recent incidents which may have caused this. I'm not carrying any spare cables because usually in France it's easy to find a bicycle shop.

My brake is holding on by threads

On this relatively flat section, I can manage, but I'm worried about the upcoming descent to the river to exit the gorge. I don't have much choice but to manage my bicycle down because there aren't any shops around here, let alone bicycle shops.

In the meantime, I will visit one of a few caves, as there are numerous ones here, so I just select one at random. After an interpretive centre with info on the gorge's history and its flora and fauna, I join an hour guided walk with an audio guide. The cave is okay, but I'm not seeing anything I haven't seen in other caves; still, it's nice to see.

Further on, there are more lookouts, but the gorge is starting to become repetitive viewing. Soon the road is further away from the edge, with fewer opportunities to look down.

Fortunately, the meandering descent is much gentler than the climb up and helpfully, there are some short uphill corner sections to slow my pace. Still, there are times when I'm strategically using my rear brake to gradually slow me down without skidding to avoid needing to use my front brake. As I meet the river, many of the canoe tours are ending, while a few cyclists are finishing their ride.

Once I'm finally safely down, I'm in the small town of Saint Martin where I find some wi-fi, but I can't find any bicycle shops which are open this Sunday. I'm also concerned that many appear to be closed tomorrow, so will see what I can find in the morning. Fortunately from here, it's a flat ride following the River Rhone north, so I should be able to manage until then.

After a busy road, I'm at the Rhone, where I help direct a couple heading in the opposite direction to the correct route for the ViaRhona. This cycle route follows the Rhone from Switzerland to the Mediterranean. From what I can see on Maps.me, there appears to be plenty of bicycle paths to cycle on this route.

The ViaRhona is well signed

After initially following a road north, a paved path takes me on a dogleg route through wheat paddocks and a small forest back to the river. Once a path is beside the Rhone, I'm able to admire this wide river with many trains racing past on the other side. Apart from a slight headwind, it's a relaxing ride as a few cyclists pass me in the opposite direction.

Every so often, there are semi-suitable places to wild camp beside the river, but none are exceptional, so I will keep going.

ViaRhona travels through farm paddocks and beside the wide Rhone

After crossing the river, a local football ground could be a suitable place to stay tonight. I'm able to sneak inside the fence, and since there is power, water and a toilet, I will camp here. I have chosen well because it's a quiet night other than one person briefly walking around the football ground.

In the morning, rather than staying on the cycle route, which soon crosses the Rhone again, I follow the railway line into the suburbs of Montelimar to find a bicycle shop. It's quiet around this suburban shopping complex as I wait for an Intersport store to open. Thankfully once inside, my brake cable is easily replaced, so I will head into the city centre.

I soon learn of a local dairy-based lolly called Nougat which has a choice of different solid objects like nuts or dried fruit embedded in it. Around the city are numerous large pieces of Nougat artwork, including on the side of buildings and large scale Nougat statues in the local parks. A few factories show how they are made and offer some varieties to purchase, so I do. This soft milk flavoured fudge has a pleasant taste.

Nougat is made in Montelimar, so Nougat artwork is around town

After using a levee bank to follow a small river back to the broad blue Rhone and then crossing this river on a road bridge, I'm back on the ViaRhona. Just like yesterday, there is a slight headwind as I begin heading north, but since I'm currently in an open landscape, there is no shelter from the wind. Visible in the distance are three tall round towers with white smoke coming out of them.

Approaching something

The ViaRhona soon leaves the river behind as it takes me to a bridge just for cyclists and walkers. After walking under a castle tower-style entrance, I'm on a narrow swing bridge which takes me across a narrower anabranch of the Rhone. A few cyclists are coming in the other direction, so I stop at the next tower to let them pass.

Once across this scenic bridge, I soon re-join a path beside the Rhone as the three round towers become more visible. As I get closer, the cycle route briefly takes me around them away from the river as signs tell me this is a Nuclear Power Plant.

On the ViaRhona, I'm constantly seeing touring cyclists, most of whom are going in the opposite direction. This is helpful for finding each turn on this route because if I'm unsure, soon another cyclist will come along and show me the correct way.

The ViaRhona takes me over a narrow bridge and pass a nuclear power plant

A cyclist with a box for his gear

I'm meeting a mixture of nationalities, including Canadians, Americans and numerous Europeans. Most are carrying a traditional pannier bag setup, but one man is riding a long bicycle with a wooden box at the front where all his gear is stored. Four of us cross the Rhone together at one stage, as half a dozen cyclists are coming in the opposite direction.

As for the actual route, the majority of the time, I'm on a cycle path, sometimes beside the river on levee banks, other times alongside a railway line and a few times through farmland. I'm also passing where a couple of rail trails branch off west of here and head into the mountains.

Besides a few issues with finding the correct route through some towns, it's a relaxing ride that takes slightly longer than expected. By the time I'm in the city of Valence, I don't have much time to explore as I need to keep going to allow enough time to get to Grenoble before tomorrow night's match against Jamaica.

Camping beside the L'Isere

After only looking around for half an hour, I leave the city. I'm still following the Rhone north for a brief period before I turn east by following the L'Isere River, which has a similar cycle path beside it. It's quieter, and I'm cycling much quicker as the day is now getting away from me. Eventually, a place beside a pedestrian bridge alongside a French cycling couple younger than me will do for a place to camp.

Following the L'Isere

Initially, my morning route to Grenoble involves crossing the L'Isere a few times on quiet dogleg roads. The further I travel, the more visible mountains are becoming as Grenoble is on the edge of the French Alps. Thankfully the last 34 kilometres is more straightforward on a flat cycle path among trees beside the river as it takes me all the way to Grenoble.

Approaching the Alps

Other than Paris, Grenoble is the first city I'm revisiting from my 2013 trip. However, since I cycled in from a different direction last time, it's initially a fresh view.

As I make my way to a town square, seemingly everywhere I look are yellow Australian shirts and as I pull up to gather my thoughts, a few Australians say hello. They remember meeting me in Montpellier, including a couple I chatted to on the tram after the match against Brazil. Having been here for a few days already, they offer me advice on things to see.

My main memory of my last time in Grenoble is of a cable car ride up to a fort on top of a hill, which provides views of the city and the surrounding mountains. This time I don't bother with going up the hill. Instead, I will just explore around the river before making my way to my Warmshowers host Serge's home in a small apartment not far from the stadium.

Grenoble

An hour before the game, I begin walking to the stadium in daylight. I pass a group of approximately ten-year-old boys around a locked bicycle. I soon realise they are stealing a wheel, and before I can stop them, they race off. Thankfully, my bike is locked in a dedicated room for bicycles in Serge's apartment building.

The football stadium is in a large park, so it's a party atmosphere outside as I make my way there. In Europe, they like matches starting at 9 pm, so as the game begins in a reasonably full stadium, an orange dusk is beginning.

The current standings in our World Cup group have Italy on six points, Australia and Brazil both on three and Jamaica on zero. With Italy playing Brazil at the same time, depending on both results, we can finish from first to fourth. Only the top two are guaranteed to make it to the next round. However, with 24 teams made up of six groups of four, there are also four positions in the knockout stage for the four best third-placed teams out of the six groups. Because of results already in other groups, even finishing third should be enough to qualify for the knockout stage.

Where we finish in our group will determine who and where Australia's next match is, which could be in a few different places all over France.

If we finish top of the group, we get to go back to Montpellier and play a team ranked in third place.

Second place will mean playing Norway, in Nice. I have been there before, so I don't want to go back because it is a busy touristy seaside city.

Finishing third will probably mean playing the host nation in Le Harve on the opposite side of the country, making it harder to get a ticket and get there, while it will also be a hard match to play. Even if we get past the French, we would more than likely have to play the defending champions, the USA, in the quarterfinals.

So going back to Montpellier is my preferred location as it will mean an easier match, easier route to the final and easier for me to get there, especially as that match is three days later than the one in Nice.

Suppose the expected result of beating Jamaica happens. In that case, Australia will finish the group stage on six points. If Brazil beats Italy, they will both also have six points, so it will come down to goal difference to decide positions. With Brazil and Italy having already beaten Jamaica by three and five goals respectively, we need to make up the goal difference to overtake them.

Thankfully, we start well with Sam Kerr scoring twice before half-time, while it's nil-all in the other match, so at this stage, we are finishing second.

As the second half begins, unexpectedly Jamaica scores their first-ever Women's World Cup goal, which leads to the crowd celebrating the underdog scoring. For the most part, Australians are okay with this as long as they don't score again. Thankfully, Kerr scores again after another twenty minutes, so the second spot is ours at this stage.

Five minutes later, it trickles through the crowd that Brazil has scored, so now we are all trying to figure out the goal difference maths because three teams are currently all on six points. I think we are behind on goal difference at this stage, so we will finish third and have to play France.

As the final ten minutes begin, thankfully, Kerr scores a fourth goal herself, but I'm still confused about where we are on the ladder. As the game finishes, I'm still uncertain, I just know by the players' reaction we are through, but I'm not sure in which position.

Fortunately, as I leave the stadium, other Australians who have internet access show me that we have finished second behind Italy on goal difference, while we have the same goal difference as Brazil, but since we have scored more goals, we are ranked higher. So we will now play Norway in Nice in four days.

Before returning to Serge's home, I find some wi-fi to purchase a ticket. Since I know from my last visit that Nice is expensive, I ask on the Matildas travelling fans Facebook group if anyone else wants to share accommodation in Nice.

With numerous Alpine mountains between Grenoble and Nice, it's nearly impossible to cycle directly in the time I have without doing big days and long climbs. I would prefer to enjoy the ride than constantly be rushing, so I'm searching for a scenic cycling route and train options to bridge any gaps. Serge thankfully has a few paper maps, and he offers me advice.

I have found a train route from Briancon via Marseille, which should work. All I have to do is just climb up and over a 2,000 metre pass.

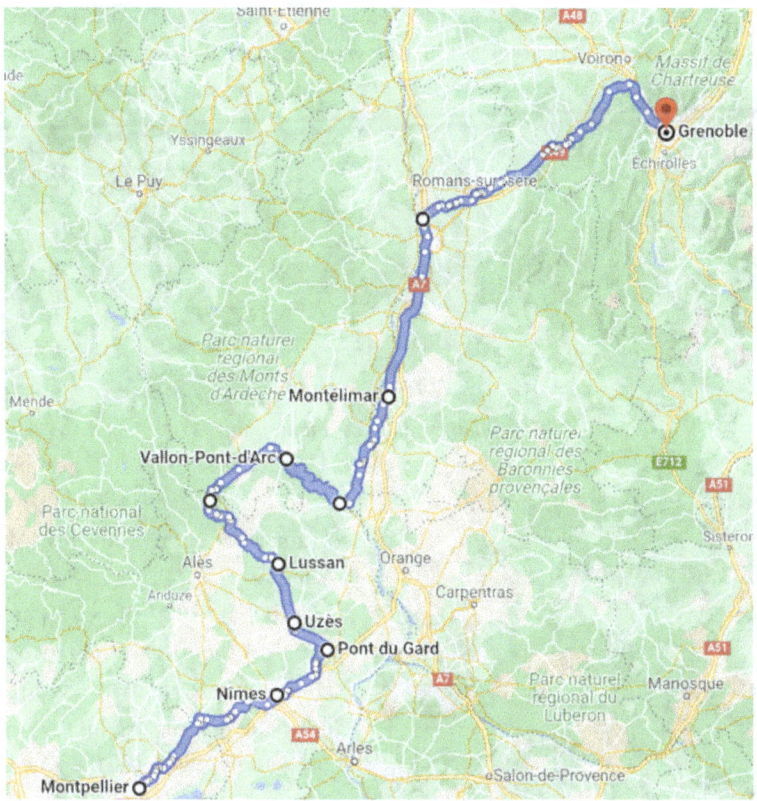

Montpellier to Grenoble (Google Maps)

Norvège

Just like in 2013, it's hard to get out of suburban Grenoble. Mercifully, the main road has a bicycle lane, so I can cycle comfortably as eventually the number of houses decreases. Thankfully, the traffic appears to be busier heading towards Grenoble.

As I'm about to leave the town of Vizille, I remember that Serge had mentioned that the Italian border is close to Briancon, so I have a look online.

It's less than 30 kilometres from Briancon to Italy, and once I'm across the border there is a railway station, so I could take a train to Nice that way via Torino. It will take a similar amount of time as going via Marseille, and be a new route for me instead of going via towns I saw in 2013. More than likely after Nice, I will go via Marseille anyway, especially if Australia makes the quarterfinals.

Also trains in Italy appear to be cheaper but it's less clear which ones allow bicycles, so regional trains just like in Spain appear to be the go. This route will mean one more climb, but I have a spare day in my schedule, so it should work. I will think about it.

As for now, I'm following a river in a gorge, which with a slight gradient is enough to be a slow ride without ever being steep. With the sun out, it's a scenic ride, but at around 30 degrees, it is a little warm, especially because I'm climbing.

Afternoon cycling in the mountains

An Australian presence in Le Bourg d'Oisans

The road flattens out just before Le Bourg d'Oisans, allowing me to comfortably cycle into this Alpine town.

Nearby is one of the famous climbs on the Tour De France *Alps d'Huez*, so there are many cycling and Alpine-themed shops in town. For those not familiar, it's the one with 21 switchbacks. It only leads to a ski village, so I won't climb it as I prefer climbing to go somewhere rather than just doing it for the sake of it. Anyway, I have other climbs I have to do in the next few days.

I have organised a Warmshower with Fred, Vero and their two-year-old daughter Charline and of course, as usual for a Warmshower host, it's up a hill. They welcome me into their home, which from their backyard provides a view of Alps d'Huez. We chat about their cycle touring experiences, including taking Charline to New Zealand. Just because you have kids doesn't mean you can't go cycling.

In the evening, while checking Twitter, I see that Scotland is 3-nil up over Argentina with 21 minutes to go, so they are about to qualify for the next round. This will be Scotland's first-ever progression to a knockout stage in international football, in either women's or men's.

However, the Scottish curse continues as they concede three late goals, including a controversial penalty retake, after the Scottish goalkeeper is judged to have come off her line after saving the first penalty. The 3-3 result means neither side qualifies for the knockout stage.

I wake knowing that for the next 40 kilometres, I will have to climb 1,300 metres to get to the Col du Lautaret pass.

The start of a climbing day

As soon as I leave town, light rain begins on a cold overcast day as the road becomes steep with a few tunnels and a deep gorge below me. It's going to be a long, cold day.

Thankfully, the road slightly flattens out after a while, and the rain has stopped, but it's still a struggle despite some reasonable scenery.

By the time I arrive into the scenic Alpine town of La Grave, it's lunchtime, and while admiring the snow-capped mountains in the distance, the sun finally appears.

Lunchtime in the Alps

After lunch, it feels like a more manageable ride despite it being steeper with a few zigzags. The open Alpine scenery seems to power me up, as it takes me just over an hour to climb the final ten kilometres to Col du Lautaret. Helpfully along the way are small signs telling me how far to the summit, the current height above sea level and what the gradient is. Presumably, these signs are for the many road cyclists who are passing me in both directions.

At the pass are some restaurants, along with cycling memorabilia because the Tour de France passes through here often on the way to an even higher pass off on a side road which I'm not doing. It's enjoyable being back in the mountains, having not done any cycling like this since New Zealand in 2016.

Elevation signs, help me climb in the Alps

Restaurants at Col du Lautaret

After putting some layers on, I begin descending. I'm flying down this scenic road, including briefly going through a long wooden snowshed. The 25 kilometres flies by without really needing to put in much effort, so I'm soon in the busy Alpine town of Briancon.

There is still enough time in the day for me to continue, but my legs are suddenly feeling tired from climbing. Anyway, I want to have a look around town. Staying will allow me to see if I can watch some World Cup matches on television tonight.

I soon find a lovely park with a lake and viaduct beside the River Durance, while up a hill is the older part of town, which is promoted for tourists. It's easy to walk around, and there are scenic views of the rest of the city below and the surrounding mountains. However, it's nothing special, just another old European town with cobblestone roads and a gutter in the middle of the street.

View of downtown Briancon from the Old Town

Below the old part is a barb wire fence memorial for people deported during the Second World War. It's hard to imagine that people from this scenic place were sent to the horrors of the Holocaust.

The rest of town feels like a typical French town that just happens to be surrounded by mountains. After the past few days of staying with Warmshower hosts, and because I will probably have indoor accommodation for the next few nights, I will stealth camp tonight, but will need to wait until dark.

Fortunately the last four matches of the World Cup group stage are on tonight to pass the time.

Initially, I find a bar busy with people more interested in drinking than the football. I end up having a couple of conversations with semi-drunk Frenchmen while keeping an eye on the Netherlands-Canada match. I'm also trying to keep up with New Zealand and Cameroon, who are playing each other to decide who will make it through to the next round. Cameroon scores a late goal to set up a round of sixteen knockout match with England.

Thankfully during the break between games, I have found a more upmarket restaurant, allowing me to sit down in peace and have dessert while the USA gets the better of Sweden.

It's now dark enough to search for a place to set up my tent. The park isn't an option because it's locked at night but on the other side of the Durance is a path that doesn't appear to lead anywhere. Once I'm past a few teenagers who are more interested in each other, there is a spot just dark enough for me to set my tent up.

After a quiet, undisturbed night, I will begin climbing to Italy.

Leaving town is the hardest part of the day as it's steep on a busy road high above the Durance, while a castle above the old town is visible.

A quiet road popular for cyclists

Thankfully after a few kilometres, I'm able to join a quiet, gentle road beside a small river that gradually climbs through an Alpine landscape full of pine trees. When I pass through a couple of small towns, every house has a pointy roof. It's a popular road for cyclists as I'm seeing more bikes than cars. Presumably, this is why there are more signs informing me of the gradient, height and distance to the summit.

The river doesn't cross the border, neither does this road which seemingly just runs out. Instead, I will join a minor side road, which for three kilometres involves using a few switchbacks to climb to the border. It reminds me of when I left Spain for France, and just like on the Spanish climb, I'm able to look back at the quiet scenic valley I just climbed up.

The pass among many pine trees isn't the Italian border, so I will keep going as the road begins descending.

Climbing to a pass

As I stop at a lookout of a valley, a group of road cyclists appear. As soon as they start talking, I can tell they are Scottish. They are doing a week of day trips in the area. After I talk about where I have been cycling and where I'm heading, they mention Scotland missing out on the next stage of the World Cup. They also provide suggestions on where I should go when I get to Scotland in August, particularly mentioning the west coast.

The descent into Italy is on a few quick switchbacks. There is no border sign to say I'm in Italy, but I can tell by other signs.

About to descend into Italy

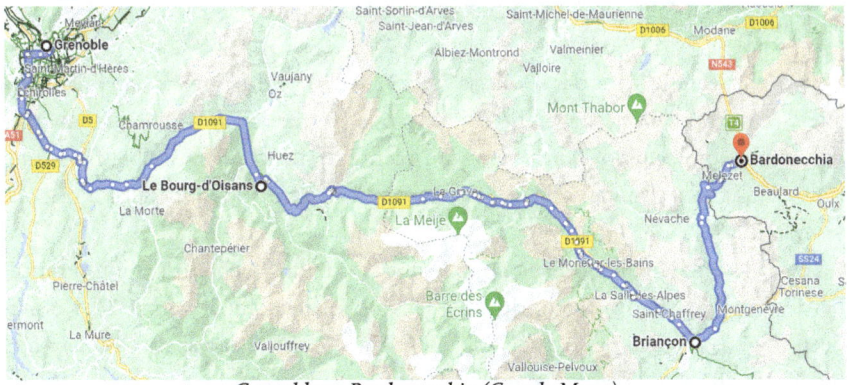

Grenoble to Bardonecchia (Google Maps)

The town of Bardonecchia is on the main railway line between France and Italy and has an hourly service to Torino. While waiting for a train, I have a quick look around town. There isn't much difference to France as it's still an Alpine town, just a language change and different varieties of chocolate shops are on offer.

This older train doesn't have a dedicated bicycle space, but is still a relaxing ride with scenic views of valleys and mountains as it descends to the city of Torino.

As soon as I wheel my bicycle out of the large railway station, a heavy thunderstorm begins, causing light flooding. Luckily, I'm near a small tourist info centre, allowing me to get some information while sheltering for a while.

Once it stops raining, it's still overcast, so as I begin exploring most surfaces are still damp.

I only have this afternoon to look around as I'm leaving tomorrow morning, so I will just see what I can find. I'm soon passing some large squares with interesting buildings and monuments.

As I begin cycling towards a market on a wet road with tram tracks, suddenly, out of nowhere, my bicycle slips under me, causing me to land hard sideways on my right side. As a stranger helps pick me up, I have a few minor scratches on my right knee and arm, and I'm feeling a little dazed. My bicycle wheels must have slipped into the gap next to the tram tracks, causing me to fall.

My right knee is aching as I move again, so I will finish my exploration early. I end my sightseeing via an ugly riverside area as I search for my Airbnb apartment.

It's a small rundown apartment up a few flights of stairs, with bicycle parking downstairs. After cooking a bolognese meal and resting my knee, I listen to the Men's Cricket World Cup match between England and Sri Lanka. England loses and is now in danger of missing the semi-finals.

This is only my second ever night in Italy, and I will be back in France tomorrow afternoon after using a couple of trains to enable me to be in Nice for tomorrow's round of sixteen knockout match against Norway. From my brief times in Italy, it feels like it is a poorer country than France, with more graffiti and rundown areas.

The train leaving Torino is scenic as we descend to the Mediterranean following a few rivers, and at one stage, the railway loops around itself. We then follow the continuous built-up coastline west with plenty of beachgoers visible from the train. This train terminates at the Italian border city of Vermingtella, a place I visited in 2013.

To get to Nice requires changing to a modern train, which crosses into France before briefly going through Monaco. Having visited Monaco in 2013, I don't need to go back. I didn't particularly enjoy Nice either as it was too touristy for me but I will see what it is like now.

Four people have got back to me about wanting to share accommodation, including Simon, who has found an apartment with four beds for the three singles and the couple who will be staying.

Simon and Dawso meet me outside the apartment, so together, we open the door to a surprisingly small apartment. Other than a small bathroom, there is just one main room which contains a double bed and a fold-out couch, which just fits two people on it.

Simon has misread the listing, so this explains why it's cheaper. It's still expensive compared to other places I have stayed at on this trip.

For me, at least, there is a small balcony to store my bicycle, and I have my Thermarest mattress. However, Dawso and Simon will have to share the couch as they decide that Rachel and Taryn should have the larger double bed.

We each have a different reason for being here. Rachel isn't particularly interested in football; instead, she is here for a holiday while supporting her girlfriend Taryn, who is interested. Simon has been criss-crossing France to watch a few non-Australian matches, particularly the Netherlands. Dawso has just flown in from Australia, and it appears he does this often, flying into a place for a few days before jetting off again.

We only have one key, so together we walk to meet up with a few more Australians as we still have time before the match starts late in the evening.

Norvège

As I hit the esplanade, it brings back memories of this busy tourist area with fancy restaurants and an ugly stone Mediterranean beach with plenty of deckchairs. As I walk along, I think about the terrorist attack with the truck on the esplanade, mainly because I know of a person from my hometown who witnessed it.

Outside a pub are about 100 Australians who have gathered for a pre-game meet up. Like me, most are wearing a yellow football shirt, with a variety of editions between us. Some have updated to the new colourful splashy Matildas specific shirt, which was only released in March, the day after I purchased the previous version.

Others are dressed up in various Australian themed attire, including a group of women dressed as crocodile hunters in safari suits. It's nice to meet up again with a few people I have met in other World Cup host cities.

While inside on televisions around this British themed pub, both the Cricket World Cup and the first knockout match of this World Cup are on, as Germany comfortably beats Nigeria.

The Nice football stadium is a fair way out of the city. Thankfully, there are dedicated buses, which I soon board. Since the stadium is so far out of the city, it has a more sterile vibe.

My seat is decent, behind a goal in a disappointingly less than half-full stadium. I'm near some Australians and Norwegian supporters, but unlike in Montpellier, the main group of Australians are in another part of the stadium.

Inside the Nice football stadium

As for the game, Australia just isn't playing that well, while Norway is creating multiple chances, so we are lucky to be only one goal down at half-time. As the end of the second half nears, we haven't played any better, so it's looking like we will be going home.

With less than ten minutes to go, we have a corner kick. As Elise Kellond-Knight once again crosses a hopeful ball into the penalty box, somehow the ball avoids touching any of the more than a dozen footballers as it goes directly into the far end of the goal.

Norway has a late chance to win the match as the ball pinballs off the post and crosses right in front of the goal without thankfully going over the line. As the final whistle sounds, the match will now go into extra time.

Norway still looks like the better team in extra time, and it becomes a harder prospect when Alanna Kennedy is sent off due to her clumsily bringing down a Norwegian attacker who was on her way to being one-on-one with our goalkeeper.

With one less player, we cannot force the issue, so we are holding on with the hope that the game will go to penalties. Despite Norway having chances, including hitting the crossbar, we manage to hold on, so penalties it will be.

I haven't been to a match with a penalty shoot-out before, so I'm interested to see how it goes, and fortunately for me, it's at my end. Thus I have a clear view as firstly Sam Kerr skies our first penalty, before Emily Gielnik's shot is saved. Alas Norway isn't missing, so eventually, they are too far in front, so the World Cup is over for Australia.

After the game, it's a sombre wait for a bus in long lines along with half the crowd. As I wait, I do at least have another chance to chat with a few fans, including the two New Zealanders I met in Valenciennes and the man I saw in both Valenciennes and Montpellier.

Our apartment is booked for two nights, so this will allow me to have a rest day and time to figure out a way to get to Lyon to attend the semi-finals and the final. I haven't had a rest day since Montpellier, so this will allow me to recharge the batteries.

After seeing the popular beach, all I really do is walk around the headland, which has a war memorial below and some average views from the top. I walk back through a long park with water fountains which are refreshing on this hot afternoon.

I end up back at the same bar as yesterday, allowing me to watch England comfortably beat Cameroon despite the Cameroonians complaining a lot about video assistant referee decisions. Particularly two offsides, one that correctly awards England a goal and one where a Cameroonian is just offside, so their goal is ruled out. At one stage, the Cameroonians briefly walk off the pitch, and by the end of the match, they are playing rough with some terrible tackles.

Thankfully, the evening match is a much better display of football as France and Brazil are evenly matched as it finishes 1-1 after 90 minutes. An extra-time French goal puts them through to a probable meeting with the USA in what should be the match of the tournament.

Someone left the oven on

With Australia out of the World Cup, I now have nine days to get to Lyon from Nice, so I will head north into the mountains again. I'm aiming to go via Gorge du Verdon, this time seeing the southern side, the opposite side to my 2013 ride.

Leaving Nice I need to climb to 1200 metres from the sea. An extra challenge is that summer has arrived with all week looking like it will be above 30 degrees Celsius and in some places, nearly 40 degrees. Hopefully, it will be cooler in the mountains.

By 9 am it's already warm as I briefly follow the coastline out of Nice past the airport using a bicycle path before heading inland. Once out of suburbia, I begin climbing in Le Loup Gorge, following two cyclists for a while before stopping for lunch. The gorge isn't too steep, but it's all uphill with a couple of tunnels. The main issue is the draining heat, but thankfully, shade is available for some of the ride.

After following the Mediterranean out of Nice, I begin climbing in Le Loup Gorge

In the gorge are a couple of waterfalls but not within touching distance. Otherwise, I'm just admiring the scenery on this slow climb before eventually, I'm on top of the gorge.

After an icy pole at Greolieres, there is more climbing but at a gentler gradient to the town of Andon located in a colourful valley. The temperature has decreased now, not sure if it's because I'm currently at 1,200 metres or because it's 5 pm.

After climbing, I'm now up following a mountain range

For the next two hours, I'm able to enjoy cycling, especially as the majority of this route is downhill and more open with mountains in the distance as it looks like I'm on a ridgeline. I just keep going until Comps, the last town before the Gorge du Verdon, which will allow me to cycle the gorge in the morning, hopefully before it warms up.

After looking around, there's nowhere suitable for wild camping, so I will pay to stay at a basic campground. Apart from a few permanent vans, I appear to be the only customer. As for facilities other than some picnic tables on a grass area and a building with showers, there isn't much here.

I wake knowing the day will be warm, and even by 7 am, it is, so after visiting the bakery in Comps, I will set off. No idea why but nearly all bakeries in this region put one dried olive in the middle of pizza buns. It isn't because there are olive plantations around here like in Spain. They are still delicious and are a better offering than what's available in most supermarkets.

Having seen the Gorge du Verdon from the opposite side in 2013, I know what to expect. However, it's still just as spectacular with sections where the road is right on the edge of this deep gorge. The varied landscape of either bare white rock or being covered in trees reminds me of Gorge de L'Ardeche, but this one looks deeper with more sharp drop-offs.

Occasionally visible across the gap is the road I cycled in 2013, while at other times I'm ducking away from the gorge for a short period to go around a side gorge. Thankfully, the only traffic to worry about are friendly tourists, including many motorcyclists, who like me are stopping to admire the various lookouts, so we briefly chat.

I recall from 2013 seeing a group of tunnels on this side, so I'm finally able to cycle through these as I meet a few touring cyclists and roadies, with most going the other way.

There are plenty of short undulating sections and times where I'm climbing for a few kilometres and then descending for a similar distance. The final climb with a switchback takes a while as the day is starting to become warm. As I begin an even longer descent, in the distance is a large lake as this road takes me into the town of Aiguines.

The only services are a couple of restaurant beside the popular for cycling Gorge du Verdon

Gorge du Verdon

It's not even midday yet, but it's already hot, so I will rest here for a bit by visiting a museum that focuses on handmade wooden carvings. This area used to specialise in this with factories set up. On display are various items they produced, particularly the ball for the game of Boules, which people often play in most towns here with dedicated parks for it. I believe it is what we call Bocce in Australia. I didn't realise until today that boules' balls are made by hammering nails around a wooden ball.

Making Boules balls

After descending to the lake, the road crosses the blue River Verdon, where on one side of the bridge is the lake, while on the other is the spectacular end of the Gorge du Verdon. It's full of people on various crafts, including stand up paddle boarders visiting this scenic deep gorge. However, I can't find a place hiring them, so I presume people have brought their own I could hire a canoe, but with too many bad experiences, especially at work, I will stay away from them.

End of Gorge du Verdon

As I follow the lake away from the gorge, I eventually see that stand up paddleboards are available to hire, but they are just too far away from the gorge for me.

In 2013, I camped at Moustiers Sainte-Marie, so as I approach this town located on the side of a mountain, I will go for a brief look in town again, mainly as an excuse to get an ice cream.

It's a tourist town with a small church built high above on the side of the mountain. With stairs carved out of the side of the mountain, it's an easy walk up.

Moustiers Sainte-Marie

Stairs leading up to a church

Admiring some rocks

It's nothing special, just another church. However, as I walk back down these slippery stairs, there is a nice view of the town and the valley stretching out in the distance. My sandals are not getting much grip on these stairs, so I soon slip causing my foot to sting.

I have cut my heel, it's only a tiny band-aid size cut, but along with my knee still being tender from the fall in Torino, I'm feeling a tad sore.

The final descent is to the town of Riez, which has some Roman history, including four connecting columns from a long-gone building and some interesting fountains, but the water is *non potable* (not drinkable). Some water fountains have had 'non potable' signs in the last few days, while others have nothing to say either way, while a minority have *'eau potable'* (water drinkable), so it's hard to judge, especially when I'm thirsty.

After watching the Netherlands prevail over Japan in a local bar, I find a wild camping spot beside the river at the local football ground.

As I make my way back into Riez's town centre this Wednesday morning, I'm surprised to find a busy street market overtaking what was a quiet space last night. After stocking up on some fruit and bread on an even warmer morning than yesterday, I begin climbing through purple lavender farms before descending to the wide River Durance valley through small towns.

While admiring some tall rock formations in the valley, two elderly British ladies on touring bicycles appear. They are going the same way as me, so I follow them for a bit on a now hot, dry heat day. We eventually separate as I briefly use a rough canal path before I make today's destination of Volonne by 1 pm.

My Warmshower host Elisabeth, won't be home until the evening. Thankfully, I have found a stone water trough in the cool shade under the overhang of a building. It's a saviour on warm days like this.

A variety of water troughs, allow me to cool off

Over the past few days, it has felt like my Thermarest mattress has been going slightly down overnight, so this trough is a perfect spot to check for leaks. I can't see any regular bubbles after regularly dunking it in the trough, so I'm assuming it doesn't have a leak.

After spending a few hours in the local library staying cool, I make my way just out of town to my Warmshower host's home. I'm soon welcomed in by a friendly elderly couple. Elisabeth speaks English much better than her husband Jack, but they still both make me feel welcome as we share a meal, and I'm given some advice on my route for tomorrow.

Today's cycling felt rushed, as all I was focusing on was staying cool and getting to my destination rather than enjoying the ride or towns I went through. With weather predicted to be getting above 40 degrees over the next few days, I'm unsure what to do. I had similar weather this time last year in Russia.

Nice to Volonne (Google Maps)

You can spend hours planning your route the night before and then suddenly, when actually cycling, find a better route you were unaware of.

Originally I planned to stop due to heat in the town of Serres, but before getting there, I spot a sign to a gorge heading west. After checking my map, I realise it's a quiet road with less climbing than my planned route. However, this will mean ending up beside the Rhone in a more southerly location than planned,

Gorge de la Meouge

but with plenty of trains heading north to Lyon, I can manage. For the most part, I don't plan my days too much, I'm free to change my route at a whim, so I will.

The Gorge de la Meouge starts with incredibly scenic layers of rock in a narrow, curvy gorge that occasionally provides shade while climbing at a gentle gradient. I'm seeing a few road cyclists on the ride and cycling signs while people are out swimming in the river, so I'm feeling good about my choice.

Unfortunately, this gorge lasts for less than ten kilometres, as it soon becomes an open valley, still with a nice gradient but without shade, while the road cyclists have nearly all disappeared.

I don't have much food as I have become used to at least one bakery in every town. However, today the few small towns I'm passing through either have shops closed, or they don't exist at all.

Earlier in the day, I had deliberately not gone into the bigger town of Sisteron because I wanted to keep going before it became too warm. I stayed in Sisteron in 2013, so it was nice to briefly see again the large rock face which dominates the town. The last time I was in this region, it was cold and raining; now it's way too warm.

Eventually, I make it to Sederon, where the supermarket is closing at 1 pm for an afternoon siesta break. In this region, it's common for both supermarkets and bakeries to take at least a two hour break, but it's normally closer to four. While this is annoying, I am enjoying bakeries being open by 7 am, allowing me a snack for breakfast.

I consider stopping here for my own siesta, but the temperature is still just reasonable at around 32 degrees, so I will continue onto the slightly larger town of Montbrun. I do have to decide between the direct route with a four-kilometre climb but with a fast descent or a longer, gentler route. Overall I will probably do the same amount of climbing, but the quicker descent will mean less time in the sun.

The climb is manageable with some switchbacks, so I just take my time to get up. After meeting some road cyclists at the top of the pass, it is indeed a quick descent on switchbacks.

The air is now feeling warm, so as soon as I make Montbrun, I find the air-conditioned Office de Tourisme and rest inside for a few hours as the temperature is now 39 degrees. The library is next door, but the librarian doesn't like me, not sure why.

A zigzagging route up and down on the way to Montbrun

The old part of Montbrun is at a high point, so late in the afternoon, I walk up a steep road to a row of old buildings and a tower, with some average views.

I'm hoping tonight to watch the first World Cup quarter-final between England and Norway, starting at 9 pm. However, all hotels and restaurants here are closing before then. Thankfully, I have learned of a sports bar in a town down the range which stays open until 11 pm. So in this late afternoon heat, I will cycle for a few hours, hopefully as the weather cools down.

Initially, descending is comfortable, with some shade and wind keeping me cool. However, when one meandering section requires climbing, I'm back in the stinking hot sun, so I'm relieved once I start descending again.

High above me throughout my evening ride on my left is Mount Ventoux, another famous Tour de France climb. Earlier on this trip, I met cyclists planning to cycle up it. It's not something I have considered as climbs just for the sake of it are not my thing, and with this weather, definitely not.

I'm in Mollans-sur-Ouveze just after 7 pm and thankfully the supermarket is still open, so I'm able to refresh my liquids and obtain more supplies.

After cooking dinner in a park, I make my way to the sports bar, where England thrashes Norway on a terrible grainy television. Norway's performance is bittersweet because if Australia had defeated Norway, we would have been playing England. With the history of Australia-England sporting rivalries, this would have been extra special and would have helped spread the Matildas brand even further to the Australian public.

After sleeping at the football ground, I'm woken at 5:30 am by sprinklers, but I'm not quick enough to get out of my tent and move it before it becomes wet. On an already warm day, it will dry quickly. With sunrise about 6 am, there is some light, so I will pack up now. I'm usually packing up my tent after 7 am and on the road after 8 am, so I'm about two hours early, but with the heat, this is fine.

My route is nearly all on an old railway line which is now a paved road, so it's an enjoyable ride to Vaison-la-Romaine, as I pass some former cement railway stations. As the name suggests, this town has Roman features throughout. On a cooler day, I would stop here but with 40 degrees predicted, I will continue

Road uses the rail formation

before it gets too hot. Besides if I stay, by the time anything opens up, it will be too hot to enjoy walking around.

Part of my route continues to follow a former railway line for another hour. At times, the road is using the rail right of way, including former rail bridges.

At Jonquieres, I have the choice to either head directly west to the city of Orange or use a developed rail trail to head east to Carpentras. Since the weather is still just reasonable to cycle I will join the paved rail trail. I'm soon passing more cement stations, going on former rail bridges, under road bridges, and through a scenic deep rail cutting.

Jonquieres Station on this rail trail which has a few road bridges

Friday market in Carpentras

By 10:30 am, it's warm as I arrive in Carpentras. Despite this, the old town centre is full of market stalls for the weekly Friday market, but I can't find any drinking water fountains. Helpfully a cycle path goes around the old part of the city, presumably where the old city walls were.

After an explore, I make my way to McDonald's to stay cool and use wi-fi to research what to do for the next few days. It's the hottest temperature ever in France, and this heatwave looks like continuing for the next few days. This weather is what I get at home during Australian summers, so I'm used to it, but I just prefer not to be cycling in it.

Perhaps I should get a train to cooler London for Australia's World Cup cricket match against New Zealand at Lords tomorrow before getting back to Lyon for the football semi-finals. There are direct trains from Lyon to London, but I needed to have booked a while ago.

It just doesn't work out financially or logistically with my bicycle, and anyway,

I'm hoping tonight to watch France play the USA on television somewhere with a group of locals. There is no point in catching a local train as it's hot nearly everywhere in France, so I will just make my way to the library to stay cool.

In the evening, after searching around, I have found a pizza bar to watch the quarter-final match alongside about two dozen locals.

It's a similar experience to last year in Russia as the emotions of the home fans ebbs and flows. Unfortunately it's a similar result, with the home team losing 1-2.

It's now dark, so it's refreshing cycling back on the rail trail in the dark, especially through the deep cutting. I'm not sure where I'm sleeping other than to find somewhere away from civilisation. When I can't see lights or hear anyone, I just set my tent up beside the trail. Since it's so hot, I won't bother putting the fly on my tent.

The first cyclist passes me on the rail trail at 6 am so there is no need for an alarm clock.

Waking up on a rail trail

It's a straightforward cycle on the trail back to Jonquieres, where despite this former railway having continued to Orange, it isn't a rail trail. However, for the most part, quiet roads follow the rail right of way until meeting an active rail line on the outskirts of Orange.

It's not even 8 am, and already warm as I arrive at the smaller than expected Orange with only the Roman theatre and Arc de Triomphe d'Orange of interest. There are other Roman-era buildings but only for admiring, as they are either just wall remains or being used privately.

The theatre is engaging as I learn how it operated with the curtain dropping rather than rising and that people were separated by class despite it being a free performance. Inside are videos showing examples of the different types of performances, from tragedies to pantomime and comedies. It is still used today for concerts and theatre shows.

In Orange is the Arc de Triomphe d'Orange and a Roman Theatre

The theatre was built on the side of a hill, and castle remains are above so I could walk up to it but by 11 am, it's hot enough to not be a priority.

Instead, I head to the railway station and catch a train to nearby Avignon, a city I enjoyed visiting in 2013. I wonder if it will still be as scenic as I recall, or having seen so many other medieval-style towns since, will it now be less impressive.

Volonne to Orange (Google Maps)

Cycling is allowed beside Avingon's wall

Pont d'Avignon

Once off the train, I see the memorable medieval walls around the city, so it's good to be back.

Also still here is the bridge that only half crosses the Rhone. Nearly 500 years ago, a flood washed away part of this bridge. Since then, subsequent floods have washed away more sections leaving only a small well maintained part, which I access after paying a fee.

In 2013 my budget was less than this trip so I missed seeing a few sites, including the Palace of the Popes, so I will take the opportunity now.

During the 1300s, Popes lived here, rather than in Rome, while Avignon wasn't a part of France then, with the French border just across the Rhone.

On this tour, I'm given a touchscreen tablet that provides audio and visual information. As I scan the tablet around, it shows me what each room used to look like centuries ago. Today the walls are plain, but according to the tablet, they were once colourfully decorated with patterns, while we see what furniture they had back then. The actual building is nothing unique as it's just like visiting any other church or castle. The touchscreen showing how it used to look will be how I remember it.

Once out of the palace, the temperature is now 40 degrees, so I make my way to my Airbnb apartment. My host is flying to Senegal, so I have the place to myself, allowing me to spend the afternoon watching the last two FIFA World Cup quarterfinals while listening to Australia beat New Zealand in the Cricket World Cup.

Touchscreen view of the Palace of the Popes

I'm not sure where to go after Avignon, as it's still too hot to cycle. I could use trains over the next few days to get to Lyon using a route via Beziers, Millau and Saint Étienne. This would allow me to see the famous high road bridge across the valley at Millau. However, from the available train schedules, it appears I will end up having to rush through some places, while other times, I will have too much time waiting for the next train.

Instead, I'm looking for anywhere around Lyon, which may be cooler in the next few days, to allow me to cycle. There aren't many places that won't be hot, but one town, Saint Agreve, has a cooler prediction. Before this heatwave, I had considered cycling a rail trail to there. With Monday looking slightly cooler, only mid-thirties, I will cycle there.

In the morning, after exploring a little more, including using cycle paths that go right around the outside of most of the medieval wall around Avignon, I catch a train north to Valence. From the train's window, I'm seeing glimpses of where I had cycled beside the Rhone about two weeks ago.

A few touring cyclists are on this train, including an Irish couple who have done the same ride as the Englishmen I met in Vallon Pont d'Arc, from Saint-Malo to Nice. They are now heading to Nantes via Lyon to cycle to Roscoff, where a ferry will take them back to Ireland. Next week I will be getting the same train to Nantes from Lyon and a different ferry from Roscoff.

While staying cool in the decent Office de Tourisme in Valence, I notice some tourist railway brochures. They are not far from me, so once again, I will adjust my route.

After waiting until 6 pm for it to cool down, I set off by retracing my route in reverse out of Valence on the ViaRhona heading south to Beauchastel. Unlike last time I'm not seeing any touring cyclists, but I do pass a few people permanently living under bridges in vans.

Once I join the Dolce Via rail trail, it's a relaxing ride with plenty of shade as I'm slowly climbing beside the River Eyrieux, west away from the Rhone. Most of this route has been carved out high above the river, sometimes on a dedicated rail trail, other times roads are using the old rail right of way. Most towns are below on the other side of the river, while a few people are swimming, but I can't find an access point to the river from the rail trail.

Random shelter shed

By 8 pm, the day is cooling down, but dark clouds soon appear, and then thunder begins, so I'm suddenly in need of shelter.

Miraculously one appears beside the trail as a heavy shower begins. It's only a small wooden shelter with just a roof, but I'm sheltered enough to stay dry. The rain eases after fifteen minutes, but I will camp here since I have found a perfect dry spot.

The Dolce Via follows a river and has a few bridges

It's clear skies in the morning, and thankfully as it continues to hug the rock, most of the rail trail is covered in shade, allowing a relaxing scenic ride through small towns as the trail crosses the river a few times on stone viaducts.

By 11 am it's warm again but slightly cooler than the previous three days, but I'm still glad to make the town of Le Cheylard to cool off.

On Maps.me, past here, the rail trail is an uncompleted dotted line to Saint Agreve. After looking more closely, I see that from Le Cheylard, a branch line went from here to Lamastre, a town I was planning to visit anyway after Sainte Agreve, so I have found a shortcut.

At the Office de Tourisme, I learn that the rail trail is now open all the way to Sainte Agreve, having been completed last year. On a cooler day, I may have done this trail but instead, I will now take the branch line to Lamastre.

It's a little trickier, with some gravel to negotiate when not on paved sections used by cars. Still, it snakes its way up on a railway grade before descending for a longer period.

As I arrive into Lamastre, the rail trail ends in a car park where a few RV's are staying. Across the road, the rails still exist as a tourist train operates on this smaller metre gauge railway. This rail line heads east back towards the Rhone, but isn't running from here today. Nearby is the option of a Velorail ride on a short section of this line. I could do it this afternoon, but it is now 36 degrees, so instead, I'm trying to stay cool in town. Thankfully, the railway station is a nice place inside to stay cool.

It's a quiet town, so in the evening, after looking around for a while, I will wild camp at the local sports ground beside the rail trail.

Pop up market in Lamastre, while the bakery has a variety of tasty items

In the morning, I'm surprised to see a market popping up in Lamastre covering the whole town square with hundreds of people around. So after some delicious food, including baked goods, I leave using a quiet meandering road. I'm trying to follow the railway line, but I'm only getting the occasional brief glimpse.

After only fourteen kilometres, I'm at Boucieu Le Roi, where I'm hoping to enjoy a Velorail ride. I have heard of this style of rail travel on old railway lines, but I'm yet to do this, so I'm looking forward to trying it.

It's busier than I expected with plenty of people around this two storey cement station in this small town. There are about 50 red four-seater Velorail cars on several rail sidings alongside a few regular railway vehicles and passenger carriages. As I ask to buy a ticket in my broken French, I'm told they are sold out.

However, one staff member who speaks English takes pity on me, allowing me to ride with another staff member. He only speaks a few words in English, but we can talk about our lives using a mixture of French and English. I explain that I'm heading to Lyon this afternoon to watch the World Cup semi-finals. However, since he is wearing St Etienne football shorts whose main rival is nearby Lyon, he naturally doesn't like Lyon.

It's heavier cycling than on a bicycle, a bit like the brakes are rubbing or when I tried a pedal kayak. This is why a downhill route is needed to operate a Velorail because they are too heavy to cycle uphill, and need momentum on the flat. We are at the back with about a dozen cars in front of us, so we often have to slow down for other customers. Still, it's a relaxing ride as we pass through a couple of tunnels, while below is a river in a gorge. Since I'm sitting down, it's a different view of the rail right of way than being on a regular train or cycling on a trail.

My first Velorail ride

I'm just not sure if I will do it again, but still, it's an experience.

We finish in the middle of nowhere, so we get off the Velorails and ride in a single-car train back up the track while this train tows all the Velorails together. I had asked if I could take my bicycle on this train and then ride from the end, which would avoid a climb, but I wasn't allowed.

The climb isn't particularly hard on this quiet road as I hear the next train go through below while I'm well above on an open rocky landscape. After descending, I'm back following the river and the railway before I soon meet the Rhone again.

I could cycle north to Lyon on the ViaRhona, but I'm out of time before the first semi-final tonight between England and the USA. Instead, I will take a train. While waiting for my train, I stream the radio coverage of the start of the Women's Ashes cricket series with a one-day international starting in Leicester.

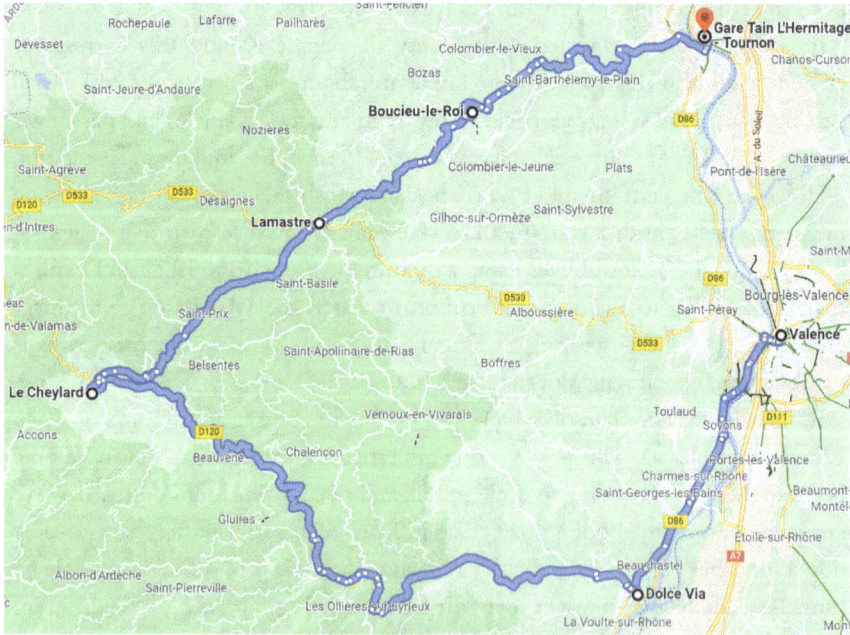

Valance to Tain (Google Maps)

Lyon, not Nathan

I'm a little overwhelmed as I exit Gare de Lyon-Perrache into one of the largest cities in France. On my way to a large square, I'm seeing so many Americans, in particular families with children, whereas most other World Cup supporters are generally adults.

This enormous open square has been turned into a giant Fan Fest with plenty of games, merchandise and a Futsal court. After obtaining information in the busy Office de Tourisme located to the side of this square, I begin making my way to my Warmshower host's home.

Lyon is located on a junction of two rivers, so there are bridges to cross on a wide river which looks more like a canal and is just as hectic as Paris. Thankfully, busy cycle paths beside the river take me to a large open park where a free zoo has foreign animals on display, including giraffes, lions, monkeys, and plenty of birds.

Gates leading to a Zoo

Nearby is my Warmshower host's home, where I'm staying with Thomas and his young family. He recommends cycling to the football stadium, which is ten kilometres out of the city, but for the first semi-final, I will try the tram system, especially as a tram stop is near his home.

I do have to change trams in the city centre, but overall it's an easy ride as the tram drops me right out the front of the stadium. The majority of the crowd are American, but there are also plenty of English supporters. I'm not the only Australian here as I'm seeing a few yellow shirts, along with many other nationalities.

Outside every World Cup stadium, there have been signs saying you can't bring in bottles of any kind. I presume this is to make people buy inside. I disagree with this, so I have tried to sneak a plastic water bottle into every stadium; sometimes I have been successful, other times not.

Out the front of this stadium, temporary metal fencing has been erected in a dogleg route allowing me to sneakily leave my bottle beside a fence, and go through security before stealthily collecting my water bottle.

As for the match, it's see-sawing with the USA going ahead before England levels the score. When Alex Morgan scores USA's second goal, she celebrates with mockingly sipping a cup of tea.

England then has a goal ruled out for offside by VAR before their captain Steph Houghton misses a penalty as the USA holds on to a 2-1 win.

After the match, with a nearly 60,000 strong crowd, everyone is lining up to get on a few trams. Since there is only one tram line back to the city, it takes me more than an hour and a half to get back, with more than half of that time spent lining up. I can now see why Thomas suggested it's easier cycling to the stadium.

Before this trip, randomly somewhere on the internet, I came across a message from Rachel Allison from the Mississippi State University, asking to interview people attending the World Cup. So I sent her an email, and she asked to meet in Lyon. Since I have time between the semi-finals, I have organised to meet her at her Airbnb apartment.

It's an interesting talk as we compare women's sport in Australia and the USA, in particular, how they are viewed in each country. There are some similarities with crowded sporting markets but also different expectations of sport, especially with performances in this World Cup. With the USA three times World Champions, they expect to be in the final, therefore many Americans have seemingly only come to France for the semi-finals and the final. Most Australian supporters have been here for the whole World Cup, and were hoping but didn't assume we would make the semi-finals.

Walking beside the River Saone

It's quiet in the suburbs as I walk alongside the River Saone back towards the city centre, with no real plan. As the streets suddenly become busier, I have seemingly ended up in a tourist pedestrian mall, where a funicular railway heads up a hill to the Basilique Notre-Dame de Fourvière.

This church was only built in the 1800s, while of more interest is the surrounding views of the city stretching out below.

It's a busy lookout with plenty of orange-shirted Dutch, bright-yellow-shirted Swedes, white-shirted Americans and yellow-shirted Australians. As I walk around, once again, I bump into the same Australian man I saw in Valenciennes, Montpellier and Nice, so we say hello again, and he talks about attending a few other World Cup matches. Despite the frequent meetings, we never exchanged names, but since returning home we have met a few times again at A-League Women's games, so I now know his name is Teddy.

I soon return to the city square because Australian and American supporters have organised a match using the futsal court in the Fan Fest. It's a warm afternoon with plenty of children playing games and sponsor souvenirs being given away. As I walk around, I meet my flatmates again from Nice along with a few other Australians.

A few different matches are being played throughout the afternoon on the Futsal court. When it's our turn, there are nearly 40 Australians here, and the majority are women, while surprisingly, there are fewer Americans, and they are nearly all men. With so many wanting to play, I will let others play because I only have my bicycle sandals with metal cleats. Still, it's an enjoyable experience cheering on my fellow Australians as we rotate our squad regularly.

Australians ready for futsal in Lyon

After all this, I only have enough time to visit one museum. The Centre d'Histoire de la Resistance et de la Deporation Musee focuses on Lyon during the Second World War. It has plenty of information and items, particularly on the impact of Jewish people deported from here and the overall population's resistance to the German occupation.

Stories on how they were able to resist the Germans while avoiding detection are inspirational. They used things like a homemade self-timer made out of a mousetrap and a tin can, to spread resistance news.

Homemade device for spreading news

However, stories of the Jewish deportations are just depressing as some locals were complicit in helping send people to concentration camps.

The only issue with this informative museum is that the English paper guides don't appear to line up well with the displays, so it takes a while to work out how it all makes sense.

After last night where it took forever to get back after the game, I will take Thomas's advice and cycle to the stadium for tonight's second semi-final. Near his house is the Rhone with a cycle path beside it, so it's an easy cycle before I leave the river and follow the tram tracks to the stadium. A few bicycles are locked to bike racks beside a path on the way to the stadium, so I will leave my bicycle here; I hope it will be okay.

I try again to sneak a plastic water bottle in, but this time, it disappears between when I leave it and when I return to it. A police officer is looking suspiciously at me, so I walk away.

The crowd is more even tonight, with bays at one end full of yellow Swedish supporters, while there are plenty of orange Dutch supporters at the other end.

As for the game, it's a lot scrappier compared to last night, with neither side looking like scoring. It's a relief once the Netherlands finally score in extra time.

Sunset view from the Lyon stadium

Mother Nature must favour the Dutch because a beautiful orange sunset takes up the whole skyline during the match.

It's much quicker leaving the stadium tonight because while most are waiting for a tram, I collect my bicycle and begin cycling back in the dark. Since my route is initially beside the tram tracks, I wave to the sardines going past in the trams. Thomas was right; the cycling is quicker as I'm back more than an hour earlier than last night.

With three days until the World Cup Final, I have plenty of spare time. So I will cycle more of the ViaRhona this time towards Genève with no real plan, except to get a train back in a few days. With more hot weather predicted, I have left my warm clothes and sleeping bag at Thomas's house, as I doubt I will need them.

I take the same signed cycle route as last night beside the Rhone as it takes me out of the suburbs of Lyon. Every so often, I have to switch sides of the river, while for the majority of the morning, I'm on a shaded tree-lined cycle path, so it's an easy, relaxing cycle. At one stage, I meet an American family of four who currently live in Germany. Like me, they have just watched the semi-finals and are now cycling until they get a train back to Lyon for the final.

There are sections of the ViaRhona not yet completed, so some road cycling is required after lunch. One road is busier than I hoped, so I will try a dotted line track near the river. It starts okay, but soon this track deteriorates and becomes narrow in a forest with some stinging needles to avoid.

Once I find my way back to a quiet road, I'm now passing through a few small scenic villages with hills to my right and the river on my left. After crossing the Rhone into the larger town of Lagnieu, a rail trail takes me back towards the river. Along the way, a tiny old yellow harvester in a small cereal paddock is harvesting the crop, while other paddocks are full of small recently bailed hay.

The ViaRhona pass a few small farms, before being beside the Rhone

After crossing the river again, it's becoming more scenic, with pleasant hills to admire while a paved path goes through a few resorts right beside the Rhone.

I'm not sure where I'm sleeping tonight, so I will just keep cycling as the ViaRhona takes some dogleg routes while crossing main roads.

As I approach the small town of Quirieu, I spot a small pavilion in an open space which presumably is an abandoned sports field. As I look closer, I see that water and power are available, but the toilets are locked. It's in a quiet spot, so I will see if anyone shows up and if no one does, I will stay.

Since no one appears, it feels safe to camp here.

In the morning, after a rail trail takes me slightly away from the river, I return to being near the Rhone and continue following it by using either trails or quiet roads. Occasionally, I have to cross the river, which is fine except for when a half-built bridge forces me to detour on a main road. It's fine as the traffic is light, while in places, it's scenic as the road goes through a few tunnels and passes a small castle under a rock.

After following a deviation canal of the Rhone for a while, as the Rhone reappears, a side canal takes me to the most scenic town of the day. There is just one problem, the canal separates me from the village, and I can only find a high pedestrian bridge to get over into Chanaz. So I will have to leave my bicycle and walk over.

On the ViaRhona route

Castle under a rock

It feels like a tourist town with restaurants and many water vessels available to hire, presumably because of nearby Lac du Bourget, which is the largest lake solely in France. The ferry south across this lake to Aix les Bains only operates on Sundays, so instead, I will continue north following the Rhone.

Beside a canal, which leads me to Chanaz

As I approach Seyssel, I pass a large public park in a corner where the small River Fier flows into the Rhone. It appears a road follows this small river east into a gorge away from the Rhone. After visiting Seyssel, I end my day at this busy park, which has a velodrome, a lake and a visitor centre, a perfect spot to cook dinner. A track that goes around the corner where the rivers meet is an excellent dark spot to camp.

For my last day before heading back to Lyon by train, I could continue following the Rhone to Genève in Switzerland. However, having already been to Genève, I will go elsewhere. Ideally, I would love to explore more of Switzerland, but I don't have enough time. With some of these sections of the ViaRhona still being developed, it's probably not worth it anyway.

Instead, I will go to Annecy via the Gorge de Fier. Initially, the small climb through a narrow gorge is scenic before becoming a more open landscape but still with more short climbs. After a few towns, I'm soon descending to the Gorge de Fier.

The walkway in Gorge De Fier

Since 1869 walking routes have been offered through this scenic gorge. Initially, this involves high walkways attached to the edge of a narrow gorge while the river is flowing below. As the walkway changes height a few times, this allows me to admire the gorge at different levels. It is incredible, and it's hard to imagine building this walkway in the first place.

It regularly floods here, including high above the walkway, causing severe damage. Photos of the 2015 floods show twisted metal. Eventually, the walk ends beside a more open space at river level with many eroded rocks.

After a few narrow walkways, the Gorge de Fier ends at an open area

Cycle beside Lake Annecy, mostly on a rail trail

A memorable day of my 2013 trip was cycling from Annecy to Ugine on a paved rail trail beside the scenic Lake Annecy on a beautiful sunny day. Today six days short of six years since I was here, it's a little more overcast but still a scenic ride. I'm passing some familiar sites while admiring the beautiful blue Alpine lake and the mountains behind it. It is still one of the most scenic rides I have done, but I'm not sure if I will ever be back.

After following a cycle route beside a canal, I'm in Albertville. I don't need to be back in Lyon until tomorrow so I could stay the night somewhere. However, with thunderstorms around, I will return to Lyon by train tonight.

After admiring some scenic mountains from a train, I have an hour stopover in Chambery between trains, so I will have a quick look around this holiday town. It's enough time to see the outside of a castle and an elephant themed fountain.

The second train is full of Americans making their way back to Lyon. So for once, I have to hang my bicycle on a bicycle rack rather than leaning it against folding seats.

In hindsight, I should have stayed another night somewhere to have a longer look around.

Elephant statue in Chambery

I have some time before needing to leave for the World Cup final, so I will do some maintenance on my bicycle. Swapping the tyres so the more worn out rear tyre is now on the front, in theory means both should now last longer. While doing this, I'm listening to Australia bat comfortably against England in the third women's one-day international cricket match in Canterbury.

Once again, I cycle to the World Cup stadium, where I finally discover dedicated bicycle parking under the stadium. The only issue is that security wants me to take all my gear off my bicycle, including my water bottles and small tool bag. Thankfully, I'm able to cloak them. There are hundreds of bicycles locked up under the stadium in a dedicated spot, showing just how appreciated bicycles are in France.

Once I'm inside the stadium, I find some wi-fi to check the cricket score, as England had started batting just as I left my Warmshower host's home. I'm shocked to see that in the time it took me to cycle to the stadium, England has been bowled out for 75, with Ellyse Perry taking seven wickets. We are now six points up in the Ashes multi-series format, so I wonder what the test match will be like when I get to Taunton.

World Cup Final 2019

As for the crowd here in Lyon, other than one lower end of the stadium full of Dutch supporters in Orange, the majority is American. It reminds me of being in Winnipeg during the 2015 World Cup when Americans outnumbered me.

As for the match, the USA appears to be comfortable most of the time despite not scoring until the second half, with Rose Lavelle's solo run goal a highlight as they win 2-0. Since the crowd is predominantly American, the celebrations feel like I'm in the USA, especially as the chant of equal pay is loudly made a few times.

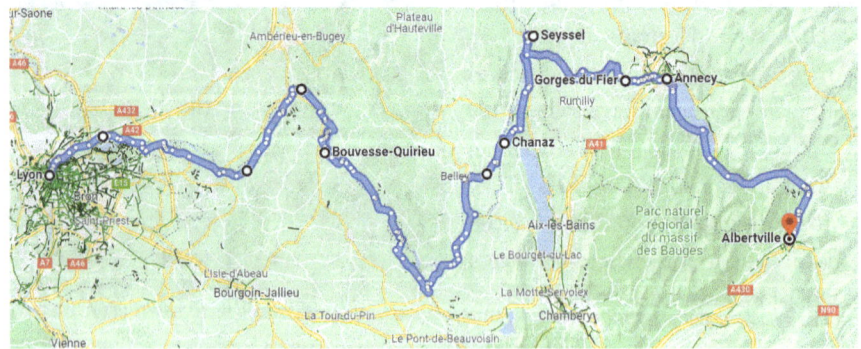

Lyon to Albertville (Google Maps)

Brittany

With the only Women's Ashes test match starting on 18 July, I knew before I left home I had ten days to get from Lyon to Taunton in southwest England. So I spend time working out how to cross the English Channel, including looking up a range of train and ferry timetables.

I could use a few trains, including Eurostar under the English Channel, a trip I did in 2013. However, the Lyon to London direct Eurostar doesn't allow bicycles, neither does the TGV service between Lyon and Paris. Instead, to get to Paris with a bicycle, you have to take a much slower train. Furthermore, since I last went on Eurostar, the price for taking a bicycle has gone up considerably.

The other option is one of a few ferries that cross the English Channel. The most sensible choice is from Roscoff in the far west of France in the Brittany region, which will take me to Plymouth, not far from Taunton.

Luckily, I booked this ferry before I left Australia because when checking in at Melbourne Airport back in April, I was asked for proof of when I was leaving Europe. As an Australian, I can spend a maximum of 90 days in the Schengen region of Europe without a visa. Strangely, last year when I flew into Moscow, I wasn't asked when I was leaving Russia, and in that instance, I had no proof of when I was leaving.

I don't have enough time to cycle to Roscoff, so I have had to find a train route that allows bicycles on board. After looking at a few options, the most sensible route involves two trains. A semi-fast Intercities train will take me on a seven-hour cross country ride to Nantes for €20. Then a local TER train will take me to Rosporden in the south of Brittany, where a rail trail will allow me to cross the Brittany Peninsula in a day.

Tunnel for non-motorised traffic under Lyon

To get to Gare Lyon Vaise in the western part of Lyon, Google Maps suggests a mile-long tunnel in the middle of city, which is unusual for a bicycle route. However, this tunnel has a dedicated lane for non-motorised vehicles next to a pedestrian path, and also a bus lane, while cars are using a separate tunnel next door. On this Monday morning it's busy with cyclists travelling between the Rhone and the Saone rivers.

It's a busy train to Nantes, with people getting on and off all day, including numerous cyclists. This makes sense since this train follows a popular cycle route beside the River Loire for the second half of the trip.

Bicycles on the train to Nantes

I couldn't pre-book a seat or bicycle space on the train to Rosporden, while strangely, it's nearly twice as expensive for this short two-hour ride than my seven-hour train earlier in the day. Plenty of people are lining up, but even so, as I board, I'm still shocked just how packed this local train is. Fortunately, I'm just able to find a space to store my bicycle, while I have to stand up the whole time.

I'm off the train at Rosporden, just before the supermarket closes, allowing me to collect some fresh supplies for dinner. After cooking by a small lake, I follow the rail trail for a short period until a spot beside a small canal not far off the trail will do as a place to set up my tent.

After visiting a delicious bakery, I set off. Despite it being a dirt surface, it's an easy enough cycle as most of this rail trail is through forests. Having been in mountainous southern France for a while, Brittany feels different as it's flatter and more rural. They also have a local language, but since I'm only spending one full day here, I won't have enough time to learn anything meaningful.

Rail museum in a former station

Along the way, I'm passing a few abandoned cement railway stations, with one now a small informative railway museum with some English information. Brittany used to have a metre gauge railway network separate from the national rail network until all lines except one closed in 1967. This rail system was nicknamed the star because it spread out from one city, so on a map, it looks like a star with pointy lines heading in every direction. Now most of these former lines are signed cycle paths.

A few cyclists and abandoned stations on this rail trail

This rail trail is split in half because the town of Carhaix still has one active rail line. The middle of the star rail network was here, but now it's just the end of a French branch line.

The second half is just as scenic as it mostly follows a river to Morlaix, where a still-active rail line exists. Throughout the day, I have been encountering cyclists, including at one stage a large group of children and adults.

A two storey high rail viaduct which crosses over the long rectangular city centre dominates Morlaix. I'm told in the Office de Tourisme that you can walk on one level of this viaduct. However, once I finally find a way up, it has just closed for the day.

Morlaix Viaduct

With Roscoff only a couple of hours ride north of here and my ferry not leaving until 3 pm tomorrow, I'm in no rush, so I can wild camp wherever I want. I'm just unsure where, so I begin cycling north using a short rail trail to leave town before cycling beside a canal.

I soon spot a church up a hill. As I make my way up there, an open grass area is across the road from the church. It's out of sight enough for me to set my tent up in fading light.

The first part of the ride to Roscoff follows a canal which gradually becomes the sea. The tide is clearly out, leaving a shallow river with high uncovered muddy green banks. I'm told when the tide is low, it's possible to access some of the numerous islands just off the coast.

Tide is out near Morlaix but is back again as I make Roscoff

However, by the time I'm near an island, the tide is back, preventing me from walking to it.

Even once I leave the coastline behind, the ride is fine as I travel through built-up coastal towns until making Roscoff. It feels like an English town with numerous English tourists, and plenty of seaside carnival attractions, while a local market is on.

With time before the ferry leaves, I listen as India loses early wickets in their chase against New Zealand in the first Men's Cricket World Cup semi-final.

As I line up for the ferry in my own dedicated lane, four touring cyclists with various pannier bag set-ups are waiting here, but we never end up chatting on the ferry.

Once onboard bicycles are tied to a rail on a car deck. As I walk upstairs, there are a few decks to explore. It reminds me of the Spirit of Tasmania, with various activities to do, including a cinema, children's games and several types of restaurants.

On one deck are four televisions showing sporting events including Wimbledon and the Tour de France, but none are showing the cricket. I ask them to change the channel, but I'm told they can't, so I listen using wi-fi as New Zealand upsets India while the French coastline disappears from view.

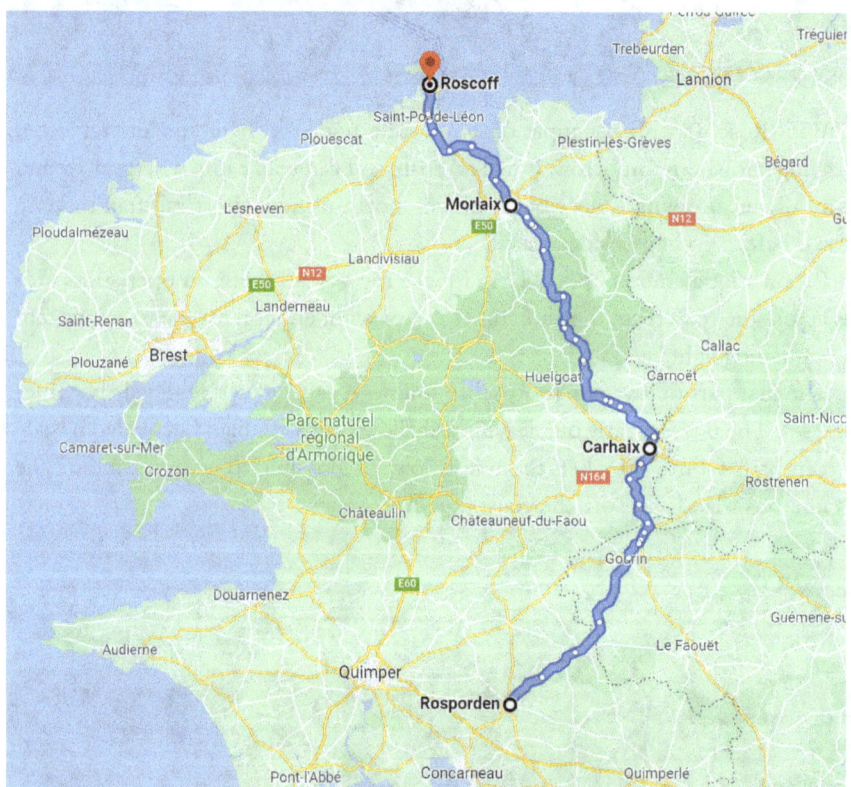

Rosporden to Roscoff (Google Maps)

Devon

After a six-hour crossing of the English Channel, the ferry arrives into overcast dull-looking Plymouth. As I make my way out of the terminal, an old man with a white beard and a bicycle asks me if I'm Joel. I say yes, and he introduces himself as Sid, my Warmshower host in Plymouth and says, 'follow me'.

He soon outpaces me up a hill to his home. So many Warmshower hosts live up a hill.

It's strange suddenly talking freely in English, but I'm often replying in French to Sid's questions as it has become a habit even when people speak to me in English.

Sid walks up to a nearby high point of Plymouth every day, so I join him in the morning.

Once we reach the top of this small grass-top hill surrounded by houses, Sid explains how there used to be battery guns stationed here from the Napoleonic Wars until the end of the Second World War. Now only the bricks and stone foundations are left, with a few information panels around. From this height, the numerous surrounding houses all look the same. Sid explains that because Plymouth was bombed during the Second World War, most buildings are from after then. He also tells me we can see Cornwall to the west, a place I thought about visiting but probably won't.

My first full day in Plymouth is about getting my bicycle and body serviced, along with exploring the city.

A few days ago, I booked a service with Evans Cycles because my bicycle hasn't been looked at since leaving Australia. Along with a general service, I'm told it will need a new brake cable and a new chain, so I will leave it here all day.

My right knee is still sore from my fall in Torino two weeks ago, so I have found an osteopath. He finds my ligaments are still swollen but thankfully no significant damage. He recommends getting the swelling down using Voltaren and ice.

Today Australia is playing England in the second Men's Cricket World Cup semi-final, so I'm searching for a transistor radio to listen to today's cricket and the six Ashes test matches coming up over the next two months. I could just use an app on my iPhone, but this will require me to get a SIM card, which will drain its battery, so a separate radio is preferred. It will also allow me to see what British radio is like.

I'm not having any luck finding one in the various electronic stores. So without a radio, throughout the day, I'm ducking into pubs to check the cricket score as Australia is batting first.

Plymouth's focus is its harbour, as many people immigrated from here to various places, including Australia. A few plaques on a stone wall refer to where people migrated to, including one for the Cornish part of South Australia, where I briefly lived a few years ago.

The most famous departure was the Mayflower to North America, so where these pilgrims left from is called the Mayflower Steps. However, I can't see anything because they are being refurbished in preparation for the 400th anniversary in 2020.

Old railway office is now a tourist office

Nearby is a four storey red-bricked building with the *London-South-Western Railway Parcel Office* name still on the outside in block letters. Plymouth's tourist information centre is on the bottom floor of this former railway building, while above is a museum focusing on the journey the Mayflower Pilgrims took. On three levels are stories of the people who migrated, why they chose to leave and the varying success of those who settled in North America. There are also items on display, including a model of the Mayflower sailing ship.

Around from this harbour, is a grass-covered headland with plenty of people out enjoying this cooler day than I'm used to.

Late in the afternoon, after randomly walking into a store called Argos, I have found a digital USB charging transistor radio with the help of a friendly staff member. However, instead of having stock on display, they just have lists of available items. You order the item, and it magically appears from the back, ten minutes later.

Throughout the day, it has been strange walking past shops that appear more franchised than France, with many selling cheap junk. Maybe because I can now read shop signs, I know what each one is selling compared to Europe, where sometimes I had no idea.

As for food, bakeries are more like Australia, with pasties and meat pies now available, while the more chocolate-based items have decreased, along with the mini pizza buns I was enjoying.

There is also less stone fruit available, and nearly all fruit in supermarkets is sold in sealed plastic bags, with half a dozen pieces often in each bag. So it's hard to get just a single piece of fruit. It also generates a lot more plastic waste. Even more annoyingly, these plastic containers aren't resealable, which means raspberries and blueberries spill easily. Thankfully, I have my Tupperware container for storing berries.

Fruit is now sold in plastic and so containers aren't resealable

While walking to collect my bicycle, I listen as England comfortably chase down Australia's total of 223. So England will now play New Zealand in the Men's Cricket World Cup Final in a few days.

It's been strange today cycling back on the left side of the road. I have gone to the right side a few times, but a more common occurrence is looking the wrong way when crossing the road or at an intersection. From previous experience in a few days, I should get used to being back on the left.

Compared to France, there appears to be less cycling infrastructure, especially bicycle lanes, and fewer cyclists.

In the evening, back at Sid's place, I spend some time working out a plan on how I will cycle to Taunton in time for the start of the Women's Test in six days. With Dartmoor National Park nearby, most of my planning involves finding a route through the park while still cycling rail trails where I can.

In the morning, after another walk with Sid up to the same hill, I will leave Plymouth by following Sustrans National Cycle Network Route 27.

In 2013 I was pleasantly surprised to discover the National Cycle Network with hundreds of numbered routes criss-crossing the country. I particularly enjoyed National Cycle Route 4 along the Kennet and Avon Canal between the River Thames and Bath, along with Route 8 through the Brecon National Park north of Cardiff.

This is the main cycling reason for returning to the UK, especially since most of these routes involve rail trails or towpaths beside canals. If there are gaps, often these signed cycle routes will take quiet roads.

I still have a National Cycle Network paper map of the UK at home, which helpfully shows sections that include off-road paths like rail trails and canal towpaths. It was useful for developing route ideas, especially in Scotland. I'm assuming more cycling routes have been developed since 2013, so looking online at the cycle network has also been useful.

Navigating the National Cycle Network is easy because these routes are well signed with white numbers on a small red square on a larger blue background. Often at junctions and in towns, there will be more prominent signs with distance markers to the next town. Helpfully sometimes tourist offices will have brochures on specific cycle routes.

The lower the number, usually the longer the route is. For example, Route Two follows the southern coastline, while Route One follows the east coast all the way to the top of Scotland. Often a route with more digits will relate to a route with fewer digits nearby, sometimes as a loop route. For example, route 339 is a loop of route 33.

It's nostalgic seeing these National Cycle Network signs again, especially one of the four types of artistically designed mile marker posts, which I recall from 2013. Apparently, there are just 1,000 of these throughout the UK. Each one is uniquely shaped, coloured, and designed for that specific location as direction and distance information is on them.

One of four types of mileposts

After crossing the River Plym on an old rail bridge, National Cycle Route 27 initially follows the shoreline of the currently broad Plym. As the river narrows, this route becomes a rail trail named after Devon local Francis Drake. For a short time beside this trail is a tourist railway which only operates on weekends. It This trail is in good condition, with a few viaducts to cycle on as I'm passing through a mixture of forests and open treeless landscapes.

Unfortunately, this route leaves the rail right of way a few times. Even then, I soon find an even older horse-drawn tramway to follow, which still has stone sleepers in the ground. The downside is that there are numerous wooden gates to open with a slide latch, as stock are on this part of the trail.

From Yelverton, I could head directly east into the Dartmoor National Park, but with the rail trail existing for four more miles north of here, I will cycle a bit further.

Gates to open on this trail which passes the remains of a tramway

It takes a while to actually be back on the rail right of way. Once I'm back on the trail, a new looking white bridge soon appears. It's located much lower than a train could get down to, while cement block remains are next to the trail. As I cross this bridge and head up a short section, an information panel explains that the bridge was demolished when the railway line closed in the 1960s, so a new bridge was opened in 2012 for rail trail users. Not long after going through a former rail tunnel, I will turn around because from here, the cycle route isn't on the rail right of way for another ten miles.

A new bridge built for rail trail

Once back at Yelverton, after visiting a familiar green Co-op grocery store, I will be heading into Dartmoor National Park. After some quiet roads, I'm near a reservoir, where I join a former rail right of way, which climbs up to Princetown, the highest town in the park.

Initially this trail has been fenced with a few wooden pine gates to open with a sliding metal hatch, while some bridges have been converted for non-motorised traffic to cross over roads. There are mile markers on this trail, but it's a rough track with the surface unimproved from when rails were removed.

Not sure why it hasn't been improved for cycling because as it becomes tree and fence less, it's a gradual climb with decent views of the surrounding rocky landscape. Despite the bumpy surface, the cold wind and the sun coming and going behind clouds, it's still an enjoyable ride.

At the start this rail trail is fenced, before it becomes an open unimproved surface to cycle

Along the way, a few mountain bikers pass me heading downhill, while there are many hikers with backpacks, including a few teenagers who aren't looking that thrilled to be here. As it's looping around a hill, occasionally, I can see where I have come from.

Today has taken a bit longer than expected, so I have just made it to Princetown before the national park visitor centre closes at 5 pm. After learning more about the park, instead of continuing on further tonight, I will stop here, enabling me to enjoy it more tomorrow. Since I'm in a national park, I will respect the no wild camping rules, so I will have to find a place to stay.

Princetown is a small town, so there are only a few options. I could pay £8 50 to camp behind a pub in a grass paddock, or I could stay at a backpackers behind a café for £13 50. If I'm going to pay for accommodation, I prefer to sleep indoors with a bed and a kitchen, rather than in a tent. So it's an easy decision to go with the warmer backpackers.

As the pound is roughly worth 50 cents Australian, I just double everything when working out prices, so $25 to sleep inside is fine by me. With only an elderly couple staying in another room, I'm able to relax here, cook a nice meal and watch the Federer-Nadal Wimbledon semi-final on the BBC.

The elderly couple from Plymouth are looking at hiking in Dartmoor for five days, having turned back previously due to heavy rain. It appears many people come to Dartmoor to go walking, so I'm wondering what I will see from my bicycle tomorrow.

Before leaving Princetown in the morning, I will visit the prison museum on the edge of town as one of the maximum-security prisons of the UK is based here. As I cycle to the museum, the entrance to a collection of stone buildings must be the prison. The museum is in a similar style of building.

Inside are rooms full of information, pictures and objects. This prison was first built to house French prisoners during the Napoleonic Wars in 1809 and then housed American prisoners from The War of 1812 before eventually becoming a prison for British criminals. After telling the story of the establishment of the prison, the museum has examples of general prison life, including talking about the attached farm, while there are a few escape stories over the years.

As I begin my ride into Dartmoor National Park, it's supposed to be a sunny day, but it's cold and overcast, despite being predicted to be above 20 degrees. I don't have a plan except to just cycle in an easterly direction. If I learn of anything interesting, I will change my route.

It looks like I'm riding in the Western District of Victoria with stone fences, small farms, and numerous farm animals. Along the way are a few popular small tourist villages with souvenir shops and restaurants. Despite the weather, people appear to be enjoying themselves, with plenty going for short walks.

Stone bridges in Dartmoor National Park

The actual cycling is mainly on narrow hedgerow roads, where I'm going up and down numerous small hills. Sometimes if cars meet, they have to reverse as the roads are so narrow.

After a steep climb, as I make my way out of the national park, suddenly the landscape becomes open and treeless, with many small scenic rocky hills. Numerous people are exploring them, while seemingly wild horses are feeding around them. So I randomly stop near a hill.

The top of this rocky hill provides a 360-degree view, including the English Channel in the distance. Once back on my bicycle, as I begin descending, I pass more rocky hills, including one that reminds me of Pride Rock from the Lion King.

One of the few rocky hills

After hearing on my radio that Simona Halep has comfortably beaten Serena Williams in the Wimbledon singles final, I depart the small town of Bovey Tracey to join a rail trail. It soon runs out despite this former railway line having continued north.

Instead, I'm trying to go around the eastern side of Dartmoor National Park by following the Dartmoor Way signed cycle route. Occasionally I'm still seeing the remains of this former rail line, in particular a few stone bridges. There are a couple of short sections of rail trail, but also short sharp hills to negotiate and narrow roads, with cars often forced to reverse.

Following the Dartmoor Way

While snacking in the town of Lustleigh, the locals learn I'm Australian, so a man asks me who I will be supporting in the cricket tomorrow. I'm unsure because I don't have personal animosity to either nation. I know an English win will be good for the locals and raise the profile of cricket here, which is less than what I'm used to in Australia. However, the underdog story of New Zealand is also compelling.

After negotiating all these short sharp hills by the time I make Okehampton, it feels like it has been a long day. This could be because I'm now cycling miles rather than kilometres, so the distance covered feels less impressive and takes longer. After more than three months of cycling, I'm used to knowing that x number of kilometres should take me a certain amount of time. Now I have to recalibrate my estimations for miles. If it's ten kilometres to the next town, I know it's probably less than an hour ride, but ten miles will be closer to an hour and a half.

I will get use to miles but I can't get my head around measuring height in feet especially using the gradient feature on Maps.me. It just sounds so much higher and doesn't relate to miles at all.

Okehampton still has a passenger rail service, while a short tourist line travels south in the other direction.

Meldon Viaduct

A paved cycle path follows this tourist line before eventually becoming a paved rail trail just before the high steel Meldon Viaduct.

Randomly in the middle of nowhere, a paper sign is saying the trail is closed ahead due to private property. To get through, I have to go around on a long detour. However, I will keep going on this trail to see what the actual situation is.

A random short rough section

As I meet an unlocked gate, ahead is an undeveloped rocky surface. Since no one is around, I open the gate and go through. After like 200 metres, there is another gate, and as I go under a cement road bridge, the paved rail trail returns. I have no idea why this situation exists because in the morning, plenty of cyclists and walkers were ignoring the signs as well.

Further on is a smaller viaduct, and just after that, there is a flat bench seat near a cement shed presumably left over from the railway. As it's now dusk, this will do as a place to cook dinner while watching a red sunset. With no one else around, I set my tent up beside the rail trail.

Camping beside the rail trail

I wake up to a busy trail this Sunday, with people cycling, running or walking their dogs. I will leave my bicycle bags in the cement shed because there is only a short section south to Lydford to finish this rail trail.

It runs out just before this small town, which has a small abandoned castle.

If I continued heading south, I would eventually connect with the route I left to head into Dartmoor National Park, but this section is not a rail trail despite a former rail line having existed. There is a gorge south of Lydford, but it isn't open for another hour, so I will return north, collecting my bags on the way.

Back in Okehampton, the rail station is now busy with a footbridge separating two bricked station buildings. Inside is an informative rail museum that helps explain where railway lines went in the southwest of England. An excellent map shows many rail lines that no longer exist as there is now only one main line with just a few branch lines. Many of these former rail lines are now rail trails.

Many railway lines in the UK closed in the 1960s after a government report by Dr Beeching recommended a third of them should close. Many of the 6,000 miles closed by the Beeching Cuts have been made into rail trails.

Nearby is the small Okehampton Castle, which is managed by English Heritage. It doesn't look worth paying to enter, especially as I'm now distracted by listening to the Men's Cricket World Cup Final, taking away my focus on anything else today. I'm also trying to keep up with the men's singles tennis at Wimbledon.

National Cycle Route 27 is called the Coast to Coast route because it connects Plymouth on the English Channel to Ilfracombe on the north coast of Devon opposite Wales. There are rail trails at both ends, but in between are some hills, especially a steep one out of Okehampton. After chatting to a 75-year-old touring cyclist, I leave him behind as he says he will walk the whole hill. I end up walking the last bit as it's at 17% gradient.

Until joining another rail trail, the rest of this route involves smaller hills. With narrow roads where the vegetation is close to the road, I have to get right off the road a few times due to tractors carting trailers full of hay coming towards me.

In the small town of Sheepwash, the local church has signs saying cyclists are welcome to have a picnic in the garden and a toilet is available. All because I'm on a cycle route.

Cyclist welcome in Sheepwash

It appears a train could still arrive at these stations

As I join a rail trail, the sun is out, and the trail is in good condition, so it's an enjoyable ride as I pass a few sculptures, and old railway stations which are now restaurants. Unlike in Spain and France, here most stations have kept railway infrastructure like seats, signals and railway gates, so it looks like a train could arrive at any time.

I'm soon following the old Rolle Canal, which became obsolete when the railway came through but still today, a stone aqueduct is visible from the trail. After crossing the River Torridge a few times on scenic former curvy rail bridges, the river begins to widen. So for a while, the rail trail follows the eastern riverbank through a couple more refurbished stations.

Crossing the River Torridge, before cycling beside it

As the cricket becomes a close game, I'm hoping to find somewhere to watch the last ten overs. Thankfully, North Devon Cricket Club is right next to the rail trail, located scenically beside the river's mouth.

A local T20 tournament is finishing, but I head inside the thatched straw roof and white clubhouse to watch on television the incredible finish in the World Cup Final.

I can't do the match justice, so I recommend watching highlights on YouTube or reading Geoff Lemon's book *The Comeback Summer*.

Anyway, from what I see, England is lucky to force a tied match with an incredible final over, including an unintentional, fortunate deflection off the bat of Ben Stokes from a fielder's throw, which runs to the boundary for four. For the final ball in the subsequent Super Over, New Zealand needs two runs to win. Martin Guptill hits the ball and attempts to run the two required, but is run out going for the win. Scores are level again, which means England has won because of an obscure rule where the team that hits more boundaries in the match wins.

Throughout the clubhouse the locals are celebrating and singing "*crickets coming home*". I'm hoping the cricket I will be attending will be just as dramatic.

As the crowd disperses, a red sunset is visible over the oval and river mouth out to the sea behind it, while this also provides a reflective glow on the clubhouse windows.

This cricket ground will do as a stealth camp, but I will temporarily leave before the last person to avoid making the locals suspicious.

After about half an hour of sitting on a beach, I return to the now quiet cricket ground, where a few marquees have been left set up. They are a perfect space to sleep under, and will allow me to be out of sight of nearby houses.

Sunset at North Devon Cricket Club

From North Devon Cricket Club, the rail trail follows the shoreline of the River Taw through to the town of Barnstaple. After heading south of town to cross the river on a former rail bridge, I turn around and head north, following the Taw by using a previous rail route into the town centre. I'm told that Barnstaple once had five railway lines spreading out from town, and there were nearly as many stations. Now there is only one passenger service, and sadly the scenic curved rail bridge over the Taw is long gone. At least there is still a nice looking old stone road bridge.

This scenic paved rail trail leaves Barnstaple by continuing beside the Taw for about three miles before heading away from the river to the town of Braunton, which feels more like a beach village with holidaymakers. Near where the long-gone railway station was, is a nature visitor centre, while across the road is the visitor information centre.

Braunton Museum

This centre is also a museum, where I learn that sandy beaches nearby were where Americans trained for the D-Day landings as they are apparently similar to Utah and Omaha beaches in Normandy. During my 2013 ride, I visited many D-Day landing sites in Normandy, so I am familiar with them.

I end up spending half an hour chatting to a man at the museum as he explains the history of Americans training here. Specific training objects like bunkers and loading ramps are still there, but mainly covered in sand. It's always enjoyable learning something new.

Since there is a gap between rail trails, I make my way via a beach to Croyde, where there are surfers and plenty of people sunbaking on actual sand. However, as the man in the visitor centre had explained, there isn't a road between all the beaches, so I will begin climbing up to join the northern part of the rail trail.

Style of houses in this region

Along the way, I'm on narrow hedgerow roads and passing picturesque houses with thatched rooftops. I'm also coming across recycling trucks going around picking up recycling and sorting by hand into individual bins in the back of the vehicle. In Australia, recycling typically goes in one bin together and is sorted later.

After climbing, I'm able to enjoy another paved rail trail which rolls nearly all the way down to Ilfracombe, another tourist town where the railway line ended until 1970. The former station was high above the town, and is now a factory. I only know where the station was because an information panel tells me about the railway lines history.

As I descend into this unremarkable town, it's busy with holidaymakers despite the ugly beaches. One is only accessible by man-made tunnels, but it's rocky and ugly, so not sure what the attraction is, especially as I have to pay to visit it.

Tunnels lead to ugly rocky beaches

From here, National Cycle Route 27 ends and route 51 starts heading east, but unlike 27, which was mainly on rail trails, 51 uses secondary roads, which appear to involve a lot more climbing.

I have heard from fellow cyclists that the southwest is a hilly part of England. This afternoon, I can confirm for Devon at least this is true. All afternoon involves numerous short steep up and down sections often descending to rivers before then climbing straight up again, without a break of any flat cycling. It is just draining and hard on my knees.

I'm covering less distance than expected, especially compared to much more mountainous Spain and France, where it was generally longer gradual climbs so I could get in more of a rhythm, therefore less stress on the knees. Thankfully, the weather is delightful, mid-twenties with little wind to worry about.

My day ends at the village of Parracombe because it has a small park with a toilet block with picnic tables, but I can't find the general store which is supposed to be here.

While relaxing after dinner, a woman comes over and locks the toilet, but doesn't comment on me clearly cooking dinner here. This locked toilet is annoying as one of the reasons for stopping here was to have a toilet in the morning for my regular morning poo. So in the morning, when no one shows up to unlock the toilet, I find a pile of old mowed grass under a tree to cover my deposit. Unlike last year I'm not carrying a mini shovel to dig a hole.

Nearby a short one mile of narrow-gauge railway has been rebuilt around the restored Woody Bay station. It's nice to go inside the cafe attached, and to learn a little more about the rail line that once went between Barnstaple and Lynmouth. Hopefully, one day a longer tourist line will be rebuilt on this former railway line. Having cycled in this landscape, I can understand why only a narrow-gauge railway line came to this region.

Restored Woody Bay Station

Suddenly just before Lynmouth, there is a 25% road to descend. So I hold tight onto my brakes for this short, fast descent into a seaside fishing village with plenty of visitors, and fish and chip shops. The tide is currently way out, leaving many boats high and dry.

It has been hard finding drinking fountains in England. Thankfully Lynmouth has one near the toilets. Around the corner is a national park visitor centre where I learn of a walking track up the hill.

Lynmouth is a twin town with Lynton located at the top of the steep hill I just rode down so much so that there is a cliff railway between the two.

This double-track railway works using gravity, where one carriage's weight going downhill lifts the other up. It's a scenic ride as I look back at a scenic open bay on this beautiful sunny day as this green carriage goes under a couple of bridges.

Cliff Railway

From Lynton, there is the Valley of Rocks walk. After walking on a bridge over the cliff railway, I'm walking on the edge of a cliff with a clear blue sea on one side and rock formations on the other, with goats sunbaking on the rocks. This is the highlight of the day, especially as I had no idea about it.

Valley of Rocks Walk

As I loop around on the way back to town, I pass a scenic cricket village ground in one of the few flat areas. It's enchanting seeing so many scenic village cricket grounds in England.

Back on my bicycle, I'm trying to avoid a straight up and down road climb by following the East Lyn River using a bridle path.

I walk past a scenic village cricket ground, while I'm soon cycling on a bridle path

Initially, it's enjoyable beside the river, but unfortunately, the track soon becomes rough. Eventually walking my bicycle becomes the only option, especially with some minor uphill sections at the end. Fortunately, it's only just over a mile of walking. When I meet the road, a sign tells me that I have missed a 25% climb.

Thankfully, the road follows the East Lyn River for a while out of Devon into Somerset, but occasionally there are still some short, steep climbs, particularly for the final climb before Porlock. However, this allows a decent descent on the scenic, quiet Toll Road with only one passing car and a few cyclists.

After more hilly cycling, I'm in the busy beachside tourist town of Minehead with an unremarkable stony beach. There is a free small museum as part of the tourist office, while a more extensive, well maintained railway station is across the road. It closed in 1970 but then became part of a tourist train line in 1979. There are a few services a day, with most being steam trains.

Minehead Railway Station

After looking around Minehead, I can't find any suitable places to camp, so I will cycle to the nearby town of Dunster.

It's quieter here with a castle I can't access dominating this town. There are a few options to wild camp, including either at the more open cricket ground or in a nearby enclosed public playground. Since no one shows up while I cook dinner in the park, I will camp here using play equipment to keep my bicycle and bags sheltered from the morning dew.

West Somerset Railway operates the longest tourist line in the UK from Minehead to Bishops Lydeard near Taunton. Since there are no quiet road options and I'm feeling in need of a rest from cycling, I will take the opportunity to ride the train.

Bishops Lydeard Railway Station

They have informative museums at the stations at both ends of the line, and from the train it appears there are also some scenic stations along the way. However, the actual ride is nothing special as the landscape is unremarkable apart from a pleasant view at the start when the rail line is beside the ocean.

The end of the tourist line is for England, at least in the middle of nowhere near some factories. This rail line is still connected to the mainline, but there is a gap to the nearest operating railway station, so I will have to cycle the short distance to Taunton.

Not long into the ride, I suddenly hear a big bang and my bicycle stops.

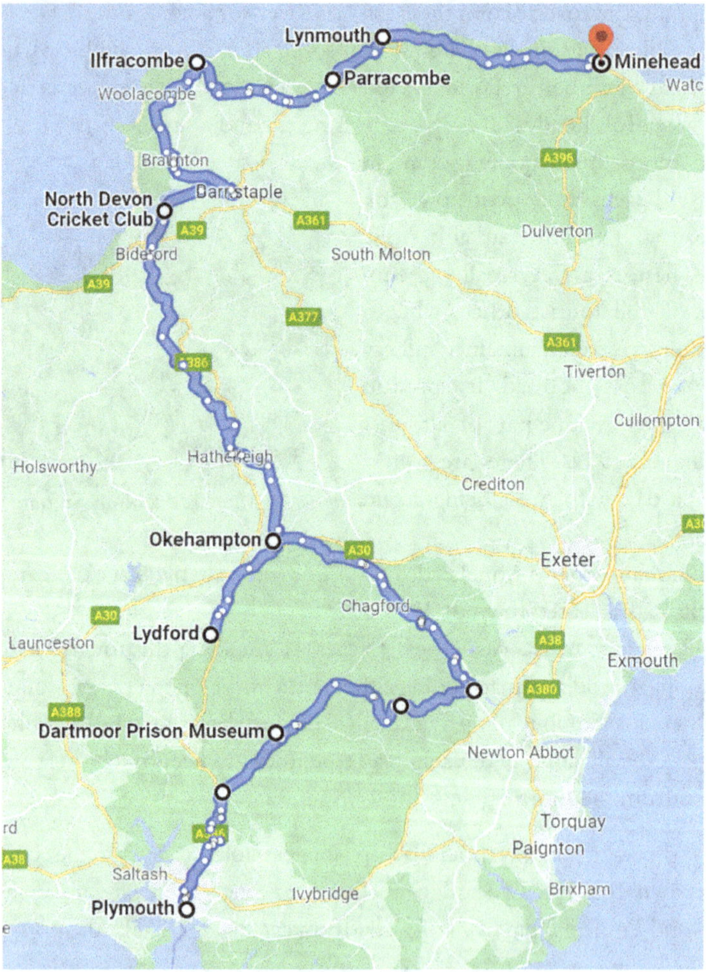

Plymouth to Minehead (Google Maps)

Taunton

It doesn't take me long to see that the rim of my rear wheel has developed a large crack, so a new wheel will be required. Yesterday I could hear my rear wheel making a noise, but couldn't figure out why, especially as my bicycle was serviced less than a week ago.

As my rear brake uses the rim, I now don't have rear braking capacity, and it could become worse, potentially causing me to fall off. It's probably safer to hitch-hike the last five miles into Taunton.

Thankfully, Englishmen are helpful, so it is easy getting a ride to a bicycle shop.

The rear wheel was last replaced in Toronto four years ago, after a crack developed on the previous wheel. It had only been replaced a month earlier, after my original wheel developed a crack after three years of cycling. I suspect that the replacement wheel didn't have enough spokes to hold me and the weight of my bags, which led to broken spokes and the wheel going out of shape. So I double-check with this bicycle shop that my new wheel has enough spokes.

The wheel fits fine on my bicycle, but when I reattach my calliper brake, it won't connect as the cable won't slide into its holder. I'm unsure what's going on, so I ask a staff member to help me out. He also struggles until we realise the new wheel's rim is wider due to no wear from braking, so we loosen the brake cable.

Taunton feels like a country town rather than a city, a bit like Adelaide compared to Melbourne. The cricket ground dominates the landscape as it's right in the centre of the city beside a small river and is the main reason for me visiting.

I can cycle directly into the cricket ground, where a few people are preparing the ground for the test match tomorrow. It's not a particularly large ground, more like a suburban cricket oval like North Sydney Oval or the Junction Oval in Melbourne, with one level of seating going around the ground along with a couple of taller cricket pavilions. Behind one side of the ground are blocks of flats where people can watch the cricket from their tiny balconies. Before leaving, I confirm with a staff member that I can park my bicycle here tomorrow.

I have had no luck with Warmshower hosts in Taunton, so instead, I have found an Airbnb host in a small house. Johnnie hosts often, so he can provide me with some local advice, including recommending I cycle the Jurassic Coast on the southern coastline of England.

We also briefly chat about Brexit, which despite him not wanting to leave, he didn't vote in. However, now he just wants to be out of Europe because the discussion will be over. This was a common view I had with people during my time in the UK, in that most weren't a fan of Brexit but now just want it over.

There is not a lot to see in Taunton as the Visitor Centre doesn't have much on offer, but there is an interesting museum which is free. Many museums around here rely on donations rather than an entry fee. It does mean I often visit these museums knowing I can leave whenever I want and donate according to how informative it is, rather than feeling like I need to get my money's worth. It also allows repeat visits.

So before the cricket starts, I spend the morning exploring this museum in an old castle. It covers a wide range of topics with many older natural features highlighted, including how the Somerset landscape formed and how people developed over millennia in this region. There are plenty of fossils and artefacts on display, including well preserved Roman mosaics and coins.

Murals and weapons are on display in the Somerset Museum

Unlike men's test cricket, women's test cricket matches are rare. Now only England and Australia play each other once every two years, alternating between host countries. (India played two test matches in 2021, one each against England and Australia, so things may be changing)

The last test match was a day-night match at North Sydney Oval in November 2017. I attended the last day of that four-day test match, which had a family atmosphere with plenty of young girls in attendance. In 2013, I spent one day at the test match at Wormsley Cricket Ground in the middle of nowhere, which had a friendly village atmosphere.

After parking my bicycle, as I walk into the Somerset County Cricket Ground, it has a noticeable lack of atmosphere. Besides family members of the Australian cricketers, it looks like I'm the only Aussie here. It's not like watching the Matildas.

Somerset County Cricket Ground

The majority of the sparse crowd are made up of retirees who regularly attend Somerset County Cricket matches. I end up spending most of the day chatting to a friendly group of them.

A similarity to North Sydney is that Ellyse Perry continues her form with the bat as she and Haynes each finish the day not out after both scoring 50. Earlier, Healy and Lanning individually got fifties before both were bowled by spinners, so Australia is on top after the first day.

During the lunch break in the cricket, the Somerset Cricket Museum is the perfect spot to explore. It's in a small separate two storey stone building with a pointy roof, just away from the oval part of the cricket ground.

Inside is a fascinating memorabilia collection from a couple of centuries of cricket here, with a wide range of items on display, from old wooden bails to numerous shirts and photos. The focus is on Somerset men's county cricket because this ground rarely hosts the England men's national team. Since England women play here regularly, there are also a few women's cricket pieces.

Somerset Cricket Museum

Initially, I was going to only attend one day of the cricket, but with occasional showers of rain predicted, I consider if it will be more enjoyable watching the cricket on day two, even with rain breaks, than cycling in the rain. After revisiting the Somerset Museum for an hour or so in the morning, I make my way to the county ground to decide if I will pay to go inside, knowing it could be rained off at any time. When a lady outside the entrance gives me a free ticket, I decide it's fate to go to the cricket today.

Some of my friends from yesterday are here again. While Australia remains on top as Perry brings up her century before both Perry and Haynes fall to Laura Marsh just before lunch.

Unfortunately, during lunchtime, light rain settles in and never looks like stopping, so by late afternoon, I cycle away from Taunton following a canal path that goes right through the city. Occasionally the showers become heavier as I pass through a few small villages. Somehow I end up taking a wrong turn and find myself late in the day in the village of North Curry, where the rain appears to have cleared. Thankfully, there is a quiet cricket ground with a small verandah to camp under.

During the Second World War, a defensive barrier designed to defend against an invasion of Cornwall was built utilising canals and railway lines from the Bristol Channel to the English Channel.

Barriers are still above Donyatt Halt

In the morning on a beautiful sunny day, I'm able to cycle alongside a small part of this former barrier on the rail trail to Chard, with a few road bridges going over the trail. Along the way are remains of this barrier, including cement blocks at the former Donyatt Halt station, while beside a road bridge in a farmer's field is a bunker from that era.

Since changing my rear wheel in Taunton, my bicycle gears haven't been changing as well. I have tried fixing it myself, but I haven't been able to get it perfect, so I will find a bicycle shop in the town of Chard.

The friendly bicycle mechanic immediately takes another bicycle off his bike rack to work on my gears; I had been prepared to wait. He also offers me water as he tells me he goes on bicycle tours himself. After a quick adjustment, he then refuses payment, so I purchase some Hydralyte tablets from him.

As I make my way south towards the coastline, I'm listening to day three of the cricket on my radio while cycling on numerous quiet narrow hedgerow roads and passing through a few small unremarkable towns.

West Bay Station is now a cafe

About to descend to Weymouth

Just before the coastline is the town of Bridport which is reasonably busy. After a short exploration of this town, a small section of rail trail takes me to West Bay on the English Channel, where the former railway station is a café. This small coastal town is busy with holidaymakers, so shops accommodate this, along with carousels and other rides. It's too busy for me, so I'm glad to leave as soon as I can.

Despite this next section beside the coastline being a secondary road, it's busy with constant holiday traffic as I climb for a bit on rolling hills. Still, it does allow some decent coastal views on this beautiful sunny day. I can now see why the National Cycle Route Two is more inland here.

After a decent quick descent, I'm in the city of Weymouth, which thankfully has some cycle paths to help me find a way into this beachside city.

Weymouth doesn't feel as busy as expected, possibly because it's later in the day, but also it's more spread out with a nice long strip of seaside waterfront to explore. There are a few sand sculptures to admire, including a war memorial next to Shrek, but most of the actual beach is made up of small pebbles.

Further along the waterfront, are some permanent memorials including a small one for Australian First World War soldiers and references to royalty who liked staying here.

A Queen Victoria memorial

As dusk begins, I look for a place to stealth camp. As I search, I find a small section of rail trail, but there's nowhere suitable for my tent. So I make my way north to a large park. After looking around, there is some space under trees for my tent to be hidden.

As I drift off to sleep, I realise I never really learned anything about the Jurassic Coastline, as I forgot to visit a dinosaur museum.

South of Weymouth is a narrow strip of land connecting with the small Portland Island, a significant departure point during both World Wars. The rail trail I found last night heads this way and is a scenic ride through a deep cutting before it closely follows the coastline.

Along the way in a well-kept garden are the remains of Sandsfoot Castle which was built during Henry VIII's time but is now a ruin.

Sandsfoot Castle

Chesil Beach

Unfortunately, as the peninsula narrows, a rail bridge is gone, so I'm forced onto the only road, which thankfully isn't that busy. Even once I'm over a couple of subsequent road bridges, I can still see where the railway line went, but it's not a rail trail, so it's not worth cycling on it.

The other side of the road is Chesil Beach, which, rather than sand is a long stretch of pebble dunes that aren't much fun to walk on, especially in my sandals.

It's also becoming cloudier and windier as I make my way to Portland, so I'm not really in the mood for exploring this hilly island. There are a few navy buildings, but I'm not finding much open that I'm allowed to explore. So I will retrace my route to Weymouth.

Somehow, I randomly find myself at Northe Fort, located beside the mouth of the River Wye opposite the main beach. This horseshoe-shaped fort was built in the 1870s and decommissioned in the 1950s. I just happen to be here during the Victorian era weekend, so people are dressed up in period costumes, including as a blind beggar. As part of this a concert is on in the bowl in the middle of the horseshoe.

Most of the underground rooms in this round fort are full of information, including Weymouth's role in the Second World War because numerous D-Day ships left from here. During the First World War many Australian soldiers recovered here.

Victoria era weekend in Northe Fort, including a man dressed as a beggar

I have learned my lesson from yesterday and will now try to stick to National Cycle Route Two, which continues to take an inland route. To join it involves following a hilly signed cycle route beside the railway line to inland Dorchester. I presume this is where the current county I'm in, Dorset, gets its name. It's smaller than Weymouth but feels like a place people live rather than holiday in.

East of Dorchester, I'm on National Cycle Route 2, which is a relaxing quiet flat route through villages, rather than yesterday's busy, hilly non-cycle route.

Since it's quiet, I'm able to listen to the final day of the cricket as it peters out to a dull draw. This is disappointing as neither team appears to be trying to win, especially Australia, who has now retained this multi-format Ashes series after having already won the three one-day internationals while I was in France. There are still three more T20 matches to go, and I have a ticket for the first match at Chelmsford in five days.

As the end of the day nears, I'm cycling on quiet farm tracks, which feels pretty remote with no one around and no houses either. I'm unsure where I'm sleeping tonight until randomly I see a temporary plastic box toilet in an open grass field. With no one else around, this will be a perfect place to camp.

Camping in a random paddock, not far from the short ferry to Bournemouth

After a peaceful night, I set off in the morning expecting to catch a ferry from Shell Bay across the sea mouth of a large lake to Bournemouth.

It's quiet as I arrive at a pier with just a short gap to the other side. However, I soon spot a notice saying the ferry service has been suspended. This means to get to Bournemouth, I will now have to cycle 25 miles around a large lake and through the city of Poole. Since I'm on National Cycle Route Two, I would have hoped someone had put a sign up earlier to inform me of this detour required, especially as I now have to backtrack the ten miles I did yesterday afternoon.

Once I have backtracked to Wareham, I learn in the local library that this ferry has only been suspended in the last few days. I suggest to locals, it would be helpful if there was a sign as I imagine other cyclists will also become caught up in this. I also send a message to Sustrans to let them know about this.

No one can suggest a sensible route that isn't on a busy road. Instead, it will be quicker and less stressful to catch a train to Poole. However, this being the UK where same-day train tickets are expensive, it cost me more than if I had booked this short train ride a few days earlier.

By the time I get through Poole and Bournemouth, which are really just one big combined city, it has taken me three hours more than if the ferry was running.

Going via Poole does allow me to visit a maritime museum, and cycle a short cycle path beside the lake. However, for the most part, it's just suburban cycling before I find myself beside a busy long beach. What slows me down even more is the requirement to walk my bicycle along most of the path beside the beach. I never felt like I got to know Bournemouth at all, as it felt like a tourist trap.

In the suburb of Christchurch, while visiting a supermarket, a lady tells me she is planning to go to Wangaratta in Australia next year. During my time in the UK, I met people who have been to Australia, but others had no idea about Victoria being a state.

Past Christchurch, the number of houses has slightly decreased, but I just hate this section because it's too busy on narrow rolling hilly roads.

It's a relief once I make Lymington, where I can join a ferry to the Isle of Wight, which hopefully will be quieter.

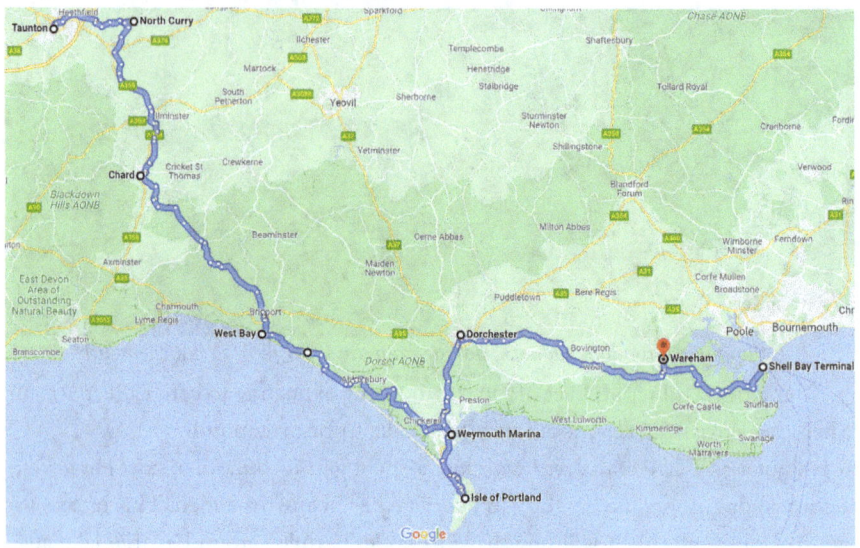

Taunton to Wareham (Google Maps)

Isle of Wight

It's a quick ferry trip with land visible the whole time as we pass numerous yachts on the way to Yarmouth on the western end of the island. After a brief look around, I make my way to the edge of this small town to where the former Yarmouth Railway Station is.

This red-bricked station is in such good condition it appears a train could still arrive anytime except that the rails have been replaced with a paved rail trail. A café is inside this station, along with a bicycle hire shop.

Inside this shop, I'm provided with a map showing numerous cycling routes, including a few rail trails, as only one

Yarmouth Station

railway line still operates on this island. However, unlike on Prince Edward Island in Canada, where all the former railway lines are rail trails, it's a mixed bag here. Some sections are developed into rail trails, but there are also many undeveloped gaps.

According to this map, east of Yarmouth, the rail trail soon ends despite the railway line having continued towards the main populated areas in the centre of the island. However in a southwest direction, this trail exists to the town of Freshwater, where my Warmshower hosts Andrew and Marianne live.

It's only a short two-mile rail trail that follows the duck-filled River Yar's shoreline through a lightly forested area before suddenly ending on the edge of town. With an hour before my Warmshower hosts are available, I will have a look around town.

Short rail trail to Freshwater

A prominent family name in my hometown of Berriwillock is Wight, so I'm on the lookout for any references to people back home like a similar name.

For example, I know a Wes Wight, so when I see a sign for West Wight, I'm able to manipulate a photo to remove the T. Unfortunately, I never

A Berriwillock name

saw any other names that worked for the rest of my time on this island.

Once I find my Warmshower host's home, I'm welcomed in by Marianne and

Andrew, who are about my parents' age. Andrew is planning on riding from France to southern Spain, but his planned route is a little west of where I went. Still, I can offer some general advice as he shows me his potential route, some of which I passed when on the train from Madrid to Burgos.

They offer for me to stay another night, so my Tuesday will be spent cycling without bags around the island. This has many positives, like less weight and less wind resistance. The downside is that I often become so focused on getting back to my accommodation that I don't take as much time to stop and appreciate where I am. If I find a fascinating place, I can't stop there for the night.

There is some hilly cycling when not on rail trails as the Isle of Wight is not flat. In particular, I follow the southern coastline in an anti-clockwise direction while passing a few white cliffs, which remind me of Dover. It's quiet with little traffic as I pass green paddocks with hay bales and go through several villages. The only issue is some wind. Otherwise, it's a relaxing ride.

An advantage of cycling is that often I can go places cars can't, including around an old minor landslide just west of Ventor, allowing me to avoid some hills as I enter a built-up beachside area.

The southern coastline includes a landslide which stops cars but not bikes

So far, the best places to find drinking water fountains in England is at beaches, which is useful on this semi-warm day for England. It's predicted to get above 30 degrees Celsius in the next few days, with some places in England getting to 39 degrees. Thirty degrees is warm for the locals, so many people are out enjoying the various beaches.

Up a steep hill was Ventor Railway Station which is now abandoned and isn't a rail trail until the next town of Wroxall. It's a nice ride on this three-mile paved trail called the Red Squirrel Trail, named after an animal forced out by non-native squirrels on the mainland, but they still exist on the Isle of Wight.

This rail trail meets the only still-active rail line on the island at Shanklin before another rail trail begins a couple of stations further along at Sandown as it branches away west from the beach toward Newport.

This is a longer paved rail trail which follows another River Yar. This time it's a much smaller river with a few ponds beside the trail. I have no idea why two unconnected rivers on the opposite sides of this island have the same name. As I leave this River Yar behind, I pass a former rail junction station at Merstone, but this branch line isn't a rail trail. As I enter the southern suburbs of Newport in the centre of this island, this rail trail unceremoniously ends near a tyre store.

Rail trail passing through Merstone Station

It's now mid-afternoon, so instead of visiting Cowes further north, I will head to Carisbrooke Castle in the western suburbs of Newport. It takes a while to find it as it's up a hill.

It's £10 to enter Carisbrooke Castle. However, since this castle is part of the English Heritage organisation, I can join this organisation and get access to hundreds of sites all over England, including Stonehenge and Hadrian's Wall. I could pay the tourist fee of about £35 which gives me sixteen days access, or I can pay £60 for a year's worth. Since I will be here for another two months, it makes economic sense to buy a yearly membership.

The only issue is that the receptionist wants to mail a card to me, but as I explain, I don't have an address as I'm moving most days.

Instead she writes on my temporary paper card that I'm travelling for two months. I hope it will be accepted until I leave the UK.

For the most part, this temporary card was accepted straight away throughout England. There were only a couple of times I had to explain why I didn't have an actual card.

Because the Isle of Wight has been threatened with invasion throughout history, the castle was strengthened a few times. Today, some parts are in ruin, but I can still walk around on a few levels of the walls, while most buildings are well kept, along with some lovely gardens.

One feature of the castle is that donkeys were used in a wooden wheel like a mouse to lift water from a well. Today, they do demonstrations, but they emphasise that each donkey only does six minutes of work each day.

Out the back is a large open lawn bowling green, where apparently Charles I played while a captive waiting to be sent to London to be beheaded.

Carisbrooke Castle

Water lifted by donkey power, while a lawn bowling green is out the back

It takes a while to cycle west back to Freshwater as the traffic is heavy in the afternoon. In a way, it is a little annoying returning west when it would have been easier to stay somewhere in Newport. Another lovely evening with Marianne and Andrew makes up for this.

At Carisbrooke, I learnt about Osborne House, which was a holiday home for Queen Victoria. So that is my goal for this Wednesday as I re-cycle the rail trail to Yarmouth before following the north coastline to Cowes.

With the first day ever of a cricket test match between England and Ireland, I'm not really concentrating on this undulating ride with a few dogleg roads. Instead, I'm listening to the cricket at Lords.

Cowes is a port town with many sailing references, including a set of mini bronze cannons beside the sea, numerous yachts and a couple of sailing museums.

Cowes is a port town

Isle of Wight

The River Medina divides Cowes in half with just a short ferry between the two.

From Cowes, there are two longer ferry services to Southampton, one on each side of the river with only one available for cyclists and foot passengers and of course, it's on the other side of the river.

However, instead of using the short ferry to Cowes East, I will begin cycling south on the rail trail beside the Medina to Newport.

The further south I cycle, the more wickets England are losing and by the time I'm in Newport, they have collapsed to 42/6, so I find a pub for lunch and enjoy watching as England is bowled out for 85. For the rest of the day, I keep an ear on the score.

The reason for cycling to Newport is to visit a museum in the Guildhall, but I'm soon told by the woman inside that she is closing soon for an hour and then only reopening for one more hour. I thought I had more time to visit by the advertised opening times, so instead, I begin making my way north, now on the eastern side of the Medina, to visit Osborne House.

An individual ticket to enter Osborne House costs £20 but it's free entry with my English Heritage card. It has nearly half paid for itself already.

Compared to Versailles, I'm surprised how quiet this place is, especially as it's school holidays. Many people are still around, including children, but it doesn't feel like I'm being herded through each room. Instead, I can take my time as there is plenty of space.

Osborne House was only used during Queen Victoria's time, so that's its focus, in particular how her nine children grew up here. It's also highlighted how the death of her husband, Prince Albert changed the time of year she visited and her overall demeanour. Just like other royal buildings, there are rooms full of portraits and fancy furniture, and because Osborne House was built when Queen Victoria was Empress of India, the dining room is full of Indian artefacts. We even end up walking through the bedroom where she died; her bed is still here.

Indian themed dining room

The gardens cover an ample space, but only a few sites were cultivated into sculptured gardens, presumably, because only 50 years of royal occupation didn't allow more expansion or the addition of buildings by other monarchs. It's not like at Versailles, where each king added their own additions to the gardens.

A set of nine wheelbarrows is still in the garden, with each of Victoria's children's royal initials on each one. There are also toy war barracks that may seem ordinary, however for many who grew up here, they or their children made actual decisions which caused wars.

Osbourne House has a small garden area

A carriage for Queen Victoria to swim inside, while there are royal war toys on display

Queen Victoria did swim in the nearby sea. However, to preserve her modesty, she used a special wooden carriage to hide her body from the people. Once she was inside, it was wheeled into the sea.

Now that I'm on the right side for the ferry to Southampton, I will spend the rest of the evening relaxing here rather than leave the Isle of Wight. It takes a while to find a place to camp. Eventually, just south of Cowes, I have found an open area behind a church with a seat that will work for camping. A few people are around, but it feels quiet.

Unfortunately, after a decent start in Ireland's batting innings, they have collapsed and have been bowled out for 207, which is still a lead of 122, but it could have been more. Anyway, it's nice to listen to happy Irish commentators on the radio after a memorable day for them.

After dinner, while walking around the church, I spot a power-point on the church's back wall, so I will begin charging my iPhone. A few minutes later, a man of subcontinent heritage suddenly appears from around the corner. Naturally, we start talking about cricket while sitting on a park bench.

Out of nowhere, he suddenly puts his hand on my leg and asks me for sex and straight away, I say no. He then says *"please"*, so I stand up and say no louder a couple of times before walking away back to my bicycle. Thankfully, he disappears, but I am a little wary for the rest of the night and have no idea why he was here. Presumably, he was being an opportunist.

In the morning, it's a simple process getting on a busy ferry to Southampton as I spend time chatting to an older man who races yachts around this island.

Isle of Wight

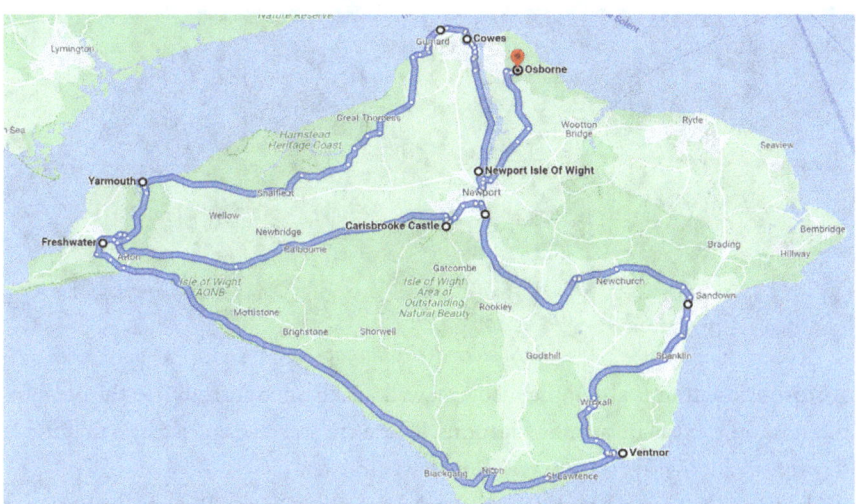

Isle of Wight, Freshwater to Cowes (Google Maps)

After departing the ferry, I can't find any information on Southampton, but I can see a medieval wall, so I begin following it.

Inside the wall is a wooden Tudor era house with its distinctive vertical black-and-white striped front where the higher floors stick out onto the street. It's a museum with interesting displays describing how the house changed throughout the centuries, from references to King John in the older stone parts of the house to marks made to protect against witches, to a Second World War bomb shelter.

Tudor era house, with a WW2 bunker inside

They have a map of Southampton, and I'm informed there is a walking tour at 1:30 pm around Southampton starting at the Bargate. The elderly gentlemen tour guides let me store my bicycle in the Bargate while I go on this tour. It's a nice looking gate which reminds me of a French church with its curvy archway entrance, religious crosses and a small statue.

Nearly everyone went through this nearly thousand-year-old gate when heading to the port of Southampton, including royalty, numerous armies and ten-pound poms heading to Australia.

Both sides of the Bargate

Most of the tour is about the medieval wall which once surrounded the old city but now only exists in specific locations. There are still clues of a castle that used to exist, including the remains of a medieval toilet.

They also show us a bomb shelter used during the Second World War because Southampton was heavily bombed, killing more than 600 people and destroying numerous buildings.

I know Southampton mainly as where the Titanic departed from, and there are a few references, including the Titanic pub and a self-guided walk. The SeaCity Museum has a display focusing on the people who worked on the Titanic, as many were recruited from Southampton, so when the ship sank, the town was devastated by the sheer number of people lost.

I have a ticket for tomorrow night's women's T20 cricket match between England and Australia in Chelmsford in Essex. Originally, I planned to cycle to Chelmsford, but having been delayed by other places of interest, I will have to go by train.

I could have taken a train via London today, but with temperatures predicted to be 38 degrees Celsius in London, trains are struggling with the heat. It's only been around 30 degrees in Southampton, so I will stay here in an Airbnb apartment before catching a couple of trains to Chelmsford tomorrow.

Unlike Spain and France, where there is basically one passenger train operator, Britain has numerous private railway companies. Often each company offers different prices even if I end up in the same place, while prices fluctuate depending on what time I'm travelling. Just like airlines, the sooner I book, usually the much cheaper the ticket.

In the evening, I spend some time working out what options are available to get me to Chelmsford. I will have to change trains in London by cycling between two of the many main London railway stations located around the city.

The train from London to Chelmsford seems to be the same price no matter when I travel during the middle of the day. However, there are a variety of prices on offer for two different routes between Southampton and London. The lower price is a slightly longer ride, but I have all day to get to Chelmsford.

Chelmsford

As I exit Victoria Station, I'm in the heart of extremely busy London, with double-decker buses everywhere and so many people. The easiest way to get to Liverpool Street Station is to follow the Thames. As I make my way there via bus lanes cyclists can use, I pass Westminster and Big Ben, before an excellent cycle path beside the Thames takes me most of the way.

As I leave my second train of the day at Chelmsford, England is bowling Ireland out in the test match for only 38. This is disappointing as they only needed 182 to win.

I haven't found much to do in Chelmsford, except for an informative museum in a park south of the city. It explains some of the history of this once Roman town, so many Roman artefacts are on display, including coins. In the 20th century, there was a Marconi radio factory here, so various radios are exhibited.

I have organised a Warmshower with Paul in the south of Chelmsford, and I think I have found his home as the wi-fi password he provided me works, but no one is home. Paul isn't responding to my messages or phone calls despite saying what time he will be home in a previous message. After an hour of waiting, time is running out before I need to head back into the city centre to the cricket.

As I'm about to give up and leave, Paul's wife Kellie shows up and explains that Paul has been delayed and his job driving fuel trucks doesn't allow him to use his mobile. She is then kind enough to drive me to the cricket.

Essex County Cricket Ground has a reputation for decent crowds for women's cricket and England dominating. So as I arrive at the ground, I pass two Australian ladies who couldn't get a ticket because the match is a sell-out.

I'm sitting next to a small group of elderly Australian ladies in this small but packed ground with a decent party atmosphere this Friday evening. It feels like people have made an effort to attend this match, whereas, in Taunton, the crowd was just retirees with nothing better to do.

Despite the local vocal crowd, Australia is dominating, especially Meg Lanning, who scores an impressive quick 100. She appears to be hitting sixes with ease while scoring 133 runs off 63 balls as Australia scores 226 off their twenty overs. It's Australia's highest ever score in women's T20 international cricket, so England shouldn't chase it, but you never know.

Australia batting at Chelmsford

Both English openers are out early for ducks, and they never recover as they end up making only 133, the same score as Lanning made herself. Australia has now won the multi-format Ashes series with two games to go, neither of which I'm attending.

Paul picks me up from the cricket, and we have a friendly chat as he apologises for the confusion.

Just before bed, I check Twitter to see the reaction to the cricket. Among the responses, I spot a post about Eliza, an Australian at the cricket tonight who is walking from Italy to Scotland to raise money for juvenile diabetes. My youngest sister suffers from this, so I message her to understand more of her journey.

Thanks Paul for the photo

I awake to steady rain, so it takes a while to motivate myself to leave Paul's home. It takes even longer to leave Chelmsford due to some delicious food at the Saturday morning markets in the central pedestrian mall.

After mostly cycling on a secondary road in light rain, I'm soon in Braintree, which still has a small branch line passenger service coming in from the southeast. This rail line once extended further, but now it's a flat dirt rail trail called the Flitch Way, which heads directly west through trees.

After only a couple of miles, the former Rayne Station appears. It's now a café, while beside the platform is a green carriage with information inside on the line's history and the subsequent rail trail development by the local community. This railway line operated for about 100 years before closing in the 1970s.

Further along the rail trail, I have to duck up to a road and then duck back down to the rail right of way, something I have done many times before.

As I re-join the trail, I just happen to see that the small bag on the top bar on my bicycle that carries my camera is empty, so it must have fallen out. I took some photos at Rayne, so it has only happened recently.

After redoing the duck up and over, I quickly spot it on the muddy trail.

As I pick it up, the LCD screen on the back of the camera has surprisingly smashed. I have had this tough camera since 2011, and it has been accidentally dropped many times without incident. Unluckily today, it appears it has just hit on the wrong angle. The rest of the camera is fine as it still takes photos, but I just can't see what I'm taking, so all my photos are now a guess if they are in focus.

Broken camera screen

I have my iPhone, but I can never keep that lens clean, and its focus often plays up. I will see once I'm in Glasgow if they can fix my camera.

The Flitch Way rail trail splits in half through the town of Great Dunmow due to sections of the rail right of way not being accessible. It only continues for a short section west before finishing near the busy Stansted Airport. Since I haven't been enjoying this rail trail, I will now begin travelling north to Saffron Walden on presumably a quiet route.

The ride to Saffron Walden is nothing memorable on this cold afternoon as I just want to get there to get out of the cold as rain could return any minute.

Thankfully, it holds off until just before I arrive into a lovely old town centre with outdoor markets finishing up. Helpfully a tiny tourist office is open, allowing me to obtain a small map of things to see, including a large church, the remains of a castle, a few sports grounds and a small hedge maze in the botanical garden.

With the rain looking like continuing all night, I would prefer to keep my bicycle and tent dry if I can because while my tent is fine in the rain, I just hate packing up a wet tent.

However, the football ground is fenced off and has people around it. While the cricket ground is open, there isn't any cover. Verandahs don't appear to be as common at sporting venues in the UK as they are in Australia, despite rain being more common. Thankfully back in town, there are some picnic tables undercover outside a bicycle-themed café which isn't open this Saturday evening. So I'm dry while cooking my pasta dinner as rain becomes more consistent.

After looking around for a while for somewhere to sleep, the best undercover solution is under a war memorial wall which I'm not comfortable with, but there isn't a better solution.

It's still overcast in the morning as I follow a National Cycle Route into Cambridge, including some sections beside a canal. Having enjoyed visiting Oxford in 2013, I will see how these famous university cities compare.

There are plenty of tourists around, and just like Oxford, many bicycles are just parked everywhere. I have found an underground parking garage just for bicycles, which is helpful on this cold rainy day.

It's a similar experience to Oxford, where I learn about university life by taking a guided tour with a student. I'm shown the outside of many colleges, each with different histories and building styles, and many have immaculate lawns. Plenty of famous people have been educated here, including Isaac Newton. He didn't get hit on the head at Cambridge, but a grafting from the apple tree that did is planted here. However, this current tree doesn't produce apples.

The River Cam goes around the western side of many colleges, with guided boat rides available, but it's a bit too cold today to interest me in going for a ride.

There are a couple of camera stores, but they can't help me with a repair.

The River Cam goes around many colleges which have immaculate lawns

Cycle path beside the busway

By mid-afternoon, I need to push on because I have to get to Huntingdon tonight as I have booked a train in the morning from there to Glasgow.

A path beside the River Cam takes me out of Cambridge before a cycleway beside a busway on a former railway line takes me to the halfway point at St Ives. Despite a slight, cold headwind, it's easy cycling, but it takes longer than I hoped.

The second half of my ride feels even longer as I'm zigzagging my way while not appreciating where I'm cycling because I just want to get there.

Since I have arrived late, I won't get a chance to see Huntingdon other than learning that Oliver Cromwell was born here. However, I do have a pleasant brief Warmshower experience with Alex and Carla.

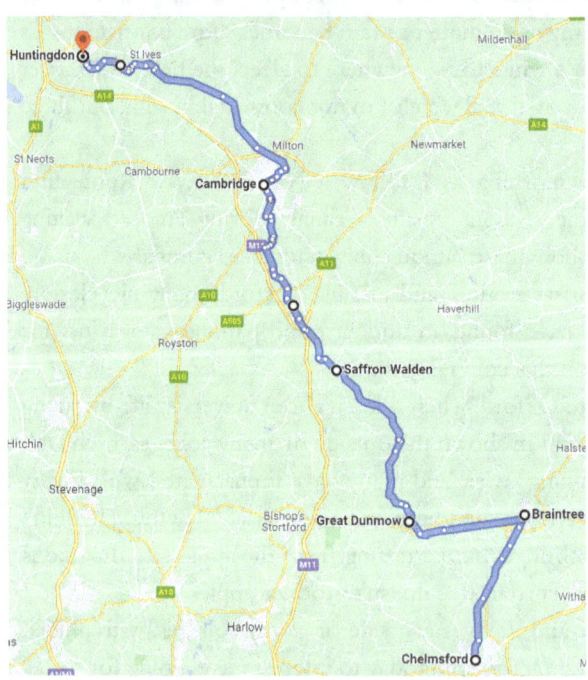

Chelmsford to Huntingdon (Google Maps)

Glasgow

If you can book a British train ticket early, they are often a lot cheaper. Two months ago, I booked a trip from Huntingdon to Glasgow via Peterborough and Edinburgh on the ScotRail website. It cost me £29 for a five-hour journey, using three different train operators. Yet it cost me £19 from Southampton to London for a much shorter trip because it was only booked the day before. Same-day trips can be even more expensive. For some smaller rail lines, it doesn't appear to matter what day I book.

I'm on a short morning train ride to Peterborough to join the LNER East Coast Main Line limited service to Scotland. For the longer trip, my bicycle is put in this red train's baggage car, while I relax for the next four hours on this clean, quick service to Edinburgh, which only stops in a couple of places. After Berwick, the train is mainly beside the scenic coastline as we cross into Scotland.

This train terminates in Edinburgh, where I'm supposed to wait for my scheduled train to Glasgow. Instead, I jump on the next service. The conductor doesn't care on this half-full train as there are so many services between Edinburgh and Glasgow. I can understand the conductor, but some passengers have a strong Scottish accent which is hard to understand; even a young girl has a strong accent.

As I exit the Queen Street Railway Station in Glasgow, the number of people is overwhelming, especially on a long pedestrian mall that goes up a hill.

After visiting a few camera stores, I have had no luck finding a place to repair the LCD screen on my camera. It's about eight years old, so they don't make the parts anymore.

Now I'm deciding between finding a new camera or just using my iPhone. I tried using just my iPhone in New Zealand, but its zoom isn't great, and when the sun is out, it's hard to see on the screen what I'm taking a photo of. Not that that is an issue so far in cloudy Scotland.

For the most part, Glasgow has been overcast, but then suddenly showers of rain will appear, while occasionally the sun will come out. I'm hoping it won't be like this the whole time I'm in Scotland.

Also, my cycling sandals are starting to fall apart, so I will begin searching bicycle shops.

Along with searching shops, I am still exploring. However, annoyingly here in Britain, most museums and other attractions are shut by 5 pm after only opening at 10 am, while often they won't let me in after 4 pm. So I have to be more selective about which ones to visit. Whereas in Europe often museums were open later in the evening, allowing me to visit after I finished my day of cycling.

West of the city centre there are some pleasant gardens and museums, including the Kelvingrove Art Gallery and Museum. Inside are numerous stuffed animals from around the world, alongside historical information on Glasgow with plenty of artefacts to admire. In the main room, a Spitfire aeroplane is above a collection of stuffed animals, including an elephant. There is also a small display about an idea of rails hanging above a vehicle. They only built a short track, and it was never taken up by anyone.

Inside Kelvingrove Museum is a spitfire flying over an elephant, and an old ladder

An idea for an overhead railway

Nearby is the Riverside Museum, which focuses on transport with many different kinds of vehicles on display from steam locomotives to bicycles and all in between, including the old tram network. Glasgow's Subway is the third oldest in the world. Initially, it was propelled by cables, as the museum shows us. Surprisingly it has never been expanded, it still makes the same one big loop around the city. Unfortunately, I never had enough spare time to ride the subway.

A model of the Glasgow subway and an old bicycle in the transport museum

Out the front of this museum are some Sustrans staff handing out information on the fabulous National Cycle Network around Britain, including cycle paths beside the Clyde, which allows me to admire the many bridges and buildings on either side of the river that divides Glasgow. I'm also seeing a range of statues of children covered in a map of Glasgow.

On the southern side of Glasgow lives my young Warmshower host Poppea. She is kind enough to share some route ideas for the western part of Scotland as

Children statues

I'm still planning my route. In particular, she suggests taking a ferry to Dunoon and riding north through some peninsulas and beside lochs to Inverness.

Just south of Poppea's home was where Mary Queen of Scots' army lost a battle that led to her losing her crown and fleeing Scotland to captivity in England. Apart from street names including Battlefield and Queen Street, there isn't much to see.

Nearby is the Hampton Park football stadium, the home of Scottish Football, which includes a basic guided tour and an engaging museum with plenty of displays. They are still waiting to correlate memorabilia from the 2019 World Cup. I ask about the 1986 men's World Cup qualifiers between Australia and Scotland, which was before my time. They have nothing on display, but I'm shown a brief mention in a book.

After further looking around, I won't change my shoes, but I will purchase a new digital camera which charges by USB and is a newer model of my Panasonic LUMIX camera.

I will go with Poppea's idea to cycle via Dunoon. I could cycle to the ferry terminal 30 miles away at Gourock on the southern shoreline of the Clyde, however, it looks like this will involve mostly cycling through suburbia. The alternative is to get a train directly to Gourock, so I can be in Dunoon tonight.

It's an easy decision, as the train allows me to research my new camera features as the landscape on the train's right becomes an open blue waterway with hills in the distance.

After a brief look around Gourock, I join a ferry next to the railway station. This is one of the many ferries in this part of Scotland that connects the numerous peninsulas which stick out in a southerly direction. Most of the narrow waterways in between the peninsulas are known as *Lochs*, which is Gaelic for both an inlet and a lake.

As we cross this scenic open waterway with plenty of high hills visible, this allows me to fiddle with my new camera. It has a few different and more advanced features than my old camera, including the ability to take wide panorama shots.

Lots of Lochs

After the hustle and bustle of Glasgow, Dunoon is quiet, so I should be able to find a place to stealth camp. It's a hilly place, and after looking around, there aren't any suitable places to camp in town, so I begin making my way into the hills behind Dunoon. As I start climbing, I spot a church on a hill.

Church camping

Once I get to this stone church with a pointy roof, no one is around, so I should be able to camp out of sight on a grass area beside it. My bicycle will be sheltered in the porch entrance of this church.

It's emotional recycling my old camera in a bin with other electronics in Dunoon in the morning. I know it's strange being attached to a camera, but having taken it on every northern hemisphere trip and many Australian adventures, it's always been there. The reason for recycling it along with its two batteries and charger is because the post office wouldn't let me mail home my lithium batteries internationally. Anyway, I doubt it would be repairable in Australia if it can't be repaired in the UK.

With the sun out, it looks like it will be a beautiful day of cycling as I'm following National Cycle Route 75. Initially, I'm following the coastline using quiet roads through a few small villages. At one stage, I pass sheepdog trials, which in this landscape reminds me of the movie *Babe*.

Even when I leave the coast behind to cross a couple of peninsulas, it's still

Occasional passing place

a reasonably gentle undulating route through a hilly green landscape with little traffic and no towns. The only minor issue is that most roads are single lane with many wider short passing places. I usually have to stop to let cars through, occasionally they stop to let me through. Most of the time, having to stop is fine, except when I have momentum during a climb.

As I meet the sea again and begin following the coastline, suddenly the road starts climbing. It begins at a 12% gradient before becoming 20%. Thankfully from the top, I'm rewarded with an incredible scenic lookout, of so many lochs and hills, while far below are a few boats.

As I descend towards a village, I pass a football pitch on a considerable slope down to the sea as there isn't much flat land here. While crossing another peninsula through the locality of Milhouse, three touring cyclists appear, but as they are all descending in the opposite direction, there isn't the opportunity to stop for a chat.

The highpoint of the day

There is only one ferry on my route today, which involves waiting for a bit before crossing to Tarbert. Many cyclists depart the ferry as I board, but I don't see any more for the rest of the day.

Above the road on the way from the pier into the small fishing town of Tarbert are the remains of a castle with a couple of sides of a small square stone tower. Still, the rise it's on provides a pleasant view of a few peninsulas and Tarbert's scenic three-sided harbour.

Above Tarbert's scenic three-sided harbour are the remains of a castle

From here, I have two choices. Either take the highway directly north along the coastline or follow the signed National Cycle Route, which loops around to the other side of the peninsula before returning to the highway. With the sun still out and having enjoyed the landscape so far, I will take the longer route.

It's undulating and feels remote as I'm only passing through a couple of tiny villages. As I begin following the sea again, this quiet route is often lined with stone fences in this green landscape. The further I travel, the more the clouds appear, and as I stop to make a sandwich at a remote school, I'm now feeling cold, but thankfully there's no rain in sight.

Quieter west side of the peninsula

Climbing back to the highway

As I begin a long climb at a gentle gradient to cross the peninsula back to the highway, the final T20 between England and Australia is starting, so I'm listening to the cricket as I cycle.

After only one short section of cycling on this highway with a few cars travelling much faster, I'm glad I took the longer route as it was relaxing.

Thankfully from Ardrishaig, there is a canal with a decent towpath to follow as I end my day by leaving the canal to head to nearby Lochgilphead at the top of Loch Gilp.

The tide is out, so the inlet is ugly. Still, there is a park to make dinner while listening as England finally win a match in the Ashes multi-format series, with Australia struggling in the chase.

I have a mini packaged Bolognese pasta meal for dinner, which is easier than buying all the individual ingredients. It also saves weight and produces less rubbish. Since it's a small meal, I have added some extra cooked pasta. I kept regularly buying these meals and adding additional pasta throughout my time in the UK, with Carbonara my favourite.

Cooking dinner at the top of an inlet

As for where I'm camping, I'm unsure yet, as I haven't found anywhere suitable in town, while the canal is my last resort because it's right beside the highway. It's now dusk, so I will check out one more possibility of a church.

In front of this church is a stone wall, but the gate is open. So I pedal into the car park, where behind the church is a quiet spot under trees. This will do for my tent. I'm then surprised to see that the church door is open and power plugs are available.

After charging my devices, I'm initially beside the same scenic canal as last night, with a few colourful flowering plants to admire and a few historical panels to read. Along the way are numerous man-made locks, which a few yachts are using to cross this peninsula. Because it takes hours for boats to get through all fifteen locks, small villages developed beside some of the locks to provide refreshments to tired travellers.

Villages developed beside a few locks

A *lock* is different to a *loch*. A *lock* is a man-made structure that allows boats to gain or lose height in a waterway which has different levels either side of the lock. Whereas a *loch* is a name for a natural body of water in Scotland. Some lochs have had locks and canals added to them to make navigation possible between lochs.

Today is the first day of the first men's Ashes cricket test match, and Australia is batting first, so I will have my radio out for most of the day.

As another inlet appears in front of me to my right is a vast open space, which will be my route north, leaving the canal behind on what looks like a quiet road. I'm hoping for an enjoyable day like yesterday.

However, after visiting the abandoned open-roofed tall stone Carnasserie Castle, the road beside Loch Awe becomes hilly with numerous short up and down roller coaster type cycling, rather than following the water closely.

There are times when there is a nice view of the loch below, while when the momentum from the descending propels me up the subsequent short rise, it is fun cycling. However, it feels like the majority of the time it's the opposite, where I'm putting in so much effort to get up a short rise before a short quick descent before starting another climb. I would prefer just one long climb that allows a consistent rhythm instead of this. The road is also narrow with passing lanes, so sometimes I have to stop to let the occasional car through, losing any momentum I had.

Undulating road

This is National Cycle Route 78, with cycling signs directing me, but it's not much fun. It also doesn't help my enthusiasm that the day has become overcast with occasional spots of rain, and it's just cold.

By the time I make it to Taynuilt, I'm sick and tired of this style of cycling, so I consider a short train ride to Connel to get to a rail trail. However, with a two-hour wait for the next train, I will keep cycling.

Passing through farms

Thankfully after a short climb, the cycle route goes through some relaxing flat green paddocks as the sun finally appears. I'm not alone as various sheep and cattle are grazing here, including some very hairy cows. Also improving my mood is that after Australia has been struggling in the cricket all day, suddenly Siddle and Smith are batting well together.

A Panorama shot of the farming area

Once I'm out of the farm area, a road takes me downhill to cross a loch using the Connel Bridge. On the North Connel side, a paved rail trail is a comfortable ride north.

However, it soon randomly ends in Benderloch, despite the formation continuing. There is a small general store and a pizza restaurant here, so I will stop for pizza. There isn't anywhere sensible to camp, so after pizza, I keep cycling as the sun is well and truly out now.

A rail cutting

National Cycle Route 78 in this section is either on the former rail right of way or beside the highway on a paved cycle path. It's mostly following the contours, so it's an enjoyable flat ride with a few large trees to admire while cycling alongside an inlet and passing a few scenic green mountains.

Near Balcaldine, the sign route drifts away from the rail right of way as it passes by a short gorge walk, so I will stop and go for an explore.

A gorge

It's a deep but narrow gorge with some beautiful large trees to look at and a lot of green moss on the ground. I could camp here, but I will keep going since it's a magical perfect evening temperature for cycling. Also, the further I get tonight, the less of a rush it will be to catch a ferry to Fort William tomorrow.

After another magical crossing of an inlet with a rainbow visible, the former Creagan Railway Station is on my right, which is now a private residence. I wish it were a rail trail as it looks delightful. Soon after this, the cycle route is back on the rail right of way, but it's now close to dusk.

Crossing a loch

As an inlet appears, a track leads off the rail trail to a quiet grassed spot. No one is around, and since I have been told in Scotland that I can camp anywhere, I will camp here.

I awake this Friday, knowing it's a short day to Fort William with a couple of ferry rides required. My only concern is that I'm unsure what times the second ferry operates to Fort William, as signs on this cycling route say there are four daily crossings, but it only mentions 16:35 as the last one.

Wild camping

I don't have to use ferries as there is a direct route on the east side of Loch Emil. However, it's a busy highway, so the recommended cycling route involves catching two ferries.

After passing a small castle on a tiny island, the cycling is just as delightful as the previous evening, with all but two miles on a cycle path and the majority on the former rail right of way. Often this path is right beside the water, providing colourful, scenic, reflective views of mountains in the distance while passing through a few railway cuttings and a couple of former stations.

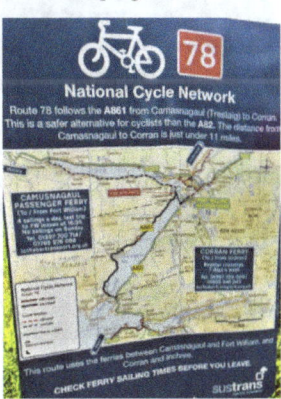
Cycle route to Fort William

The rail trail follows water for a while and passes former stations

Where the railway line ended at Ballachulish is two miles off the cycle route, but with a supermarket and potential wi-fi, I will head there to check it out. Rather than continuing on the rail right of way, I'm on a path right beside the busy, noisy highway.

Besides a former quarry that was the primary traffic for the railway, there is not much to see in Ballachulish. I have at least found out that the second last ferry is at 12:30 pm. It's now 10:45, and with another more regular ferry to take in the meantime, along with fifteen miles to cycle, I will probably have to settle for the last ferry.

As I make my way to the first ferry on cement paths, the noise from the busy highway is deafening. As two touring cyclists appear, we have a brief chat. They have just cycled on the highway from Fort William, and they don't recommend it. So it's an easy decision to take the ferry to the hopefully quieter west side, even if I have to wait a few hours for the second ferry to Fort William.

The first ferry runs every half-hour, so it's not too long to wait for this car ferry. Once on the west side, it's a relaxing quiet scenic ride at shoreline level, with the only traffic a few sheep.

First ferry, leads to a quieter side

As Britain's highest mountain Ben Nevis appears across the water, I have arrived at a quiet pier. Having just missed the 12:30 ferry, I will have to wait four hours. Since the cycling was so relaxing, I'm glad I took the ferry across to the quiet west side even if I had to wait. A sign says that a cycle path will soon be developed beside the highway on the east side. However, having cycled the quiet flat west side, I don't think they need to bother; they just need more regular ferry services.

I could keep cycling west around this bay and then take a highway back east to Fort William, but by the time I did this, the ferry would be arriving anyway.

Admiring Ben Nevis, while waiting for the ferry

Instead, I spend this beautiful sunny afternoon admiring Ben Nevis while listening to the cricket on my radio. Occasionally, I can hear and briefly glimpse a steam train going past in the distance across the water.

By the time the small ferry arrives, six cyclists have shown up, including two Austrians and a couple from Spain, along with some pedestrians. Thankfully, the ferry staff are used to cyclists, and so they end up hanging all the bicycles off the roof of the boat.

This small boat is use to taking cyclists

Fort William was only named in the late 1600s, which feels young for Scotland, while there are only small low remains of stone walls among the grass of the actual Fort.

Remains of the Fort in Fort William

This town is famous as the outdoor capital of the UK, so there are numerous outdoor shops in the long pedestrian mall as well as plenty of people with hiking backpacks or touring bicycles.

At night while staying with my nice Warmshower host Hana, I discover a few ticks on my body, so I remove them with special tweezers that Hana has. Since I will be in their habitat for the next few weeks, in the morning, I search for a spray in the many outdoor shops for preventing ticks and also midges.

While admiring a metal sculpture of a model T-Ford in the pedestrian mall, two Australian ladies recognise me and my bicycle from the World Cup in France. I met them in Grenoble and Nice, and as they say, it's such a small world.

The model T-Ford sculpture is here because in 1911, a man drove a T-Ford up Ben Nevis, an impressive feat considering even today, there isn't a road to

Model of a T-Ford

Undergarment that could be used as rope   *A secret image*

the top. I have considered climbing this mountain, but I don't really have the equipment for hiking that far, especially with my deteriorating sandals. Anyway, it's not that tall as I was cycling higher places in the French Alps.

The West Highland Museum doesn't open until 10 am, but it's worth it because it's engaging with two focuses. Firstly, the commandos training facility nearby trained men to an elite level during the Second World War. On display are numerous items used by them including many multi-use items like warm clothing, which could be used as rope.

Secondly is the Jacobite Rising of 1745, led by Bonnie Prince Charles and supported by many Highland clans, which failed to get the Catholic Stuarts back on the throne. It was hard to know who to trust during this period, so on display are a few items that secretly show who was friendly, including some reflective objects which at a certain angle shows a secret image.

It's a beautiful sunny morning as I leave Fort William, passing by a tourist steam train which presumably was what I heard yesterday. This train heads west towards Mallaig on a scenic British National railway line. I sort of follow this railway line west on an off-road path until meeting a canal where numerous locks are close together going uphill. This allows boats to eventually travel all the way north to Inverness by using a few lochs that are connected by a few canals.

So many lochs at the southern end of the Great Glen Way

Following these canals and lochs is both a cycle route and a hiking path called the Great Glen Way. They take the same route to Fort Augustus before taking a different route to Inverness. It's a popular route, so I'm encountering numerous cyclists on this route, including the Spanish couple I met yesterday on the ferry to Fort William, along with a few hikers.

This first canal section is excellent for cycling, with a decent surface as I follow it for a while until the path beside the canal runs out close to Loch Lochy. From here, I have to return to a road that thankfully is quiet and paved as it goes around close to the edge of Loch Lochy.

I follow the Spanish cyclists on the canal, before I'm beside Loch Lochy

Just off the road is a sign to a clan museum, so I will head there to learn more about the Cameron clan. Along the way, I pass some remains of a commandos training site, including a derelict landing boat.

The museum is small but explains how the clan system, which still operates today, works. It's just like a mini royal family with leadership

Remains of a Commando's training boat

passed down from father to son, reminding me of the houses in Game of Thrones. Like the British Royal family, the titles are more symbolic now than having any official power.

Once I'm back beside Loch Lochy, the paved road soon runs out, so the cycle route is now on a four wheel drive track. It's rough and undulating in some sections, but manageable.

After a sunny day so far, around 3 pm unexpectedly, rain begins. I'm in the middle of a pine forest, so I race to the northern end of Loch Lochy, where a dozen cyclists are huddling under a café's shelter beside a canal. This allows the exchange of experiences with people coming from both directions. Most are just on a short weekend ride, with some aiming to cycle far tonight to find indoor accommodation as apparently, it's hard to find in Fort Augustus.

Following Loch Lochy to it's northern end

I could camp here, but as the rain clears, people begin leaving, so I will continue towards Fort Augustus by following another canal.

It's only a short canal as I soon meet another loch, so the cycle route joins a rail trail at Invergarry, where there is still an intact railway platform. This is part of the former railway line to Fort Augustus, which only now begins to follow this water route.

Starting a rail trail at Invergarry

Once I'm on the rail trail, the rain returns, so once a former rail tunnel appears, I will stop here as the rain has become heavier. Thankfully, I have the cricket on the radio to distract me.

The rain eases after half an hour, so I will continue on this trail beside Loch Olch. Once I'm past the Loch, the trail leaves the rail right of way to return to a canal path that will take me into Fort Augustus. Along the way, I pass a man wearing an Essendon Aussie Rules hat, so I ask him why and he says in his Scottish accent that his wife is from Australia.

As I arrive in Fort Augustus on a cold, overcast evening, I pass numerous locks into a scenic town where the only supermarket is in a service station with tourist prices. Whereas Fort William felt like a place outdoor people visit for various adventures, here at the bottom of Loch Ness, it feels touristy with a few buses around.

There is a hostel, but it's full of international tourists, so it's too busy for me; I would rather camp. The caravan park doesn't appeal to me as it appears to be more set up for caravans and RVs as there doesn't appear to be any shelter for cooking or storing my gear.

Thankfully, I have found a wooden shelter shed on the local school grounds, so I should stay dry. Since it's the school holidays, no one is around this Saturday evening, so I'm assuming I won't be discovered.

On the way into Fort Augusta, I pass many locks

Camping in a wooden school shed, not far from Loch Ness

Various ideas had been made about building a direct railway line between Fort William and Inverness. However, only a section to Fort Augustus from the south was ever built. It lasted until the end of the Second World War.

This means there isn't a flat path beside Loch Ness other than the busy highway on the west side, so the recommended cycle route is on a secondary road on the hillier east side. There are mountain bike tracks, but they are even hillier.

From Fort Augustus, the road climbs 400 metres before descending back to Loch Ness. I'm finding the actual climbing part okay, unlike an older couple who are walking their bicycles nearly the whole way up. The further I climb, the foggier it's becoming, so once I'm at the pass, I can't see anything.

While the fog is annoying and cold, what becomes a more significant challenge is that rain soon begins and stays for the next three hours, so the rest of my ride to Inverness becomes about getting there rather than enjoying the ride or appreciating Loch Ness.

If Nessie had been visible today, I probably wouldn't have even noticed. I had expected Scotland to have this type of weather, and Monday is looking similar.

My view at the pass

I made date scones

After searching around, I have managed to find a hostel in the southern suburbs of Inverness. They have a room out the back just for me with a small kitchen with some leftover food, including self-raising flour. So I end up making some date scones.

In the morning, I island-hop through a few forested islands in the River Ness before following the Ness back to the city centre past the castle. Inverness Castle is still used by the courts and has plenty of information on historical events, including a memorial to Flora MacDonald, who helped Bonnie Prince Charles escape after his final defeat at nearby Culloden.

I have a full day here, so I will cycle east out to Culloden to see where the last Jacobite battle was. It's about six miles of suburban cycling to get there, so I'm trying to take a quiet route using bicycle paths where I can.

It's reasonably busy at the new looking Culloden Battlefield Visitor Centre. Inside is plenty of information on the lead up to the battle, including why Bonnie Prince Charles was here. He was trying to reclaim the British throne for the house of Stuart, who were Catholic and had been expelled from the throne in favour of the Protestant Hanoverians from modern-day Germany.

Initially, the Jacobites were victorious in a few battles as they travelled south before they ran out of support in England and retreated before being defeated here in a short battle. Afterwards, Bonnie Prince Charles fled the country, which ended any Stuart claim to the throne and caused many Scottish clans to lose their political influence.

The actual battle site is an open field with high grass and a few red flags informing us where the government front line was. Close by are blue flags, representing the Jacobite front line before they charged to the red flags, where the fighting happened. This battle is explained on a guided group tour, and we are shown mass graves with a few stones having names of a few clans on each.

Around the Culloden Battlefield, are memorial stones for clan families

It's informative learning about the battle, but the actual site isn't that interesting as I have to use my imagination to understand what happened.

The rest of my afternoon back in Inverness is spent doing a few jobs, including seeing if I can find a decent pair of cycling shoes. None are what I'm after, so I will continue with my sandals which are still just holding together.

In the evening, while waiting at the Inverness Railway Station, I learn there have been a few washouts of railway lines in Scotland, particularly west of Glasgow. This may change my plans to catch some scenic railway lines in the future as I will need to utilise trains somewhere to get to Leeds in time for the 3rd Ashes test match. While waiting for my train, I briefly consider not catching a train to Kyle of Lochalsh to head to the Isle of Skye. Instead, I could head east towards Aberdeen.

After some consideration, I will take the train to Kyle of Lochalsh while waiting to see what happens with other rail services. If I have to cycle back there from the Isle of Skye and get the train back to Inverness, I will.

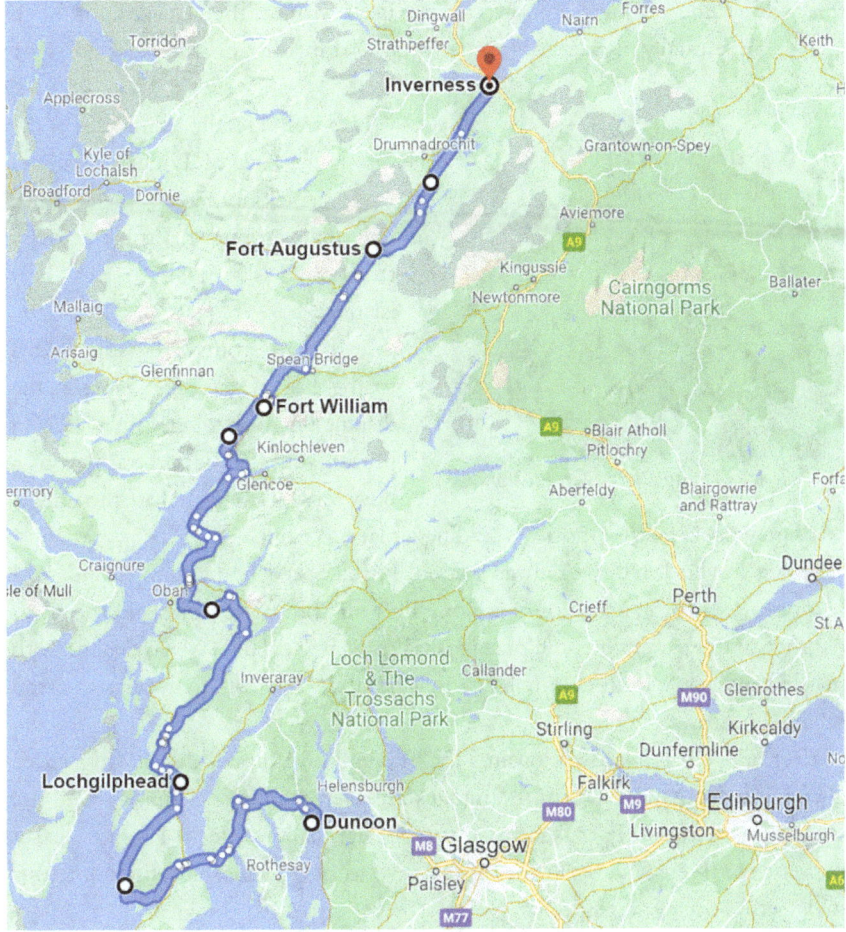

Dunoon to Inverness (Google Maps)

Skye

The train to Kyle of Lochalsh is nearly empty as we leave the suburbs of Inverness with glimpses of the sea every so often. I'm soon chatting to a young woman about how her parents live in a remote town operating a pub beside this railway line. It has taken her all day to travel from England to here.

As the train begins heading in a south-westerly direction, we leave the sea behind and begin following a river with a few scenic lakes. We are passing through the occasional small village, while there is barely a car on the single road that follows this railway line. It feels remote, especially for the UK. In a way, it reminds me of the remote rural lifestyle which is common in Australia.

As I admire the scenery, I consider that this may be a scenic cycling route to do one day. I just wasn't sure what the traffic would be like with only one road here. Anyway, I enjoy scenic train rides.

After the young woman leaves the train at Strathcarron, the final section of this railway line begins scenically curving itself around the shoreline of Loch Carron. Eventually, it becomes more open as I'm now on the west coast of Scotland.

Kyle of Lochalsh Railway Station

This train literally terminates at the sea, as the Kyle of Lochalsh Railway Station sticks out on a pier, with a few boats around it. Visible across a small strait is a mostly treeless hilly island.

As I scan around, the sole bridge to the Isle of Skye is visible in the distance. It only opened in 1995, so presumably, this station was part of a busy ferry terminal before the bridge.

It's now dusk, so my priority is finding a place to camp.

Before I even leave the railway station, I'm attacked by numerous midges. I had been told to be aware of these tiny flies that bite. Their bite and the sheer number of them reminds me of sandflies in New Zealand. While dealing with my first midges, a local man tells me that he often suggests to cyclists to camp on a hill nearby.

After briefly leaving town towards the bridge, I head up a side path to a space covered in vegetation, where the midges are even worse. So I quickly find the spray I purchased in Fort William, but it doesn't really work, so I frantically set my tent up. Even once I zip the tent, I have to begin squashing the numerous midges that have got inside.

There is a rail museum in the Kyle of Lochalsh Railway Station, so I go back to see if it's open in the morning, but it's not. I do at least check for an update on rail services in Scotland after the recent flooding. They are still figuring out what services will be operating, including from Mallaig, the railway station I'm hoping to catch a train from after visiting the Isle of Skye.

As I make my way to the bridge using a cycle path beside the road, I pass a warning of heavy rain forecast for Friday. Fortunately, it's only overcast this Tuesday as the cycle path takes me onto this high cement bridge to the Isle of Skye.

Once on Skye, the cycle path finishes and with no other road options, I have no choice but to join the surprisingly busy main road as I make my way to the town of Broadford. With so much traffic, no road shoulder and cold weather, my focus is on cycling rather than the scenery.

After stopping for a cheeseburger in a food van and looking inside an art space, the road continues following the coastline. On my left are high surrounding hills of various shapes and heights. At lower levels, these hills are covered in green shrubs, while higher up, it appears they are treeless. Today most hills are covered in clouds.

I would love to get off this busy road, but there appears to be only one short loop secondary road option on my way to Portree, so I'm relieved when I can take it.

However, not long after leaving the busy, noisy main road, there is string across Moll Road and a closed road sign. Since the alternative is a busy road with a high climb, I will duck under the string and see why it's closed as this route will give me a seven mile break from traffic.

Moll Road was once paved, but now it's deteriorating yet it's still comfortable to ride, especially with no traffic to worry about. With the road often close to the edge of the shoreline, this allows me to admire a bay that contains a few groups of sizeable circular fishing pots.

Soon a large closed road sign appears in front of a pile of gravel. As I approach closer, I can see a small section of the road has been washed away, leaving a deep drop off. While a car can't get through, thankfully, a bicycle can walk around it.

A bicycle can get around this hole in the road

Soon I duck under more string and pass a couple of houses, allowing the rest of Moll Road to be straightforward and relaxing.

As I meet the main road again, the sheer amount of traffic is overwhelming. Despite some nice scenery beside a bay at the start, it is just a horrible cold ride for the next twelve miles to Portree.

At one stage, I thought there may be another loop road option at Sligachan, but it looks like a hiking track, from what I can see. It's a longer route anyway, and I just want to get to Portree to hopefully find somewhere warm.

Busy and scenic Sligachan

The reason for cycling firstly to Portree is there is a tourist office, which allows me to learn about things to see on the island. I'm told that both the road and town are so busy today because the Skye Highland Games are being held here tomorrow. So I now have some plans for tomorrow morning.

Since it's so cold, I will make my way to the library to stay warm and research where to go for the next couple of weeks.

Isle of Skye Band

The Isle of Skye band plays each Tuesday night in Portree's main square. Tonight there are plenty of people around watching as this band marches up and down the square. There are a dozen men and women of various ages all dressed in tartan skirts and carrying a wide range of musical instruments, including bagpipes. The older leader is carrying a large pole that he is twirling while shouting instructions to the band and the crowd.

Afterwards, I make my way to the Shinty sports ground on the edge of town as I presume all accommodation options are sold out tonight.

There is a large clubhouse here in front of the field. With no one around, I will look to see if there is a spot to keep my bicycle dry. I'm surprised to find an unlocked door, so I sneak inside. There is plenty of room for me to sleep inside on the floor and store my bicycle in a change-room. Since it's so cold, I will take the chance of hoping I won't be discovered inside.

Other than hearing a couple of dog walkers outside, it's a quiet night inside the clubhouse. Since it's still cold outside in the morning, I'm comfortable with my decision to sneak inside.

One of the reasons for calling this book *'It's not about the how far I cycle'* is that often the best days are where I don't cycle at all. It's also a reminder to me and other potential touring cyclists not to focus on just cycling. Attending the Skye Highland Games was one of those days.

The games arena is located at the bottom of a small peninsula just south of the tourist office, so the sea is visible on three sides. The small, grassed, circular playing arena is surrounded by a few rocky grass-covered hills, which fill up throughout the day as the crowd builds.

The marching band in the Arena

It's a cold overcast day with light rain every so often, so I'm grateful to be experiencing a local cultural event rather than cycling.

Except during both World Wars, the Skye Highland Games have been going on since 1877. It has many cliché Scottish activities from participants and referees wearing kilts, bagpipes being played all day and Scottish dances. The same local marching band kicks off the games by marching in, and they end the day by marching out. They are a larger group today, while the same leader is dressed even fancier with a kilt cape and a tall black fur hat.

As for the games, it's split between events in the morning where only locals are allowed to compete and afternoon events open to everyone. There are four different types of events; local dances of various ages, bagpipe competitions, various running events and a strong man competition.

The final running event involves a race out of the arena and up a large hill across the bay and back, where tiny dots can only just be seen moving on a hill across the bay. The first back is an Australian man from Canberra.

In the open strong man competition, the competitors are from many places, including Austria, the Czech Republic, the Netherlands, Poland and the USA. Presumably, these men travel to all the highland events around Scotland, as they are familiar with each other.

As well as regular athletic field events, including shot put, high jump and triple jump, they throw an actual sledgehammer in the hammer throw. A few years ago, they had to make the sledgehammer heavier because it was being thrown too far, endangering the crowd.

Throwing weight over a high bar, and throwing a telephone pole over end

Another event involves throwing a 56-pound weight (25kg) over their shoulder and over a high bar from a standing position. The winner throws it over 16 feet for a new record at this event.

The last heavy man competition involves balancing a large, power pole size log off the ground upright and then attempting to throw it tip over end. The aim is to get it to land as close as it can to being straight like it is at the position of twelve on an imaginary clock on the ground.

Because the games have gone all day, it's an easy decision in the evening to return to the Shinty ground and stay warm inside again. After settling in, a group of young men come inside for a few minutes. So I end up hiding in one of the change rooms as I don't want anyone to know I'm sleeping here. Otherwise, it's another quiet night.

Road north of Portree

As I head north of Portree, it's a treeless landscape on this cold, windy, overcast day as I climb past a few small lakes. There are so many cars travelling north this morning, it's dangerous at times on this single lane road with numerous blind hills and only a few passing lanes.

At one stage, there is a busy hiking path to a natural feature called the Storr, but since it is covered in fog, it doesn't look like it's worth going.

When I re-meet the sea at a lookout, it's busy again as apparently dinosaurs were found here, but all I can see are high cliffs. Past the dinosaurs, it's thankfully a little quieter with some scenic rock faces to look at as this remote road crosses a peninsula past a few small villages. As I meet the sea again, the remains of a stone castle at Duntulm appear, but rather than being preserved, sheep are grazing around it.

Crossing a peninsula to Duntulm Castle

Further down the road is the Skye Museum of Island Life, which has six thatched roofed houses, along with farming and household items from yesteryear. There are also plenty of stories of Skye life, as it was even more remote back then. It reminds me of outback Australian stories of having to rely on yourself.

Skye Museum of Island Life

By now, the sun is out, so it's an enjoyable scenic cycle with the sea looking particularly blue as I bypass the town of Uig down below in a wide bay. Since it's a short one-way road, I won't head down to where I could catch a ferry to the Outer Hebrides Islands located further out in the sea.

Going around Uig

I had considered going out to these islands, but it just doesn't work logistically with me needing to get back to England in time for the third test match. It makes more sense to come back another time to visit the Outer Hebrides properly. Instead, I will see more of the Isle of Skye rather than only visiting half of this island.

As the road begins looping its way west, I stop for a break in Edinbane, where a telephone box has been converted to a free food box. I have seen this for books, but not for food before. Just in case I don't make Dunvegan tonight, I pick up some food and leave behind a couple of non-food items I haven't been using.

Wild camping in a paddock

Thankfully, I do make the small town of Dunvegan which has a few small shops. There is a campground, but it's packed, and since you can camp anywhere in Scotland, I just randomly walk my bicycle into a grass-covered paddock and begin cooking dinner. Once the sun disappears, thousands of biting midges suddenly appear, so I cover as much of my skin as I can and hurriedly cook dinner. Once I'm in my tent, I begin killing as many midges as I can that have got in my now zipped up tent.

I awake to consistent rain, which doesn't look like going away, so I head briefly north to Dunvegan Castle. It must see many tourists as it has plenty of parking places, including for large buses, while there are people here early lining up.

This unremarkable castle is still owned by a wealthy family and inside is information on how the castle was built, including a dungeon. While it has some lovely gardens, heavy rain means I don't get to appreciate it as much. If it hadn't been raining, I probably wouldn't have visited.

Model of Angus MacAskill next to a little person

In 1825, on an island nearby, Angus MacAskill was born. He grew up to be 236 centimetres tall. He became a circus attraction as a strongman but died aged 38, so a relative has set up a museum for him in Dunvegan. Inside are large items used by Angus, including clothing and furniture, along with a life-size model of him, while newspaper articles tell of his short life.

After waiting the heavy rain out in a local café, it looks like it has finally eased by early afternoon, so I will leave Dunvegan. However, it's still a cold, windy day with mostly a horrible headwind. Adding to my woes, randomly my bicycle stand has become loose. With the tools I have, I can neither tighten it properly nor take it off completely. Instead, I'm trying to tighten it enough to balance it to not hit the pedals or the spokes in my rear wheel. However, it keeps coming loose repeatedly, forcing me to stop, so I'm not getting any momentum on this cold day.

It's a shame that the weather and bicycle stand issues mean I'm not appreciating the ride as the landscape is scenic with few hills often on my left side. A few times, this quiet road dips down to cross inlets while passing through a few small villages with just a few houses and a church. Along the way, cars are randomly stopping to look at sheep.

Amazing scenery, just a shame it's so cold

When I re-meet my previous route at Sligachan, I ask for a spanner in the hotel, but they can't help me. Thankfully, the nearby campground can.

From here, I have no choice but to retrace my route from my first day on the Isle of Skye.

There is a little more sun this time, but with a cold headwind, it's a horrible ride with slightly less traffic than last time. As I redo the secondary Moll Road, near the washout part, I pass a touring cyclist who appears to be camping here, but I will keep going.

By the time I'm back in Broadford, I'm freezing, so I begin searching for warm indoor accommodation, but they are all booked out while the campground is apparently full. I ask anyway, and I'm allowed to stay, yet when a couple in a car shows up, he turns them away. This is my first paid campground in the UK, so I'm not sure what to expect.

As I make my way to where I'm supposed to set up my tent, I'm surprised to see less than a dozen tents in an area that could hold three times this amount. Apparently, they don't want this healthy-looking grass to die off. Compared to Australia, it looks very green to me and back home, people would be packed in.

There aren't many facilities here, no picnic tables or a camp kitchen, just bathrooms with showers and a room with small sinks. There is at least a warm drying room, which is useful for my wet clothes. I'm not sure it's worth paying for this. It does make me consider if I should bother with paid campgrounds again in the UK.

Apparently a packed campground

Having not seen many touring cyclists on Skye, in the morning, I pass a few who have come by the ferry I will be catching soon on the way to Armidale.

It's a scenic sunny ride to Armidale, where there is a small farmer's market beside the castle entrance. Inside are some beautiful gardens surrounding an abandoned ruin. This abandoned castle was the home of the Macdonald Clan.

A clan map in the museum near the ruins of Armidale Castle

Helpfully there is a museum explaining the clan system even more, especially how certain families were subservient to others. An informative clan map reminds me of indigenous maps of Australia. In the gardens, an American says to me, the word 'clan' has a negative meaning in the United States, which I hadn't considered until now.

Overall, Skye has a fascinating history, with a variety of historic buildings to explore, friendly people and a green scenic landscape. However, with many interesting places on long one-way roads and the mixed weather, it would be better by car.

Isle of Skye (Google Maps)

The Other Perth

A few touring cyclists and a group of older American women, are on the ferry to Mallaig, which is taking me back to the mainland.

Due to the smell and the number of boats, Mallaig is clearly a fishing village, while the railway station appears to be the reason why the town exists as it's right in the centre of town. A tourist steam train is leaving now, but I will wait for the regular train later in the day.

The small museum next door confirms my impressions, as there are stories about the fishing lifestyle here, while this rail line has been threatened with closure a couple of times.

There are a few reasons for taking the train; firstly I'm told it's a scenic ride, secondly at times there is only one road option, and thirdly I'm running out of time to get to Leeds for the cricket, so this is a perfect way to skip ahead.

I try buying a ticket at the station, but they won't sell me one because I have a bicycle. Instead, I'm told to wait until the conductor is back. Thankfully, the conductor lets me on to a surprisingly packed train full of tourist groups, so I have to stand up.

I presume it's so busy because we cross the famous Glenfinnan Viaduct. Anyone who has seen the film Harry Potter and the Chamber of Secrets will recognise this viaduct from when Ron and Harry in the flying car were chasing the Hogwarts Express. Since it's so packed, I don't get much of a view. I thought about getting off in the town of Glenfinnan, but I'm concerned about getting my bicycle back on another train.

On the way into Fort William, we pass the same set of locks I saw a week ago. Most people are getting off the train here, and since Fort William is a dead-end station, we are preparing to change direction. However the train has broken down, so we hurriedly change trains.

I'm enjoying the second half of this less packed train ride more as the train climbs through a treeless alpine landscape up to 500 metres. In particular, I enjoy the view from the train when it does a few long curves nearly back on itself. Despite the remoteness, at a random station, a couple of mountain bikers board the train. All the tourist groups missed this spectacular section.

Second half of the train ride

As we approach Crianlarich, the branch line from Oban is visible below in a valley as we gradually descend to a junction station.

Usually, this train continues to Glasgow, but after some flooding caused a few washouts, trains are not running between Crianlarich and Glasgow. I will miss some cycling routes northwest of Glasgow, but this will allow me to take a shortcut and save time with a more direct route to Perth.

I'm not sure where to sleep in this small town until stumbling on a free camping spot beside the River Fillan. I'm not alone, as a few hikers are camped here, presumably because I'm near the West Highland Way hiking route.

A regular camping spot beside a river and railway line near Crianlarich

My morning ride

Today Crianlarich is a railway junction town, but it used to be that two railway companies crossed here as separate lines. The line east of Crianlarich is long gone, so on this overcast Sunday morning, I'm hoping to follow this former rail line, which is also National Cycle Route 7.

Initially, the former railway line is visible from the road, but it soon disappears from view. As another small section of dirt rail trail appears near some fast-flowing water at Falls of Dochart, I'm assuming the rail line continued further east.

The cycle route passes Falls of Dochart and remains of a rail bridge

However, the rail trail ends beside Loch Tay. Instead, the cycling route is now on a quiet undulating road that follows the southern side of the long narrow Loch Tay. As I meet a family of cyclists with teenagers, they explain they have just come from the south where they cycled the rail trail I was looking for.

It turns out that the railway line at Falls of Dochart was a branch line, so there was never a railway line beside Loch Tay. By the time I have figured this out, I'm already halfway along Loch Tay and as this current route will get me to Perth, I will continue.

Loch Tay, is quite long

Near the eastern end of Loch Tay is the Scottish Crannog Centre, which has three different aspects to see. Firstly a small museum is showing heritage objects found here. Secondly, there is an outdoor area with numerous old school skills being demonstrated by people dressed in period attire, including dying wool by hand, making tools out of wood or old cooking skills.

The memorable aspect of this museum is a replica of a Crannog, located on Loch Tay. This Iron Age building was built on top of the water by jamming logs into the bottom of the loch. Then built on top was a round wooden hut, with a pointy thatch roof that has a chimney hole. A wooden walkway connects it back to land. Our guide explains they are unsure why they were built.

It's cosy inside, with places to store animals alongside their cooking and sleeping areas. Inside is a lot of straw and wood, alongside animal skins to keep themselves warm, while there are many handmade items they assume they had.

A replica Crannog

Once abandoned, as the centuries went by, they became covered in so much soil and tree litter they eventually created what looks like a natural island on a loch. However, they are in fact, former Crannogs.

The further I cycle, the colder the day is becoming, and as I pass through the locality of Dull, this sums up the weather.

Just as I make the town of Aberfeldy, light rain begins. It's becoming heavy, so I'm sheltering in a supermarket. It looks like it has settled in from the radar, so I will search online for a dry place to stay tonight. Dunkeld, about seventeen miles away, looks like the best spot.

Since it's terrible weather, with my rain jacket hoody on, it feels like I'm wearing blinkers, preventing me from appreciating the landscape. East of Aberfeldy, there was a railway line, but only a short section is a rail trail which is overgrown and muddy.

After crossing the River Tay on a former rail bridge, I have to return to the road as there are only bridge supports left of the rail bridge across the nearby River Tummel. From here, I join a skinny path right next to the noisy A9 motorway, the main road to Inverness. Along with the combination of now heavy rain, it's a struggle. Even when a road takes me away from the motorway, the rain is just as heavy.

Thankfully in Dunkeld, I'm able to find a hostel with a friendly lady who gives me a room to myself, allowing me and my clothes to dry off while seeing what UK television has on offer. It's similar reality junk as we get in Australia.

Beatrix Potter gardens in Dunkeld

Dunkeld has an association with Beatrix Potter, so there are statues of her characters in a public park, including Peter Rabbit. There is a museum nearby, but it's not enough of an interest for me to pay to go inside.

Instead, I begin making my way south to Perth by following a cycling route that has some cycle paths, but for the most part, involves quiet back roads, which take a longer route away from the motorway and the railway line. Closer to Perth, the cycle route loops back using paths beside a small river before passing through some open parks next to the larger River Tay.

Perth is a tiny city, much smaller than the city of the same name in Australia. There is not much to see, even the tourist information staff don't have much to offer. I'm visiting Perth because across the river is Scone Palace, where Scottish monarchs were crowned.

After a busy road, Scone Palace is among gardens and smaller than I imagine. Inside the palace, most of the focus is on the family who owns this castle. I learn more about how they keep shovels VIP's used to plant trees here, rather than any Scottish royal history.

Scottish Monarch's were crowned here

Outside on a small hill is a replica of the Stone of Scone in front of a church. It is just a horizontal stone slab on top of two vertical blocks of stone. Only one basic sign informs me this is where Scottish monarchs were crowned. Otherwise apart from some well-kept gardens there isn't much else to see, so don't bother visiting.

After re-crossing the River Tay on a curvy railway bridge back into Perth, I begin following a cycle route south.

Throughout the afternoon, a few short rain showers appear, enough to make me slightly damp before the sun returns.

Once I find a way out of suburbia, signs are saying I'm on cycle-friendly roads. However, often this route involves short steep sections, which aren't the best gradient for cycling.

It takes a while to get to Kinross, a town with a large round scenic lake called Loch Leven. Apparently, I can cycle right around the whole lake, but it's fifteen miles, which is too far for me to do tonight. Instead, I will relax by the lake while cooking dinner. However, I soon run out of fuel for my stove, so I will have to walk back into town.

Loch Leven

It's now after 7 pm, so only a Co-op supermarket is open. They don't have my usual fuel source of methylated spirits, but I have learned that nail polish is flammable. It works in my Trangia, but I'm just not sure how safe the fumes are.

Not far south of Kinross is the larger Dunfermline, which I'm finding more interesting than Perth, including the local library, which has a small but interesting local history museum.

My English Heritage Card allows me half-price access to the large Dunfermline Abbey, surrounded by gardens. At different moments in history, Dunfermline had a royal presence going back a thousand years, so it's interesting to see how it changed over time. The large Abbey which is still used, has obviously been expanded over the years with a change in architecture style halfway along and plenty of supporting columns inside.

Right next to the abbey was the smaller Dunfermline Palace, which today is in ruin. A small middle part of the castle is mostly intact, with a few levels to walk on, giving me access to the now more open-aired wings on either side.

The roof is gone on both the longer open wings, while the outer wall away from the abbey is still standing, unlike the top half of the closer side. The bottom half of the closer wall was built into the side of a hill, so I can look down into an open courtyard from the outside, at ground level.

From numerous markings and because there are windows at three different levels on the outer wall, it's easy to tell that this castle once had a few levels. They were accessed by spiral staircases, some of which still exist. Helpfully, info panels show how the castle operated with different tasks on each level.

I feel like I could spend longer exploring here, including the attractive gardens, but with Warmshower hosts already organised in Stirling tonight and Edinburgh tomorrow, I need to move on. It's always hard to judge beforehand how long to spend at each location I'm passing through.

Next to Dunfermline Abbey are the remains of the castle

Spiral staircases connected different levels of Dunfermline Castle

With rail trails on both sides of where the main Dunfermline Station once was, I can leave on a rail trail. It's sunny as I leave, but soon, the weather is becoming less stable with rain interruptions every so often for a few minutes at a time. When not on a rail trail, a cycle path takes me past a few random castle towers, including in the town of Alloa.

Even when another rail trail ends, a signed off-road cycle route takes me towards Stirling as the William Wallace memorial comes into view, dominating the landscape on a hill.

It takes a while to find the busy entrance to this memorial built in the late 1800s, centuries after William Wallace lived. After walking up a hill on a forested track, I can more closely see that it's shaped like a square lighthouse. Inside are narrow stairs leading to rooms on a few levels, where information helps explain the successful Stirling Bridge battle against the English. There are also a few pieces of artwork on the Scottish leaders involved, including colourful glass windows.

The 360-degree views of Stirling from the open-top level, allow me to see where the Stirling Bridge battle was, which is now just a normal part of this spread out city.

After only an hour, I have seen enough as while there are interesting things to see, there isn't a lot. Half of that hour was spent walking up both

Where the Battle of Stirling Bridge Battle was, is visible from the Wallace Memorial

the hill and then the stairs inside this memorial. It's also a bit more expensive than other sites with a similar amount of information. Still, it does explain why Stirling was a critical location between northern and southern Scotland.

Inside the Wallace Memorial is a tapestry of the memorial and a few glass windows

After crossing over the River Forth near where Stirling Bridge was back in William Wallace's time, I begin climbing up to Stirling Castle, my third historical site, this Tuesday.

As I arrive, a guided tour has just started, so I will join it.

The Stewart era of Scottish Monarchs dominates the architecture of Stirling Castle because this was their home base until James VI abandoned Stirling when he went south to become James I of England. Each King James added their own touch to this castle, clearly evident by a couple of creamy yellow buildings that stand out as more modern than most of this grey stone castle. Many of these buildings have decorative wooden ceilings, including one which has many caricatures of VIPs during the Stewart era, with most royalty, including rival English monarchs.

Another enjoyable aspect about this castle is that there are rooms showing the various tasks undertaken to run this castle, from the kitchens to the blacksmiths. Even just the view from Stirling Castle is worth it, as most of the city is visible below, while the Wallace Monument can be seen in the distance on a hill.

What I will take away the most is that it took thirteen years for weavers to make replicas of seven tapestries they think used to be here. They each have a unicorn focus as they symbolise Scottish royalty, something to do with them being a representative of God.

A mixture of grey and cream at Stirling Castle

A newer part of Stirling Castle has a scenic ceiling

Pictorials on the ceiling, while there are a few replica tapestries with a unicorn focus

Due to arriving mid-afternoon, I only have two hours to be here, which was just enough time to see it all but a little more time would have been nicer.

I end this enjoyable day sleeping on a couch in a share-house where my Warmshower host Hamish lives. His visiting brother is sleeping on another couch.

South of Stirling is Bannockburn which I know as a famous Scottish battle. This small memorial is located in a suburb of Stirling in an open grass field. The heritage centre is larger than the outside memorial, and there are films about the battle, but I'm told they are sold out. So after looking at the limited information provided outside around this small memorial, I will begin making my way to Edinburgh.

From Crianlarich towards Edinburgh (Google Maps)

Edinburgh

Cycling towards a large city often takes longer than it should, and the ride on National Cycle Route 76 to Edinburgh is no exception. Fortunately on this overcast day, I have the distraction of the first day of the second men's Ashes test match at Lords to listen to.

The Kelpies

While trying to get through built-up Falkirk, there is a lot of zigzagging as I have to cross rivers, the Forth-Clyde canal, major roads and railway lines. After passing two giant horse head statues near a busy recreation space near a canal, the cycle route eventually heads back towards the River Forth, where it's a little quieter.

A tourist railway line is beside the now wide Forth Bay at Bo'ness, and soon, a cycle path goes around the Museum of Scottish Railways, so I will stop here and head inside.

It's like many typical railway museums with carriages and locomotives on display. Of most interest is a map showing where railway lines used to go in Scotland, with a number having disappeared, particularly in the border area south of Edinburgh.

It's less populated from the railway museum as the cycle route travels through a couple of private estates with some wooden gates to open.

As the Forth appears again, soon ahead of me are three different styled high bridges which all cross this now vast bay. Instead of continuing towards Edinburgh, I find a way up to this 1964 road bridge and begin cycling north across the Forth. On my left is the 2017 road bridge, while the famous red 1890 rail bridge is on my right. It reminds me of the Sydney Harbour Bridge in scale and size. However, it's a different style as it looks like a few squashed diamonds rather than a single coat hanger.

Three bridges cross the Forth, including the Forth Rail Bridge

It's now 3:30 pm, so I will get the train back across the Forth Rail Bridge to Edinburgh. Along with experiencing a crossing of this rail bridge, this will save me time getting into Edinburgh, and allow me time to learn about what to see in Edinburgh over the next couple of days. I'm also just sick of cycling through built-up areas.

North Queensberry Railway Station reminds me of Milsons Point on the northern side of Sydney Harbour Bridge because it is similarly high on an embankment. On the opposite platform is a mural of the rail bridge and various water activities in Forth Bay, which reminds me of the numerous station murals in Russia.

North Queensferry Railway Station

Once I'm out of Edinburgh Waverley Station, the sheer number of people is overwhelming; it's a lot busier than Glasgow. It's even worse when I make it to the main street, where I'm squeezing me and my bicycle through packed crowds. I'm assuming it's this busy because the Edinburgh Fringe Festival is on.

Along with streets full of performers, there are even more people handing out flyers for shows, while every free surface is covered in numerous posters. In various open spots are many food vendors and mini outdoor stages, so I spend some time just soaking in the atmosphere by watching a few street performers, who often get unaware bystanders involved in their comedic acts.

There are so many signs of the fringe in Edinburgh

In a tourist information office, I have found a one-page map of all of the National Cycle Network routes in the UK, which is helpful for future planning.

Because of the Fringe, so many Warmshower hosts turned me down as they are busy hosting other people visiting for the Fringe. Thankfully, Gillian and Grant are available and welcoming as they share their experience with cycling in South America. They show me a phonebook sized list of the seemingly thousands of Fringe shows, so I will choose a few with different styles that fit tomorrow's schedule.

Edinburgh Tattoo is held here

For my rest day, I begin with catching a red double-decker bus into the city centre to visit Edinburgh Castle. Walking to the entrance involves going past two large temporary stands on both sides. This is where the Edinburgh Tattoo is held. It's popular, so I couldn't find any tickets.

There is plenty of royal history to learn, but over time the castle becomes too busy. Despite this, it's still engaging with its primary focus on military history because the Scottish National War Memorial is here, so there are a few army museums. The biggest impression is a display on conscientious objectors during the Second World War, with different stories on how they made their personal moral choices. I didn't realise until now that Britain had conscription during the Second World War.

The roof of the royal building in Edinburgh Castle

My first excellent Fringe show is Crime Scene Improv, where the audience decides the victim's name, their occupation (window cleaner) and how they died (hairspray) and then the cast act out various characters. In the end, the audience decides who the murderer is.

My second show is a Harry Potter musical parody of Voldemort's time at Hogwarts, which is okay. I end my day by watching a stand up show by Lucy Porter on scouts, which is okay too. Today was the first day since being in the UK I haven't cycled at all.

Over the past month, my old sandals gradually began to fall apart, with one cleat basically tearing away from the sole of the sandal. So a week ago, I organised a new pair of sandals to be mailed to Grant and Gillian's home. This new Shimano pair is a different brand and has a different style of straps, which cross over on another part of my feet. Hopefully, they will last longer than the Exustar pair I have been wearing.

The state of my sandals after only four months of cycling

After farewelling the helpful Gillian and Grant in the morning, my first point of call is to swap the cleats from my old sandals to my new ones. However, they are too tightly screwed in, so they won't come off, while the cleats are so worn they have become that sharp I have to be careful not to cut myself. Even with the help of a bicycle shop assistant, it takes a while to get them off. Once he gets the cleats off, he tells me they are too worn and it's not worth using them again, so I purchase a new set.

Along with my old sandals, I have a few items I don't need anymore, including my bicycle stand I took off after it wouldn't stay on tight enough while on the Isle of Skye. I haven't missed it because I often find something to lean my bicycle against, which is usually sturdier. With a loaded bicycle, perfectly balancing my bike using the stand is often challenging, as it can easily fall over if it's not.

I have considered posting home my old sandals, but this will cost me extra due to weight, and since I doubt they can be repaired, I won't post them.

As I ask to post the other items, the lady at the counter is grumpy and unhelpful with providing an address strip or tape to tape up the package. This is a vastly different experience to posting items in Spain or Estonia where staff were friendly and understood I was travelling and didn't have experience with how to post items in their country. A downside of speaking the same language is that often people think you understand the protocols in their country.

After spending most of my rest day attending Fringe shows, today I will visit a few museums before cycling to a Warmshower host on the edge of Edinburgh.

I end up spending three hours looking around the free National Museum of Scotland because there is so much detail inside including a vast range of topics, such as royalty, industry and natural history. The impact of Scottish people migrating worldwide is also explained, including the effect on Scotland from a large demographic of people leaving. Many industries lost experienced workers, which is not something I have considered before.

On display are various vehicles over the years, dinosaur bones and many stuffed animals, including Dolly the sheep, the first cloned animal. One of the many vehicles includes an 1813 locomotive, one of the oldest in the world that still exists. It has normal-looking train wheels, but on top, it looks much older as it's made out of large metal barrels with pipes sticking out of many places.

Scottish Parliament has a wooden roof

I had to pre-book a tour of the Scottish Parliament House, but it's worth it as it's interesting. Scotland only got its parliament in 1999, nearly 300 years after it was dissolved due to the Act of Union. The building is built specifically for parliamentary purposes and only opened in 2004, so it's well worth a visit even just to see the architecture, especially the curvy wooden ceiling of the chamber.

It's fascinating how members are elected to get a representative body. There are two methods: one way is by individual seats all over Scotland using the first-past-the-post method to elect one member, and the other is by proportional regions, where a group of members are elected together. Still, voters only get just one vote, no preferential voting here. All these elected members sit in one chamber together. It's a bit like combining the, Senate and House of Representatives to vote together.

Nearby is the Palace of Holyroodhouse, the official home of the royal family in Scotland. The Queen visits once a week each July, while I'm surprised to learn that between 1651 and 1822, no British monarch visited Scotland. Obviously back then transport took longer but still that is a long time between visits.

Inside I'm given a visual audio guide that is useful in explaining the history of each room. Mary Queen of Scots is the most prominent historical figure as the murder of her secretary happened here while she was pregnant with the future James VI. A plaque marks the murder spot.

Outside among the gardens are the remains of the large stone Abbey which is missing its roof. This was where James IV of Scotland married Margaret, the daughter of Henry VII of England. A century later, this led to Scotland and England having the same monarch and eventually a combined country.

Behind Holyrood Abbey is Arthur's Seat

From the Holyroodhouse gardens, a bald hill is visible in the distance. I recall Grant suggesting a visit, so I make my way there. A three-mile one-way paved road goes clockwise right around this hill known as Arthur's Seat.

On this sunny evening, this loop drive road is busy with road cyclists, while people are walking up to the summit in the middle of this hill. So halfway around, I leave my bicycle beside the small Dunstaple Loch and walk up a volcanic red rocky track to an unremarkable bare summit. It does at least provide a 360-degree view of the suburbs of Edinburgh, along with an expansive view of Forth Bay stretching to the horizon.

I both cycled around Arthur's Seat and climbed to its summit

Once back down after cycling nearly completely around Arthur's Seat, there is a short rail trail just off Queen's Drive. The Innocent Railway was Scotland's first rail line. This short branch line includes a tunnel and small bridge before I leave the cycle path to head to my Warmshower with Robert and his family in a suburb of Edinburgh.

A bridge on the Innocent Railway

I'm camping in their small backyard, which has a trampoline for me to relax on in the evening.

I have considered staying in Edinburgh another day to attend a men's Scottish football club match today, but after two days of not really cycling, I'm itching to cycle. Anyway I need to keep moving as I have to be in Leeds in about a week.

Berwick

Since I'm in the suburbs of Edinburgh, it's easy leaving using parts of the Innocent Railway to take me to the eastern coastline, known as the Golf Coast.

I'm soon seeing plenty of golf courses, and at one stage, I accidentally cycled through one when I thought a cycle route went through it. I end up having to find a way out by crossing over a couple of fairways to get back to a road.

Following the coastline

Thankfully the rest of the time navigation involves following cycling signs, allowing me to relax and enjoy the scenery on a sunny day with a strong tailwind. For the most part, I'm right beside the sea; other times, the cycle route takes me inland for a bit.

Grant suggested visiting North Berwick to see some seabirds that nest off the coast on a few islands. Unfortunately, all the boat cruises are either sold out or cancelled, so instead I will visit the seabird museum.

Birds nest on these islands

Inside are live videos from a few nests on the offshore islands and some films on various birds that visit here. I probably haven't missed seeing many birds because most of them have already left for the season, including the Puffins.

So far, the cycle route has been paved, but as I leave the coastline east of North Berwick, the cycle route takes a few dogleg roads before it becomes a narrow muddy track in between paddocks, which is part of the John Muir cycle route. This name is familiar to me from my time cycling in the Sierras in California, but I wasn't aware he was born in nearby Dunbar and grew up in this region.

On a trail named after John Muir, who was born in this region

Sometimes I'm cycling beside a railway, other times just the coastline

It's a mixed afternoon, with the cycle route changing between secondary roads, muddy farm tracks and the occasional cycle path beside the noisy motorway. Sometimes I'm near the railway line I caught to Scotland, with trains racing.

When I finally get well away from the motorway and begin climbing on a quiet secondary road beside the sea, clouds return, the temperature drops and light rain begins.

Eventually, I arrive in the seaside town of Eyemouth, which is a fishing village with plenty of boats around. With light rain looking like continuing, I begin searching for a place to camp.

There appears to be plenty of open space on the other side of the Eye Water river, which splits part of the town from the rest. Finding a pedestrian bridge to cross to the other side takes a while with the river wide here. The majority of the potential open space is a golf course which isn't suitable because it's visible from the currently occupied clubhouse on a hill. The football pitch is fenced off, so I will return to the town centre and search for another option.

I soon spot an open park behind the school.

After going around the back, there is a hexagon-shaped wooden gazebo with a picnic table. It's a perfect place to camp beside especially as it's still school holidays. A few dog walkers are around, but either no one notices me or cares, so I will camp here.

Camping behind a school

After a few dogleg roads through small towns, my final road in Scotland shares the border with England. So farewell Scotland, not sure when I will return, but I will be back because there are many places I didn't see.

The National Cycle Route continues as it takes me into Berwick on the Tweed, using secondary roads which take me past the railway station. Most of Berwick Castle was demolished to make way for the station as only some small remains and a garden are left.

The Tweed is wide here, therefore to cross it, a large stone railway viaduct with many arches carries the majority of trains between Edinburgh and England. It's one of now only two railway routes still open between England and Scotland. The other line is on the west coast through Carlisle.

Also, in Berwick are two lower scenic road bridges across the Tweed, one which is much older with wider arches than the rail viaduct. Apparently, James VI paid for this stone bridge after seeing the state of a wooden bridge on his way south to become the King of England.

Rail viaduct is on the edge of Berwick, while the oldest bridge is in the centre of town

Before James became King of both Scotland and England, Berwick on the Tweed changed hands numerous times between England and Scotland. I'm told at least thirteen times, while at certain times, Berwick was regarded as a separate entity. It was technically still at war with Russia for over a century because it was referred to when war was declared but not when the Crimean War treaty was signed.

Since it was a border town, the remains of high fort walls still go right around the centre of town. Today I can cycle right on top of these now grass-covered fort remains, with a few moats and plenty of old brickwork and tunnels to look at. Because it's high, this allows me to see the mouth of the Tweed and the sea, along with some veggie gardens presumably being grown by the community.

Among the fort is the former Berwick Barracks, which includes an army museum that focuses on the Crimean War period.

Fort remains around Berwick

Signs are telling me that a few National Cycle Network Routes spread out from Berwick. So from here, I will leave the coastline behind to go west for a while before heading south to meet a section of Hadrian's Wall.

So many bicycle signs

After crossing on the old road bridge, I begin heading west inland. However, the wind has picked up, and it's a strong headwind. I soon realise it's a waste of time trying to cycle into it so I will return to Berwick to join National Cycle Route One and begin heading south following the coastline towards Newcastle. Along with seeing Newcastle, this route change will allow me to see more of Hadrian's Wall, although more suburban cycling will be required.

In places south of Berwick, the National Cycle Route is a muddy goat track with a few gates to open as it follows the railway line while overlooking the North Sea below. In other sections, it takes a quiet route through grassland using gravel tracks. Along the way, I briefly cycle with a few fellow touring cyclists, each with their own plans, including a Dutchman heading to a place called Holy Island. I'm unsure what is to see there, so I will continue south.

A few gates to open as this cycle route uses a rough track

Distracting me on my ride is the final day of the second test match, as Australia hangs on for a draw with six wickets down.

Near the end of the day, as I arrive in the seaside town of Bamburgh, I'm pleasantly surprised to see a large castle on a hill coming into view.

As I get closer, it's even more spectacular because a local cricket match is finishing on a well-mowed ground in front of it. In the evening, lights come on around the castle, providing a lit-up view.

Cricket ground in front of a castle

Once it's dark enough, I begin setting up my tent beside the cricket clubhouse. However, I can't find the small middle pole of my tent. I must have left it at Eyemouth. I lost this same pole in New Hampshire on my penultimate day camping on my 2015 North American cycling trip. Since then, I have been vigilant about it. The tent sets up without this pole, it will just mean that the tent's roof is floppy, so dew can easily soak in.

As I consider returning to nearby town to use wi-fi to search for possible trains to catch in the morning to Eyemouth, I have another look around the clubhouse in the dark. As I move my tent fly, I spot the small two-piece pole hidden under it.

Bamburgh Castle doesn't open until 11 am, so I am considering if I should wait around for it to open or just leave in the morning. Another consideration is that I have hastily organised a Warmshower in Newcastle, so it will be a long day of cycling.

At times, I find it hard to balance the desire between cycling and exploring the places I'm passing through. What's the point in rushing to get to one place if I miss seeing where I already am.

After finding another museum in town which is open earlier, I will stay.

The Grace Darling Museum is named after a young woman who in 1838 at the age of 22, alongside her father William, helped rescue nine people from a sinking ship off the coast using a rowboat. On display alongside the boat are many other objects related to the shipwreck and also some personal items of Grace. The story of the rescue and Grace's short life is told, including that sadly, four years after the rescue, she died of an unrelated illness.

Bamburgh Castle has a large courtyard and is high enough to provide views of the flat sea. Outside in the backyard are a few people dressed up in medieval attire for our amusement, while inside are portraits of the wealthy family who own this castle. It's well-kept, and with photos from more than a century ago, it doesn't appear to have changed much.

Bamburgh Castle hasn't changed much

By the time I leave Bamburgh, it's midday, and with Newcastle 60 miles away, I know this afternoon will be a long ride. Of course, as soon as I begin closely following the coastline south, I get a flat tyre before the next town of Seahouses.

After changing tubes, I set off again, knowing it will now be an even later night as I'm passing through many small but busy beachside towns.

Once National Cycle Route One goes a little inland, I'm passing through open farmland, which is a slower ride than expected, especially with some side winds. As the route returns towards the sea, it has become a grassy track with a few wooden gates to open. At one stage, right next to the sea, I have to negotiate a narrow track and small pedestrian bridge over a creek. If I weren't in a hurry, I'm sure I would be enjoying this car and town free section right next to the sea.

The cycle route follows a grassy track

Unfortunately, as soon as I re-join a road, I get another flat tyre. By the time I have patched a couple of tubes, it's now mid-afternoon, so the day has got away from me. I probably now won't make Newcastle tonight. I shouldn't have visited Bamburgh Castle, especially as it wasn't that impressive inside.

In the UK, I'm often overestimating how far I can cycle in a day because I'm forgetting to include time to look around. Sometimes I'm also forgetting that miles take longer to cycle than kilometres.

I could just cancel my Warmshower in Newcastle, but I feel bad doing that, especially as I only organised it last night. Instead, I will catch a train from Alnwick to Newcastle. Since I buy a ticket at the railway station just before the train leaves, it is an expensive half-hour trip, which costs more than some longer train rides I have taken. In those other cases, I was able to book days or even weeks earlier.

Edinburgh to Alnwick (Google Maps)

Hadrian

Newcastle's Town Moor

Cracks in my bicycle frame

While cycling to my Warmshower host's house in a northern suburb, I pass through a vast open grass space known as the Town Moor. Cattle are grazing here, close to the city centre, a relic of when Newcastle was much smaller.

Over the past few days, my water bottle cage attached to the bottom tube of my bicycle's frame has been rocking slightly. It holds my one and a half litre Nalgene water bottle. After unscrewing both bolts to remove the cage, I can see that cracks have developed around both holes where the bolts screw in on the frame. I am not sure if it's because of rust or if the water bottle is too big, however, I did carry this same size bottle in the same spot on last year's trip. Only this cage can carry my Nalgene as the rest are too small.

I'm not sure how to fix it, but I have found a welding shop to see if they can. A helpful man tells me it's not possible to weld it, but he does try using some sealant to fill the cracks. In the meantime, he gives me cable ties to allow me to switch around my various water bottle cages.

My bicycle came with three dedicated spots to store bottles, one of which carries my methylated spirits fuel bottle. The other will now carry my Nalgene. However, I also have regular-sized water bottle cages zip-tied to both sides of my front fork, so I still have some capacity. Anyway, with the cooler weather and towns close together in the UK, I don't need to carry much water. I may need more capacity once I'm back in more remote and warmer Australia.

Before leaving Newcastle, I visit a few bicycle shops to see if they have any advice on the cracks on my frame, but they are no help. Some are quite frankly indifferent to my issue.

My biggest takeaway from Newcastle is that so many bridges cross the River Tyne.

After seeing parts of the small remains of the castle in Newcastle, I will begin cycling west. Initially, I'm following a cycle route beside the Tyne, but as it leaves the river, it's becoming a little confusing exactly where I'm supposed to be cycling. A former railway line ran parallel to the river, but only occasionally is it a cycle path. Other times, the cycle route drifts away from it and returns closer to the Tyne.

Once I'm out of the suburbs, I'm more constantly cycling on one of the first railway lines in the world, built to transport coal. Along the way right beside the rail line is the birthplace of George Stephenson, the man who built the first main railway line in the world between Liverpool and Manchester and one of the first locomotives: Rocket. The small double-storey white house which his family shared with three other families isn't open today.

After crossing the Tyne on a former railway bridge, this rail trail ends as it meets a still-active rail line. From here, a path takes me beside the Tyne before I cross to the north of the river and join a quiet road which takes me to Corbridge.

Corbridge is the first place I'm seeing signs of Roman heritage, including a busy tourist office in this town with fancy bakeries. I'm told nearby is the remains of a Roman town of the same name.

It's not far out of town, and I can use my English Heritage card, so it's free for me to enter. I'm provided with an audio guide to learn more about this two-part site. Firstly there is a room full of artefacts found around here, along with information on how they believe people lived.

This audio guide is more useful outside among the numerous remains of this former town, which was set out in a grid pattern, over about a 100-metre by 100-metre site. The remains of a few straight gravel roads are still visible, while what is left of the various buildings are mostly knee-high. This allows me to get an impression of what it must have looked like, but plenty of imagination is still required.

The audio guide is handy as it explains what they believe each building was used for. Some housed people, others stored grain or was a bathroom. Some buildings only have the knee-high outside walls left and steps leading to the entrance, while a building that stored grain has numerous stone abutments inside, presumably to keep the grain off the ground.

Remains of a Roman town at Corbridge

By the time I'm in the next town of Hexham, it's too late to visit the following Roman site, so I will stop here and do some research about fixing the cracks in my frame. My bicycle's designer Noel, who is Australian, replies to my email saying he hasn't seen this happen before and doesn't have any suggestions on how to fix it.

The sealant never closed the cracks, so these holes stayed unused for the rest of this tour. Once I got home, the cracks were professionally fixed with a new plate put on where they developed.

It takes a while to find a wild camp in Hexham as it's a busy town. Eventually, I have found what appears to be an abandoned oval near a school on the edge of town. As I begin cooking dinner, a couple of cyclists appear and begin racing around and around this oval. Once they finish, they explain they are training for a bicycle race.

Hadrian's Wall was built by the Romans following an east-west ridgeline, which has been north of me since Newcastle. While I have missed a few sites, there is still plenty of Hadrian's Wall to see because Roman towns were built to house soldiers every so often along the wall. Today they are often museums to visit, each with slightly different information, and usually next to uncovered remains of Roman buildings. Presumably, it was an inspiration for '*the Wall*' in Game of Thrones.

After a short climb to a ridgeline, my first stop is Chesters Roman Fort and Museum, where cyclists are appreciated with dedicated bicycle parking spaces made of timber. Once again, my English Heritage card allows me free entry to a site that only exists because a man in the 1800s purchased land around Hadrian's Wall and then began exploring. He found numerous items, which are now on display in a building, including engraved cream stones in a wide range of sizes, including archways.

Outside in a large field are human-high stone wall remains to explore, including Roman Baths, while visible across the North Tyne River are remains of a Roman bridge. Often only a tiny part of a once significant building like a military gate still exists. Helpfully, information panels with descriptions and drawings inform me what they imagine each room looked like.

Bicycle parking at Chesters museum, where various items have been found

Roman remains at Chesters

From Chesters, Military Road mostly follows this ridgeline, with the remains of Hadrian's Wall sometimes close to the road. Often long stretches of stones are located in otherwise normal grassy paddocks. Occasionally, hikers are beside the small remains of the wall, which seems to be a better experience than cycling as the marked cycling route doesn't always follow it.

Remains of Hadrian's Wall in a paddock

Now that I'm on top of this ridgeline with little cover, it's windy. It doesn't take me long to realise that I have made the mistake of trying to cycle west into the prevailing wind on this cold, overcast afternoon.

After visiting some free small sites just off the road, my next busy spot is Housesteads Roman Fort, with a car park at the bottom of a hill. It's a short walk up to the ridgeline to another small museum.

The fort remains take up a larger space than previous sites, and helpfully a guided tour is available. With 800 men living here, it was clearly a busy place in its day, as there are many outlines of former buildings to see on this side of a hill. Wall remains can be seen snaking their way east across the landscape.

A guided tour shows us a large Roman fort, which had many barracks

We are shown a wide range of buildings, including the communal toilets for the soldiers, housed in the various barracks. The drainage system is still here in this well-built stone structure, along with handwashing bowls that still hold water, and the bottom remains of a larger water tank. Information panel drawings show how men sat facing each other while doing their business.

Remains of a barn and a communal toilet

It's now mid-afternoon, and the wind is getting stronger and colder, so I will leave Hadrian's Wall early to get down into some cover. There is another sizeable Roman site in the distance as I duck down, and I know I have missed a few further west.

With rain around, I have found an Airbnb in Haltwhistle with an older lady as the rain becomes heavy overnight.

Over the past few days, the strap on my new sandals, which goes over the top of my left foot, has gradually become painful. It feels like the strap is pushing down on my foot. Adjusting it doesn't seem to reduce the pain. Wearing socks makes it slightly less sore, but I will have to look for new shoes.

I have had worse pain in my life; it's more that it hurts nearly all the time when both walking and cycling in these sandals, so it's wearing me down physically and mentally. I'm at the stage where I feel like I need a break from cycling, and perhaps I should do something else until I fly home in mid-September. The cold rainy weather isn't helping, nor is the issue with my bicycle frame.

With it still raining in the morning and looking like continuing all day, I'm not in the mood for cycling. I can't wait the weather out because I need to be in Leeds in less than four days, so I will have to catch a couple of trains as it's too far to cycle. It's an easy choice to catch a train to Carlisle.

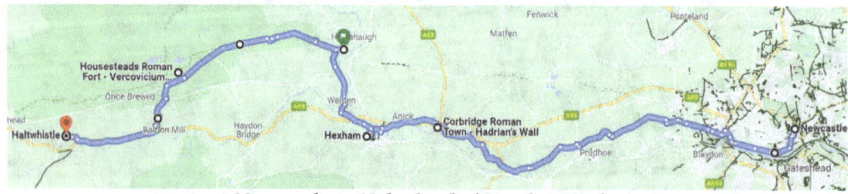

Newcastle to Haltwhistle (Google Maps)

A brief look at lakes

If you're going to visit Carlisle, do it on a Thursday because that is when a two and a half-hour guided tour of this scenic town is available. The Guildhall Museum is also open and a local market is on in the Y shape main pedestrian streets.

Thursday markets in Carlisle

Before this tour begins, I have time to explore Carlisle in light rain including its cathedral, with a blue ceiling with and yellow stars.

On the northern side of the old city centre is the red-bricked Carlisle Castle. A section is still an active military barrack, while most of the rest I can explore, including a military museum. Many unused parts of this castle are available to look around, including a tower with a few levels where there is some historic pictorial graffiti on the brick walls. It reminds me of Australian indigenous artwork, in that there are lots of hand-drawn pictures of people and animals interacting with each other.

Carlisle Cathedral

Pictorial graffiti inside a part of Carlisle Castle

Unlike in Europe, many guided tours in the UK require an upfront payment rather than relying on tips. So only a handful of people are on this informative tour as we walk around an overcast Carlisle, learning about its history as a border town.

Preserved Guildhall

One of our focuses is the wooden Guildhall building from the 1400s, which has a slight lean. Inside it isn't square, which adds to its charm. The second floor has been preserved as it was centuries ago, with old equipment from a few trades, including shoemakers and butchers. These objects make sense because if your job involves a trade, you could be a guild member who would meet in this hall.

As the guided walk finishes the weather is deteriorating, so I will catch another train. Because Carlisle is on the main railway route to Glasgow from London via Manchester, there are plenty of trains. I'm only on for a short ride as the rain becomes heavy while I listen to the first day of the third test match in Leeds.

In rainy Penrith, I cycle past the remains of a castle to a hostel set up for cyclists and hikers as I'm now near the Lake District. Strangely the owner doesn't sell all the available beds on his website. Instead, he keeps beds available for Airbnb as I had to book there instead.

Bike repair station in the basement

In the basement is an open space to store a few bicycles with tools and bicycle repair stands available as well. Many fellow adventure travellers are staying here, including a few cyclists and even a long-distance hiker, as we chat about our respective journeys. Many are heading east to cross England, as this is the narrowest part of England from coast to coast. The main cycling route ends up in Newcastle but takes a more southerly route than what I took.

During an evening physiotherapist visit, he has some recommendations for exercises to try to reduce the pain in my foot. He also suggests I keep wearing socks, but says the best thing to do is get new shoes.

With needing to be in Leeds for the cricket in 2 days, I only have enough time to spend a day in the Lake District. I have considered following a former railway line to Keswick, but I'm unsure how much is a rail trail especially near the start, where the alternative is a motorway.

Instead, I begin heading in a south-westerly direction to Ullswater Lake, where the road follows the lake

Along the way are some popular waterfalls, including the fast-flowing Aria Force, which has a couple of scenic stone bridges allowing different views. As I walk around, my feet are still sore.

Following Ullswater

Aria Force has a few stone bridges to admire the falls from

So far throughout the day, England has been collapsing in the cricket, but as I leave the lake behind, I lose radio reception.

While it was sunny in the valley, as I begin slowly climbing to Kirkstone Pass, it's now foggy and cold. Despite the fog and the steepness, it is a spectacular, enjoyable climb with little traffic in a treeless landscape with stone fences. It's a lower climb than anything I did in the French Alps, but it feels a more arduous, steeper climb.

Climbing to Kirkstone Pass

Once I'm up, I have a choice of roads to descend. The direct route to Windermere, or a longer ride via Ambleside. Since I have time, I will try to see as much of the Lake District as possible today.

It's a quick descent to the bustling tourist town of Ambleside, where the sun is out, however with so many people around, it's suffocating. It's the Friday before a bank (public) holiday long weekend, so it's not the best time to be here.

It's at least quiet in the museum, with stories about how this area used to be farming particularly sheep based before the national park developed. It reminds me of the Western District in Victoria, especially with the numerous stone fences.

There are a few bicycle shops in Ambleside, but they all have racing shoes which I can't walk in, so I will stick with my socks and sandals for now.

The western side of Windermere Lake is less developed, so I'm able to relax as I follow the lake on a path, while the other side looks more like a busy seaside town.

Plenty of stone fences in this region, while it's quieter this side of Lake Windermere

After a short ferry, I'm back in a busy overpopulated area, where my focus is just getting out of here. The Lake District is a place to revisit one day but not on a public holiday weekend.

I'm only able to relax once I join a cycle path that takes me out of Windermere before a quiet road leads me to a farm where I meet my Warmshower host Daniel.

It's a relaxing evening as Daniel explains his farm, which sounds a lot smaller than back home in Australia. We also talk about the cricket as England has been bowled out for 67.

He shares some ideas on where I can ride tomorrow as I have booked a train from Lancaster to Leeds tomorrow afternoon. This will enable me to attend the fourth day of the test match at Headingley on Sunday, so I will have limited time to get to Lancaster tomorrow.

However, by the way the cricket is going, I do wonder if it's worth going to Leeds at all because it may be over before Sunday. Instead, I could spend more time in the Lakes District.

After thinking overnight, I will cycle to Lancaster today, and by the time the train is due to leave, if the cricket is nearly over, I won't bother catching the train to Leeds.

My route out of the Lakes District is still scenic cycling, including a short section where I'm on top of a filled-in section of the former Lancaster Canal which went through Kendal. Even though the canal is filled in, some of the bridges which went over it still remain, leaving it looking like a mini railway line went through here instead.

Once out of Kendal, the former canal's route isn't a trail, so I'm back on quiet roads, where I'm passing many stone wall fences and hedgerows.

Remains of a canal in Kendal

Eventually, after some hilly cycling, I'm in Carnforth, which has a large junction railway station, where my train will be going through in a few hours. Inside this station is an engaging heritage museum explaining the rail history of this area, including some lines that don't exist anymore and the one I'm going on this afternoon.

My original plan was to visit Lancaster further south, as it sounds like an interesting city. However, it makes more sense to catch a train leaving soon from Carnforth, which will get me into Leeds two hours earlier than planned. This will allow me the opportunity to see if I can get into the cricket this afternoon as there is a chance Australia could win the Ashes tonight with England chasing an unlikely 359 to win.

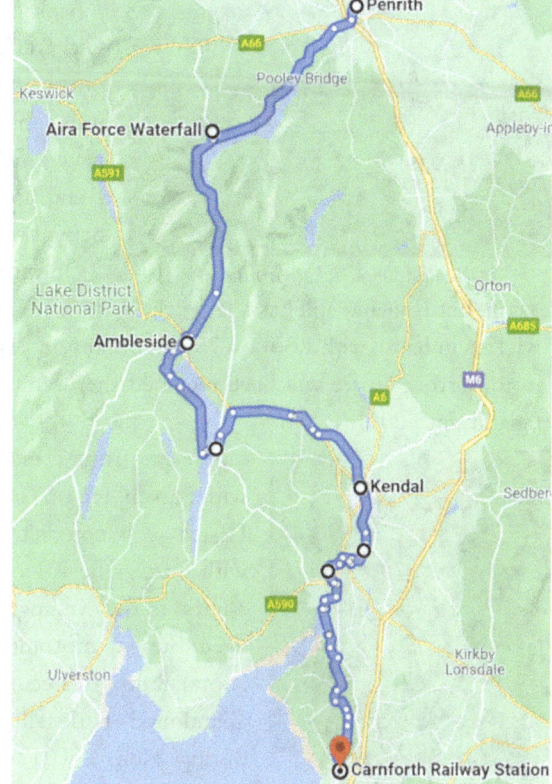

Penrith to Carnforth (Google Maps)

Headingley

The only issue with taking an earlier train is that I'm supposed to catch the specific train on my ticket. If I want to change the time I'm travelling, I'm charged an extra fee which can be expensive.

With no dedicated bicycle space, my bicycle is blocking a small collection of seats on this half-full train, which unintentionally discourages the conductor from checking my ticket. I'm still letting through the occasional passenger who needs a seat.

From the train window, I can see the potential of a future cycle route following a canal.

I'm two hours early into Leeds, so there is enough time left in the cricket today for me to cycle to Headingley, located in a suburb of the same name.

As I arrive at this large cricket stadium, I'm directed to a dedicated bicycle parking shelter in a private car park behind the rugby stadium. The rugby stadium shares a stand with the cricket ground as they are back to back to each other. From here, I'm able to sneak into the cricket for the last session of the day. Unlike in Australia, in England with smaller grounds, matches sell out fast, so I doubt I could have purchased a ticket.

Headingley Cricket Ground

Back in 2013, I purchased a ticket at Old Trafford just before rain washed out the final day, so in my mind, I'm using that ticket now. Since I don't have a ticket, I don't have a seat, so I end up finding spare seats before being moved on a few times.

Only one wicket falls in the last session, but England still has a large chase of more than 200 runs required with 7 wickets in hand, with Root on 75 and Stokes on 2. I'm assuming Australia will win tomorrow, so we will have regained the Men's Ashes for the first time in England since 2001.

My guide Stephen

Not far from Headingley is my Warmshower with Steven. He isn't an official host but his friend Ursula who couldn't host me, suggested I stay with him, as he is looking at bicycle touring one day. So in the evening, I share some advice.

On Sunday morning, Steven guides me around some suburbs of Leeds by bicycle, including nearby abandoned Kirkstall Abbey. It was destroyed during Henry VIII's time when the country's religion changed from Catholic to Protestant.

It's still in ruin but looks interesting, with many large walls intact while the roof is gone. It reminds me of similarly abandoned Holyrood Abbey in Edinburgh.

Behind the abbey, we briefly cycle on a canal which Steven explains goes right through Leeds.

After breakfast at his friend's

Remains of Kirkstall Abbey

place, Steven drops me off at the cricket before he heads off to play tennis.

My ticket is for sitting directly in the sun, so instead, I have found a spot standing up behind the bowler's arm in the shaded football stand end. I'm among a mixture of both English and Australian supporters with good banter between us all.

It starts well for us early with their captain Root caught by a diving Warner's catch behind the wicketkeeper, off Lyon's bowling for 77. It's a little nerving as Stokes and Bairstow put on nearly a 100 run partnership, but as Bairstow departs, closely followed by a mix up leading to Buttler being run out, I'm feeling confident that the Ashes are ours. As the following three batsmen fall quickly, Australia now only needs one more wicket, while England still needs 73 runs, so the English supporters are congratulating us.

Yesterday Stokes had batted slowly, only scoring two runs in twelve overs of defending. Now, as the last English batsman Leach joins him, he suddenly decides to go ballistic and begins playing some incredible shots and quite a few ridiculous ones, including a reverse sweep for six and another that is scooped behind the wicket straight towards me. Naturally, the English supporters are becoming delirious, but it still feels like he could get out at any minute as he is taking many risks. The ball is just sailing over the fielders' heads a few times, while Harris has a diving chance, but he drops it.

As England get within two runs, it's now incredibly intense as both sides can still win. As Lyon bowls to Stokes, he reverse-sweeps straight to a fielder, but Leach takes off for a run anyway. However, Stokes isn't looking, so Leach has to hurriedly retreat back to the bowler's end. In the meantime, the Australian fielder throws the ball back to Lyon, where all he has to do is take the throw cleanly to allow him to comfortably run Leach out.

Lyon fumbles the ball allowing Leach to safely make it back. At this moment, with England within two runs, that was probably our last chance, so the match is probably lost.

However, the next ball, Stokes plays a regular sweep which he misses and is struck in front of the stumps, so every Australian appeals, but the umpire turns us down. On television replay, it was out, but we have no reviews left.

It feels inevitable the next over when Stokes hits the winning runs as the vocal crowd erupts in jubilation.

I'm glad I went even if we lost. I can't believe yesterday morning I genuinely considered not catching a train to Leeds as I thought the cricket would be over before I arrived.

After the match, English supporters are celebrating on the streets, but it feels safe as I cycle back to Steven's house.

Reflective canal

In the morning, after passing Kirkstall Abbey, I begin following the Leeds and Liverpool Canal into Leeds city centre with the sunlight allowing a scenic reflection on the canal. Along the way, I'm leaving the canal to visit bicycle shops to see if they have shoes as I'm sick of my new sandals. So far, all these shops appear closed on this Monday bank holiday.

Beside the canal were many mills with a couple now museums, so I will visit one. Leeds Industrial Museum informs me about how this woollen mill worked with large machines powered by steam engines; some still operating today for demonstrations. As a long weaving machine with numerous strands of wool moves constantly sideways back and forwards, I'm told that young children were an essential part of the workforce because their size was needed to fit in small places under these large machines to fix any breaks in the woven wool. These machines continued moving while they fixed things, so accidents were common, with people occasionally losing fingers or limbs. Workplace health and safety wasn't regarded as being as important back then.

Thankfully as I arrive into the city centre via the canal, it appears most shops are open, which allows me to search for new shoes. It takes a while to find a comfortable pair and when I finally find a pair I like, staff forcefully don't want me to try them by walking around the store as I would in Australia. I'm also having

My new shoes

issues with the online store where I purchased my sandals, letting me send them back. Perhaps there are different consumer laws in the UK.

After trying a few types of shoes, I have found a green pair of more traditional proper bicycle shoes. They are more like sneakers with cleats in them, so I will have to wear socks all the time.

A different canal takes me out of Leeds, so I'm soon beside another old mill.

Thwaite Mills was powered by water and it still works

Thwaite Mills was powered by two waterwheels, which look like those on paddle steamers. Water still turns these wheels, and so do many of the connected cogs and belts throughout a three storey building, allowing various machines to still move.

Out of Leeds, National Cycle Route 67 continues following the Aire and Calder Canal as I'm passing plenty of colourful wooden narrowboats. Along the way are plenty of people out enjoying this sunny public holiday.

As the cycle route leaves the canal behind, for the next few hours, it's a mixture between short rail trails, on-road cycling and other sections through green spaces.

Eventually, I'm beside the remains of the abandoned Barnsley Canal. The trail is adventurous here as it passes through a forested area where at times, it looks like I'm cycling beside a dry creek, while in other places, bridges, culverts, and other parts of this former canal are just visible as they are slowly being reclaimed by nature.

Remains of Barnsley Canals

This former canal randomly ends on the edge of Barnsley, so once I have negotiated some suburban cycling, I have arrived in Barnsley on dusk.

I'm not sure where is best to stealth camp, until at a cricket oval, I spot a wheeled cricket cover off to the side in a dark corner of this sports ground. This long dome-shaped cover is designed to be easily manoeuvred to protect a cricket pitch from rain. It looks like something that is put over plants in an outdoor nursery to protect them from birds but instead, it keeps the rain off. There is a gap between the cover and the ground, which I should be able to squeeze under.

It's a tight squeeze, but once I'm under, there is enough room for me to lie on my inflated mattress without hitting my head, so I don't have to set my tent up, nor worry about dew in the morning. It's just like sleeping under a tarp.

Only my bicycle locked to a nearby tree is a sign that I'm here, so hopefully, no one will notice me.

Camping under a cricket cover

I'm not sure why but Barnsley has a different feel to many other cities in the UK. It does have a nice pedestrian mall and a refurbished indoor permanent market. Nearby inside the large, multistorey town hall is an informative museum on Barnsley's history, including their brief single season in the Premier League, along with plenty of mining history.

Rehabilitated mine

An annoying barrier on this cycle route

With many former coal mines in the surrounding countryside, there were numerous railway lines to service them; many are now rail trails. As I leave Barnsley by rail trail, I'm passing a few rehabilitated mining sites with information panels about mining, including a couple of fatal disasters. Otherwise, there is not much evidence of a mine.

There are gates of various widths on a few of these rail trails, presumably to prevent motorbikes from getting through. However, sometimes it's difficult getting my handlebars through, requiring me to either twist them or lift the bicycle to get over this narrow gap.

After a couple of dogleg roads in a hilly landscape, a short rail trail takes me to the River Don in the suburbs of Sheffield. From here, the Five Weir Walk beside this river takes me into Sheffield using several bridges while passing a few weirs. One of these bridges is a Bailey Bridge because Donald Bailey, the inventor of this Second World War replacement bridge, was born in this region and trained at a local university.

Bailey Bridge

Sheffield used to be the leading centre for producing cutlery in the UK, so a few cutlery displays exist.

With the anniversary of the first moon landing this year, a LEGO-themed treasure hunt has been set up in a few shops. So with time before meeting my Warmshower host, I search for each one. There are a range of human-sized fully assembled displays to find, including rockets, astronauts and the Apollo 11 badge.

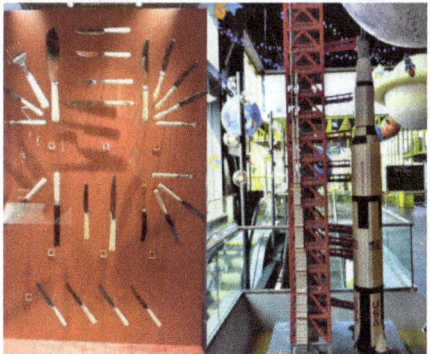

Sheffield is famous for cutlery

Space LEGO is on display in shops

My Warmshower is with Felix, a young man at his home with his parents. Once again, I'm offered food, but his brother's spicy meal is too hot for me.

Since I happened to be in Sheffield when a men's League Cup match is on, Felix and I are dropped off at Bramall Lane to watch this knockout match against Blackburn. It's not a packed stadium, but still a reasonable crowd as the more highly ranked Sheffield United wins comfortably. A downside of this match is that a small group of the home crowd are particularly feral towards one opposition player, which takes away from my experience.

It takes a while in the morning to get east out of the suburban sprawl of Sheffield because I'm constantly having to check my route at each turn as I'm using a mixture of cycle paths and quiet roads. Eventually, I'm enjoying a gradual descent on quiet roads through the countryside. As I briefly join a canal through Worksop, light rain begins but soon dissipates, leaving an overcast sky. As I leave the canal behind, this well signed relaxing cycle route takes me through a forest just north of Robin Hood's home Sherwood Forest.

After a few more quiet dogleg roads, in the middle of nowhere is a rail trail. As I begin cycling it, I'm soon on a man-made embankment above paddocks with a metal fence on either side. Ahead is a large metal bridge with high walls, stretching high above the River Trent and the flood plain on either side. It appears to be one of the longest rail trail bridges I have ever cycled over.

A long rail trail bridge

The rest of this trail is unremarkable as it takes me to another canal, which in turn takes me into Lincoln as rain returns and it's soon heavy.

Another men's League Cup match is on tonight, so I make my way to the small but modern looking football stadium in the southern suburbs. However, the match is sold out against more highly ranked Everton.

So after looking around for shelter, I have found a cricket pavilion on the edge of Lincoln with a tiny verandah that just shelters me. While cooking dinner, I listen to the Lincoln City-Everton League Cup match on my radio, as lowly Lincoln City scores in the first minute. Halfway through the second half, it's two all, before Everton scores two late goals.

The business I purchased my uncomfortable sandals from on eBay has been very uncooperative about me returning them, despite offering returns on their eBay listing. They say I can't return them since I wore them, but I argue how could I know they are uncomfortable unless I did.

Thankfully, I have worked out that eBay's return policy says I can send my sandals back to them. All I need to do is print a shipping label and drop them off at a convenience store. So on a sunny morning, I'm distracted with sorting out the mailing of my sandals.

The canal through Lincoln

Inside Lincoln Cathedral

Lincoln is a scenic city with two parts; the newer part is based around the canal and railway line, while the older part is up a steep hill. It's steep enough that I'm walking my bicycle up.

A large medieval castle and a cathedral dominate the old town, so staff in the visitor centre are dressed in medieval attire. Restoration work is being done on the front of this enormous cathedral, but it's still impressive from both outside and inside. However, since it looks like many others in the UK which are free to visit, I won't bother paying to have an extended look inside. Across the road is a small tower which I can visit for free because it's part of English Heritage.

Across the road from the cathedral is the castle, which has a display on the Magna Carta, however, to visit it, I have to pay for a tour of the castle walls as well. I can just visit the walls for a lower price, but they won't let me pay to just visit the Magna Carta exhibit. So I will leave as the castle feels touristy and I have already walked around enough castle walls elsewhere.

The nearby museum of Lincolnshire life focuses on the last 200 years. It reminds me of the majority of Australian museums, in that their history only starts in the late 1700s. Despite plenty of young children around this museum, many informative items for adults are on display.

In particular, there are a few tanks as Lincoln was where most of the development of the first tank during the Great War happened.

One of the tanks is called Daphne; she was injured during the First World War. Until now, I didn't know that tanks have a gender based on the number and type of guns they have.

Tanks were developed in Lincoln and they have genders

My route north to Hull is all by road, so there is less variety, and with only small towns, it's feeling repetitive. Helpfully with some tailwinds, it's an easy cycle to Barton, located on the southern side of the wide Humber Estuary, which separates Lincolnshire and Yorkshire.

After camping among trees near the shoreline of the Humber, I cross to Hull on a sizeable high cable bridge which only opened in 1980.

Sunset over the Humber

Hull is more interesting than expected, with numerous museums and attractive streets to explore. A display on the slave trade is a reminder of a dark part of British history. On a lighter note, a cycling display in the Transport Museum shows how bicycles changed from an essential new form of transport in the late 1800s to a recreational vehicle. There is also plenty of railway information, including a couple of trains.

Bicycles in the transport museum

Leaving Hull, I find my way to another rail trail by crossing the River Hull on a pink swing bridge formerly used by a railway.

After previously cycling some excellent rail trails, I'm disappointed with the one to Hornsea. The surface is rough in places, particularly with roots growing under the pavement, while there isn't any information provided on the history of this line. As I approach Hornsea, the surface improves, and at the former railway station, there are information panels on the rail history and the location of the turntable is preserved in brick.

Former swing rail bridge in Hull and where the turntable was in Hornsea

The town isn't that interesting as it's just another beachside town. It is, however, the eastern end of the Trans-Pennine Trail, which crosses over the Pennine mountain range in the middle of England to the west coast in Lancashire.

As I leave town in a northerly direction, the wind has picked up, so the rest of my afternoon involves side winds in an uninspiring landscape, so it isn't much fun. Initially, I'm on a busy road just away from the coastline with the occasional cycle path before quieter roads take me through farmland with harvest in progress.

My Warmshower host's home is in the town of Hunmanby, where I'm sleeping outside in the backyard, but Jonathan allows me to do some laundry.

In the morning, I try taking a track out of Hunmanby, but it runs out, so I will have to turn around and take a longer route via a busier road. Thankfully, I'm not on this road for long as a side road takes me through a caravan park to Filey, where there is a lovely small ravine to explore.

Fortunately, there is a narrow path beside the busy road to Scarborough, and even better is when a secondary road becomes available, including a small section of a closed road before a cycle path takes me into suburbia. Scarborough is, as expected, a popular beachside town, with plenty of seaside attractions on show.

Besides some ruined walls, there isn't much to see of the castle, which dominates a headland between two beaches, as it was bombed by the German Navy during the First World War. I should have taken an audio guide to learn more, but they often distract me from admiring the sites, especially when I have to wait for them to catch up.

I arrived in Scarborough on a beautiful sunny day, but dark clouds appear as I finish exploring the castle. Thankfully looking at the weather radar, it should only be for an hour at most, with a storm due to arrive around 2 pm.

Remains of Scarborough Castle

The former railway line between Scarborough and Whitby is now a rail trail called the Cinder Trail. The name comes from a volcanic rock called Cinder, used on this line instead of the standard crushed stone to hold the rail sleepers. I have been told it's rough in places, but this gravelly black dirt surface is a pleasurable ride compared to yesterday's rail trail to Hornsea.

Information on the Cinder Trail

The trail is semi-busy with a few cyclists and even more day walkers, however, too many walkers have their dogs off their leash, forcing me to suddenly stop for stray dogs.

As the rain finally arrives, I'm fortunately near a former station, which is now a tearoom, allowing me to stay dry. Helpfully, inside there are a few books and articles on the history of the many railway lines in this region. Most of them are long gone, with only one national rail network service still running, while there is a tourist train from Pickering to Whitby.

Once the sun reappears, it thankfully stays out for the rest of the day.

Past the tearoom, the Cinder Trail continues slowly climbing as a view of the sea appears, near the remains of a Second World War radar station at Ravenscar. I'm able to walk out to a couple of abandoned cement buildings, where there is a high coastline view.

A bridge over the Cinder Trail, while along the way is the former Ravenscar Radar Station

Back on my bicycle, the Cinder Trail dips down past Robin Hood Bay before climbing up again. After passing a well looked after former railway station, a long, high brick viaduct takes me over the River Esk and the still-active rail line, while in the distance, a large Abbey is visible on a hill.

Whitby is remarkably busy on the last weekend of the summer school holidays, and it appears that every third shop is selling fish and chips, so dinner is sorted. From nearly every point in town, the abbey dominates the landscape high above.

Whitby is where James Cook trained to be a sailor, so there is a statue of him here, paid for by the Australian government. It says Cook discovered Australia, which is now a controversial issue in Australia due to more respect for indigenous history.

The Endeavour, the sailing ship Cook used on the voyage that visited Australia, was built in Whitby, so there is a full-scale replica in the harbour, with a tall, empty mast.

In the evening, I make my way back along the rail trail, searching for a place to sleep. It doesn't take me long to find an open sports ground behind a school to set up my tent.

Replica of the Endeavour in Whitby Harbour, while the abbey is high above

Under the viaduct

On this Sunday morning, I'm aiming to go under the rail trail viaduct by following the old connecting rail line between the trail and the still-active railway. Initially, the track is easy to cycle as it curves under the viaduct, but it's gradually narrowing, so I have to walk. This now faint track is covered in blackberries and stinging nettles which are scratching my now itchy legs. I should turn around as I can see the bottom of this red-bricked viaduct. However, a narrow walking path visible across the active rail line is tempting me, so I will search for a way to get across.

Eventually, I'm able to drag my bicycle through the scratchy plants and across a gap in the railway fence, allowing me to ride back into Whitby to the tourist information centre.

The James Cook Museum is informative as it focuses on his scientific achievements and interactions with the local population rather than purely discovering and conquering places.

Along with fish and chip shops in the narrow streets, there are plenty of busy heritage looking tourists shops, with the black Whitby Jet of particular interest. This fossilised tree is made into a hard jewellery stone of various sizes and styles, with a wide range of jewellery items to purchase.

Jewellery is made out of Whitby Jet

Above this street on a prominent flat hill beside the sea is Whitby Abbey. It was destroyed during Henry VIII's reign, so it's a ruin. The walls that are still standing have large open spaces where presumably glass windows once were. It has a few things to see, with the highlight being a three-person play performing a Dracula story because the inventor of Dracula was from Whitby. The three actors have multiple roles, and they are using the whole Abbey to tell a story as the crowd is told to move every so often to a new location, where the story will continue.

A Dracula play moves around Whitby Abbey

Until the 1960s, numerous railway lines connected Whitby to the rest of the country, but now only the line to Middlesbrough is open. The first line, initially built to operate by horsepower, is now a steam train tourist line.

There aren't many road options in the hilly North Moors, so I will go train ride rather than cycle the busy roads. However, the tourist train isn't running from Whitby due to train delays, so I will have to cycle to Grosmont to catch the train from there. Initially, I follow the railway line using the path beside it before some short, steep, up and down roads take me to Grosmont.

This is a junction station between the tourist line and the still-active network line, so it's busy. Its style reminds me of a typical station seen on jigsaw puzzles, including white railway crossing gates, a footbridge, and many heritage items on display. Trains are still delayed, so I have enough time to visit the railway workshops through a tunnel for a horse-drawn railway built by the father of railways, George Stephenson.

Tunnel built for a horse tramway is near Grosmont Railway Station

The railway follows a valley

Eventually, I catch this 1:30 pm train at 2:30 pm, as it passes through unremarkable scenery. I had been expecting to be crossing rivers often from what I had read, but the train just stays in a valley.

The terminus town of Pickering is charming, including the remains of a small castle, which has a moat that surrounds the semi-intact outside stone walls. Inside are a few small buildings and another moat, but plenty of the castle is in ruin. I'm only visiting because my English Heritage card provides me free access. Otherwise, this and other similarly small sites that can easily be seen in less than an hour are not worth paying an entry fee of £6-10 each time.

Moat inside Pickering Castle

Consequently I have prioritised visiting English Heritage sites over other similar places, which I would have to pay to enter.

Pickering Castle

As I finish exploring the castle, heavy rain begins, so I spend some time sheltering instead of leaving Pickering. Once it finally eases it's now late afternoon, so it makes sense to stay here tonight just in case the rain returns.

However, after looking around town, there aren't many stealth camping options. There is a path around the back of the castle, but it's covered in stinging nettles. So since I can't find anywhere else to camp, I end up late in the evening finding a place to sleep outside the entrance of Pickering Castle.

Camping beside Pickering Castle

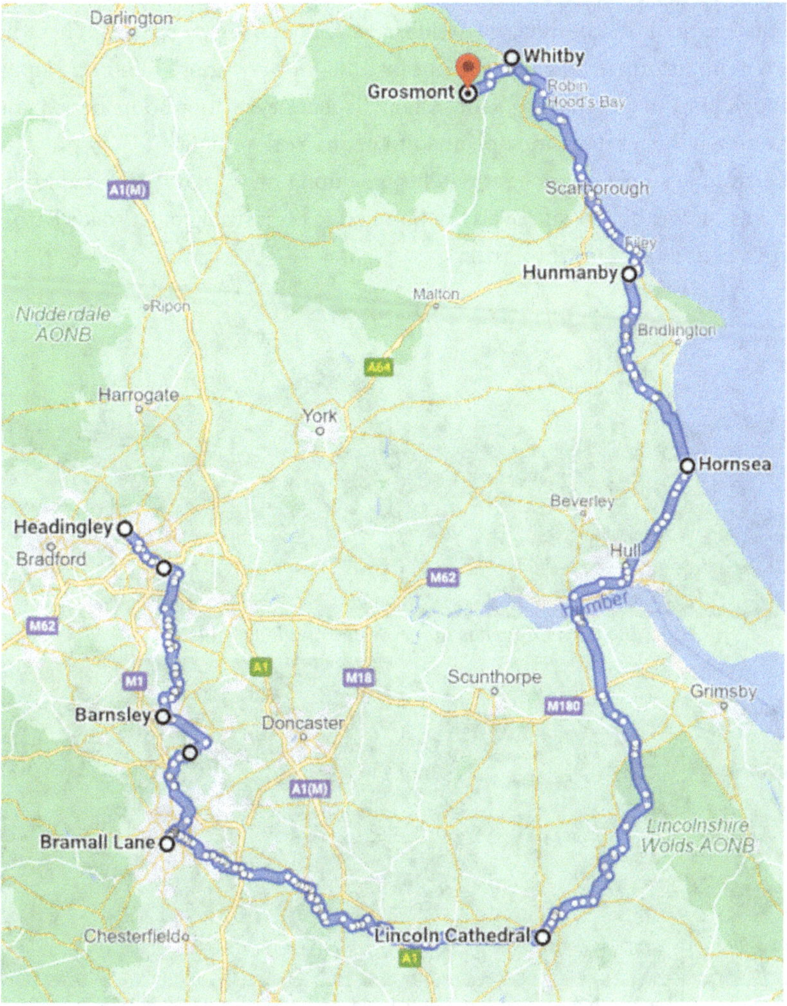

Headingley to Grosmont (Google Maps)

Old Trafford

In Whitby visitor information centre, I learnt of a former Second World War POW camp near Malton, so I will stop in at the Eden Camp on the way to York.

It's a well-preserved former camp that held Italian and German Prisoners of War with more than 30 huts still here. Many military vehicles are on display around these huts, including tanks, artillery guns, planes, and a German V1 rocket bomb, which looks like a glider with an engine. Until today, I didn't realise that it's a vastly different model and shape compared to the more rocket-designed V2.

These preserved huts have been converted to display various aspects of the Second World War, most of which have nothing to do with this camp. Many have too much information, which often feels like it has come from Wikipedia. Other huts have been set up with sound and light shows of different historical events like the London Blitz, POW life, and *The Great Escape* tunnels. These huts were more informative, while the ones with a lot of writing, I end up skipping through but I'm still learning a lot. All up, I spent nearly four hours here. I could have stayed longer if I hadn't planned to get to York tonight.

I arrived in sunlight, but light rain begins during my stay at Eden, thankfully it eases as I leave, but it's still overcast. So my ride is dry using quiet roads before a short rail trail takes me into York.

Eden Camp has numerous former POW huts

German V1 rocket bomb outside a hut, while inside many huts are World War Two displays

York has a decent visitor information centre unlike many other places in England, which often have nothing or just brochures with no one providing assistance. Whitby had a small one, but Scarborough only had brochures. Scotland was more consistent with tourist information offices well signed and located where expected, while nearly every town in France has an Office de Tourisme.

Apparently York still has a medieval wall around the city, with only one significant gap. Instead that section was deliberately flooded for centuries and just happens to be where I entered the city.

It's now 4:30 pm, so most interesting places are soon closing, but with the National Railway Museum free and open until 6pm, I will make my way there. Along the way are parts of the medieval wall as I cross the River Ouse. On the other side of the wall is the enormous busy York Railway Station with a large roof. Once I find my way through it to the other side, I can see that the railway museum is located in a few former railway buildings among a larger complex.

This museum appears to be more about collecting locomotives rather than information on specific railway lines or the history of any of the various railway companies. It's still engaging with plenty of information covering the last 200 years of rail in the UK, with a wide range of trains: from a yellow model of Rocket, the first train on the first main railway line in the world between Liverpool and Manchester with its horse-drawn style passenger carriages, to the front part of the much larger Eurostar, which travels from London to Paris in two hours.

There is so much to see that I revisited this museum the following evening. My highlight is a room full of numerous smaller historical pieces yet to be adequately organised, with various items used to help run a railway like signalling equipment, signs, clocks and items with different railway companies' initials on them.

For the next two nights, I have a Warmshower with Greg, who has spent time cycling on an extended tour, predominantly in North America and Asia. So we talk about our respective cycle tours.

Style of the first trains, while a room is full of railway items

I'm having a day off my bicycle, so I will start by walking on top of the medieval city wall. Along the wall were a few city gates, including Redgate, which as the name suggests, is a red brick gate, which looks like a small house. Most gates are more medieval in style, with the classic turret towers on each of the four corners and an open archway below to walk through, along with various coats of arms on these much taller towers. For a fee, some can be visited inside.

A medieval wall with a few gates, still goes around most of York

Clifford Tower

In the south of the old part of York is a small round tower on a dirt mound known as Clifford, the only remains of the once enormous York Castle. It's well intact, and once again, by using my English Heritage card, I'm able to walk inside and climb to a 360-degree view of York.

Outside the enormous Minster Cathedral at 11 am, is a free three-hour walking tour. Our guide Alan, keeps it engaging and varied as York has been an important location for 2,000 years, including for the Romans, the Vikings, the Normans, the Tudors, and during the English Civil War.

Alan shows us how the medieval wall was either built on top of the Roman era wall or next to it in certain locations. He also points to a tall church tower known as the Lantern, which was used like a lighthouse to tell people in the surrounding area where the town centre was.

Lantern Tower

He takes us to Shambles Street, to show us where numerous butchers used to operate on a street designed to make it easier to clean away the meat waste thrown onto it. Many older wooden buildings still have objects designed for meat to be displayed or hung. These days it's full of tourist shops instead of butchers.

One of a few Tudor-era buildings in York, while Shambles Street is touristy

York also has a Viking-based museum which is really two experiences in one. Firstly, there is a collection of artefacts uncovered during a dig in the 1980s and secondly, a slow ride on an overhead roller coaster type set up through an interpretation of this Viking City.

My next destination is Manchester because the fourth men's Ashes test match is there. I don't have a ticket yet as I'm unsure which day to attend because with rain predicted, I'm not sure how much cricket will be on. However, I do have a ticket for the first-ever Manchester derby in the Women's Super League. I'm thinking it will take me two days of cycling to get to Manchester following the Trans-Pennine Trail, including going near Barnsley again.

South of York, I find myself at a rail trail which was once part of the Main East Coast railway line between London and Edinburgh until 1983 when a mine forced the rail line to be moved. Along this trail, planets have been lined up to the relative scale of the solar system, no idea why. They are close together at the start before the planets spread out more as the trail goes away from the sun.

Saturn on the rail trail

Along the way, the former swing rail bridge over the River Ouse has a few fishing statues on top of it. Shortly afterwards, beside the trail is a rest station, with water, fruit and snacks available for donation in an honesty box. I can even boil a kettle to make tea or coffee. Surprisingly, I haven't seen a rest stations beside any other rail trails in the UK.

Near the former rail swing bridge, is a rest station for rail trail users

Sadly, this trail finishes at Riccall because the former rail right of way is now a motorway. For a while, a cycle path is beside the motorway before a secondary road, and then a path beside the River Ouse takes me into Selby. After crossing the Ouse again, a large Abbey dominates the town centre, so I leave my bicycle outside and go for a look.

Selby Abbey

As I open the door, I'm surprised to see bicycles inside the Abbey, as a group is having morning tea here. Unlike in Lincoln or York, I'm allowed to freely look around inside. My advice is unless you have a particular interest in a specific cathedral, don't line up for hours to pay to enter one. Instead, visit a smaller town because they are generally free to visit, along with being quieter.

After briefly using the Shelby canal to take me out of town, the signed National Cycle Route soon leaves the canal behind. For a while, I'm on quiet roads through flat farmland with the cycle route taking many doglegs, allowing me to listen to the first day of the cricket in Manchester.

Lost

As I find myself on a green levee bank in a paddock with fences blocking my path, I must have taken a wrong turn. I can see a road bridge ahead of me, so I lift my bicycle over a barbed wire fence and drag it through prickly weeds instead of retracing my route.

Eventually, I arrive at the New Junction canal, which has a poor towpath surface for cycling. However, I do briefly meet a few touring cyclists, while being near a canal allows me to observe people on a narrowboat operating a lift road bridge over the canal themselves.

Following New Junction Canal, where boaters have to operate bridge lifts themselves

Soon the cycle route leaves the canal and takes a few doglegs, including crossing on the same level an active double-track railway line where I have to open gates.

With a rail trail going around the western side of Doncaster, I won't head into the city centre. Just as the trail ends with a large bridge over the River Don, a thunderstorm begins. So instead of crossing this bridge, I quickly head down on a cycle path to the River Don, where the path goes under the former rail bridge and a nearby motorway. As the rain becomes heavier, I spend time sheltering under both bridges.

Once the rain eases, the paved cycle path follows the River Don, including a short canal section. The sun returns as I go under a still-active railway line, providing a shiny reflection on this wet path. Soon an even more enormous rail viaduct is in front of me. Rather than going under it, a loop path begins climbing up to an end of this viaduct. The top of the Conisbrough Viaduct is broad and has high walls, so as I cycle east over the Don, I can't see much.

Conisbrough Viaduct

According to Maps.me, this rail trail just ends in the southern suburbs of Doncaster, so at the end of the viaduct, I turn around and recross it. From here, the cycle path follows the smaller River Dearne, sometimes on the rail formation but often just near this former railway line. Other times I'm on a path right next to the Dearne.

Eventually, I end up crossing paths with myself just south of Barnsley on a brief section of rail trail I have already cycled. However, instead of heading back to Barnsley, I turn left at a rail trail junction and begin travelling through the southern suburbs. By now, darkness has caught up with me, so as I see a park beside this rail trail, this will do for camping.

Nearby is Boatman's Rest Hotel, so in the evening, I go for a look. I soon learn that tonight a pub quiz is on. It's okay and gives me something to do in the evening.

It's a beautiful sunny day on this Thursday on the Yorkshire side of the Pennines. For the most part, I'm using rail trails with a small gap where a still-active railway line is in the middle between two parts of the Trans-Pennine Trail. Thankfully, this detour is all on quiet roads.

Nature is reclaiming the former rail route including turntable remains at Penistone

As I approach the still-active Penistone Railway Station, occasional rail remains are visible, including a turntable pit. At the actual station, there is obvious evidence of a previous, much larger railway station with abandoned platforms.

So far, today's been a relaxing scenic ride with plenty of trees on both sides of the rail trail, along with road bridges over the former rail formation. There have also been a few cyclists and walkers. However, when the rail trail ends, they are all seemingly turning around rather than continuing on the Trans-Pennine Trail. Presumably, this is because from here to cross the Pennines, this former railway line went through three-mile-long tunnels. The entrance of a couple of tunnels is visible from a distance, but they are blocked off with high gates and signs saying danger, no entry. Instead, I will have to climb over the Pennines.

As I begin climbing on quiet roads, the landscape is becoming treeless, the temperature has dropped, and a few clouds have appeared. Soon in front of me is a busy motorway, but thankfully there is a narrow walking path with stone fences and a few wooden gates to open.

Crossing the Pennines

As I gradually descend, the path is covered in puddles, but is manageable until suddenly it becomes a steep zigzag path where I'm holding tightly onto my brakes while sliding down on a track covered in small stones.

As I finally make it down safely, the entrance to three former rail tunnels next to each other are blocked off. The two older single-width rail tunnels were closed for a newer, wider tunnel built in the 1950s before all rail services closed in 1981.

Descending to the western end of the Woodhead Tunnels

Instead, high powered electrical lines now go through all three tunnels, which is why they are not open for cyclists.

It's much colder on this side of the Pennines as a dirt rail trail follows a series of man-made lakes. Eventually, the trail ends at Hadfield as an active rail line still exists here.

I should have just caught the train from here because the cycling to Manchester involves a lot of zigzagging through suburbia, with a few small rail trails in-between bits of hilly cycling. It feels like it takes forever to get through to the former loop railway line, which is now a rail trail that goes around the southern suburbs of Manchester. Helpfully my Warmshowers host's home is near this rail trail. However, since he won't be home for a few hours, I will continue on it, as it gets me close to Old Trafford's Cricket Ground.

It's now around 4:30 pm, so I try sneaking into the cricket using someone else's ticket who has left early, but it isn't being accepted by the scanner. As I begin looking for a weak point in security, suddenly, just after 5 pm, an hour before the scheduled end of the day's play, they open the gates to let everyone leave. So I lock my bicycle to a metal fence and sneak in against the flow of the leaving crowd.

As soon as I find a seat, Steve Smith gets himself out with a terrible reverse sweep shot after making more than 200 runs. The Australian tail continues batting. However, I soon have to leave as Dimitry, my Warmshower host messages me to say he will be home soon, and it's about a half-hour ride back.

I have no idea what Dimitry looks like until a tall skinny man on a bicycle shows up. I soon learn that he grew up in Russia and his father still lives there. I mention that I cycled in Russia last year, so I ask where his father lives. When he mentions Samara, I surprise Dimitry by saying that I visited there. He then rings his father and tells him in Russian about me visiting Samara.

Dimitry then surprises me by offering his bed

Dimitry

while he sleeps on a mattress on the floor. I try to persuade him that I have my Thermarest mattress, but he insists. This isn't the first time someone has sacrificed their bed for me on a bicycle tour.

It's an overcast Friday morning, so I'm unsure if I should go to the cricket today. The last time I was here in 2013, it started raining as soon as I purchased a ticket. However, with the weather forecast looking better and no rain yet, I will see if I can find one.

After searching Twitter, I have found a person who has a spare ticket for £60. Of course, as soon as I start cycling to the ground, it starts raining. Thankfully by the start time of 11 am, the rain has eased slightly, but the covers are still on. It looks like the rain will clear up after lunch.

Play does begin after lunch on this cold, overcast day, where I'm seated high up in the temporary stand, which is freezing, so my sleeping bag is helping to keep me warm. It appears to be the party stand as the predominantly English crowd are sarcastically cheering every time Nathan Lyon catches the ball, in reference to Headingley, where he dropped the ball on that run out chance. As for the day's play, England mostly bat okay before we take a few late wickets, so this match is still in the balance.

It's cold at Old Trafford Cricket Ground

With the first-ever Manchester derby in women's football not until 3 pm, I have some time this Saturday morning to look around Manchester, a city I only briefly visited in 2013.

The People's History Museum focuses on political protests as it goes through 200 years of political change in the UK. It's in Manchester because this was the site of the Peterloo Massacre in 1819. Eighteen protesters died after the army broke up a demonstration for more voting rights. In 1819 very few men had that right, particularly in Manchester, while it would be a 100 years before any women could vote. Throughout the museum, there are also references to more recent political issues like Brexit and the UK's involvement in selling missiles to Saudi Arabia, which are then dropped on Yemen.

1830 Station

The science museum is located on the site of Manchester's first railway station, which opened in 1830 as part of the first main railway line in the world to Liverpool. I can explore both outside and inside the original red-bricked station and a railway warehouse from that period. Throughout the site, rails are still on the ground among paved paths.

Rocket; a very early locomotive

Apparently, they have the actual Rocket locomotive used in the Rainhill Trials in 1829 to determine which train they would use on the line, yet I thought the rail museum in York had a Rocket as well.

The City of Manchester Stadium was built for the Commonwealth Games in 2002 and is about three miles from the city centre. Ashton Canal goes right past the stadium, so it's easy getting there by bicycle. After asking around, I'm unsure if there is bicycle parking at the stadium, so I end up parking it at a bicycle rack near a tennis court beside the canal. Of course, as soon as I walk over the canal and enter the stadium forecourt, people are parking their bicycles at dedicated parking spots near the stadium.

With this being a women's football match, there are families with young children, many of whom I presume can't afford to or don't usually attend men's football. It's easy getting inside the stadium, which feels about half full but still has a decent atmosphere with a good amount of both sets of supporters in attendance. During the second half of the match, the attendance of 31,213 is announced, which is now a record for domestic women's football in England.

Manchester Derby is about to kick-off

As for the match, it's a tight first half before Caroline Weir scores a volley early in the second half for City. Noticeably with ten minutes still to go, many people start leaving the stadium despite United having some chances.

After the match, since I'm in the eastern part of Manchester, I will use the loop rail trail to return to Dimitry's home. It takes a while, especially as I briefly miss a turn near Gorton Lower Reservoir.

While I have been away from the cricket today, England has been bowled out before lunch, and Australia has set them 382 runs to win. It's been a good start from us as we have already taken two wickets in the first over of their batting innings.

On the fifth day of the cricket, we will need eight wickets to retain the men's Ashes while England will need an unlikely 364 runs in a day. So I have purchased a ticket for the cricket tomorrow.

At the same time I have been cycling, Eliza Bartlett from Adelaide has been walking from Italy to the UK raising money for diabetes, which she and my youngest sister both have. Once in England, she has been attending many days of cricket, while still hiking in between matches. I was first made aware of her journey on Twitter after seeing a post mentioning her walk when she was at Chelmsford when Lanning went berserk.

Since then, I have been following her journey on social media because it's interesting to see a different perspective on travelling through the UK. Eliza's hike has made me realise that I haven't done many walks at all on this trip. I have done a few day hikes on previous bicycle tours, but I just haven't on this tour.

Seeing Eliza's occasional struggles have been a motivator for me because no matter how hard my cycling is going, at least I'm not walking. Making her hike more challenging, is that she isn't carrying sleeping gear, so she has to find indoor accommodation each night. This isn't as much of an issue for me as I can set up my tent wherever.

Her social media posts have shown she has had some late nights to make indoor accommodation, while some of the places she has stayed haven't been great. One night, she arrived late to find no bed linen available, so she had to sleep in all her clothing. Another night, she booked a hotel miles away in the wrong direction and so had to hike the wrong way.

I thought I fleetingly saw Eliza at Headingley after Ben Stokes heroics, while up until today, we ended up going to different days of the cricket at Old Trafford. Thankfully on this sunny Sunday, our paths have finally crossed.

Eliza is cricket-obsessed as she wicket-keeps for Sturt in the Adelaide Women's Premier Grade Cricket, alongside cricketers who play for South Australia and even represent Australia. Apparently, she played underage cricket for South Australia just a year above when my middle sister played for Victoria.

Also at the cricket are her sister Clara and Clara's Russian boyfriend Sergey, who have travelled to the UK from Singapore to walk for a few days with Eliza. However, after one day of walking 38 kilometres with Eliza, they are giving up on walking. I end up spending most of the day talking to Sergey, as it appears I'm more interested in Eliza's walk than she is in my cycling. She still has about three weeks to get to Aberdeen.

Unlike in France, where I spent plenty of time with fellow Australians following the Matildas, here in England, I haven't got to know anyone despite many Australians attending the cricket. It was nice today being able to briefly get to know people from home.

As for the cricket, we are getting regular wickets throughout the day, but there are a few nervy moments with England holding on for a while, delaying the inevitable. However, the English weather may save them as late in the day, with two wickets still to get, it's beginning to get a little dark, so they may go off for bad light.

Thankfully with a change of bowling to part-timer Labuschagne, his spin bowling removes Australia's Headingley nemesis, Jack Leach. Shortly afterwards, Hazlewood hits Overton on his pads, trapping him leg before wicket. However, our celebrations are briefly postponed as Overton reviews the decision. Everyone's attention now turns to the big screen. As the three red lights appear, every Australian in the ground erupts as we have finally retained the men's Ashes in England for the first time since 2001.

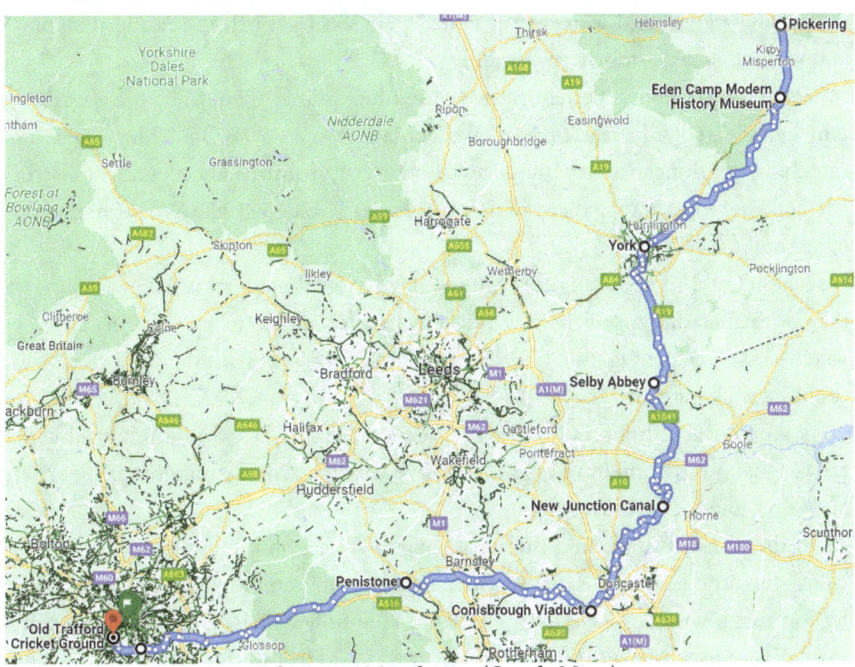

Pickering to Manchester (Google Maps)

Ashleworth

With only a week left until I leave the UK, I have worked out a route to London via a few places of interest, including an English Premier League match at Brighton. To get there in time, I will have to use a few trains in between. Knowing how built-up it is around Manchester, getting out by train makes sense.

After looking at train options and cycle routes, a train to Wolverhampton via the 1830 rail line to Liverpool makes sense, allowing me to join a rail trail, which goes west around the built-up surrounds of Birmingham. I have visited Birmingham before, so I'm not missing anything. While at Liverpool, I only have a short break between trains, so I won't have a chance to look around in the city which I started the UK part of my 2013 tour.

I have just made it to Liverpool with enough time to catch a train leaving half an hour earlier than the train I'm supposed to be on. Since it's only just over an hour ride to Wolverhampton, I will join this train.

Halfway through the trip, the conductor comes through on this half-full mid-morning train. When she scans my ticket, she tells me angrily I'm on the wrong train. Since I got early into Liverpool, I explain that I thought it was okay to get this train as it's precisely the same schedule, just half an hour early. However, she tells me to stay on this train for the final half-hour to Wolverhampton I have to pay a fee, which is more than my original ticket cost. Otherwise, I have to get off at the next station and wait for my actual train. So I get off at a random station and waste half an hour of my time.

After arriving in Wolverhampton around lunchtime, thankfully, the morning rain has cleared. My last time in Wolverhampton in 2013 is a blur, so I try searching for things to see, but I can't find a visitor information centre to offer advice. There is an art gallery which is unremarkable, just like Wolverhampton in general.

The rail trail I'm searching for is in the northern suburbs. Along the way, I pass the football stadium, which now hosts a premier league team. Back in 2013, I watched Wolves play against Crawley Town when they were in the third tier; how times have changed.

It's an enjoyable brief rail trail with a decent dirt surface and a few well-kept railway stations. As the trail begins to curve east towards Birmingham, I leave it and soon join a canal towpath.

On this canal, I'm passing numerous narrowboats and a few scenic locks. As I pass the junction for a canal to Birmingham, this reminds me they were built to connect towns before railways existed. Helpfully canals usually still go right through towns as it does through the centre of Kidderminster, whereas rail trails sometimes end before town centres for various reasons, often because either the rail infrastructure still exists or the rail right of way has been built over.

Following a canal

As it's late in the afternoon now, rather than explore Kidderminster, I will continue as the canal makes its way to the River Severn. Just before the Severn, the signed cycle route leaves the canal for a short rail trail, before some dogleg roads take me to Droitwich Spa. It's now early evening, so I'm considering camping here, but despite plenty of green spaces, I can't find anywhere suitable, so I will continue.

As dusk appears, the cycle route joins a canal taking me into Worcester, but rather than going all the way tonight, I will try to find somewhere to camp. The canal is near a motorway interchange and the massive lit up Worcester Warriors Rugby Stadium, so I'm concerned about finding a quiet spot.

I soon spot a small pedestrian bridge across the canal, so I leave my bicycle at the bridge, walk over the canal, and go through a gate in a metal fence to some rugby fields. It's quiet here, so in the corner of one of these rugby fields, it should be a quiet out of the way spot to camp.

I awake to a curator in his tractor, angry that I have camped on one of his rugby fields. So I quickly leave.

My route into Worcester is all by this canal, allowing me to comfortably arrive in a scenic city on the Severn. All I know about this city is that one of the smallest men's county cricket teams plays here.

Helpfully the Worcester visitor information centre is in the large scenic Guildhall in the centre of town, where I'm informed about a daily guided tour at 11 am for £7.

I nicely ask while I'm on this tour if I can leave my iPhone to charge here. As the lady I have been talking to goes to say yes, another woman suddenly grumpily says no. Her tone makes me annoyed with English people in general, especially after the unfriendly conductor yesterday and the rugby curator this morning.

Guildhall with royal statues

Worcester Cathedral

I have some time before my tour, so I will go for a ride along the cycle path beside the Severn, allowing me to see numerous white swans on the river, the impressive cathedral and the county cricket ground across the river. Compared to Old Trafford, it's a much smaller cricket ground with only a few stands, so the cricket pitch is visible from a road.

The guided two-hour tour of Worcester covers so much, especially as the English Civil War's first and last battles were here. Worcester supported the King, so on either side of the main door of the fancy Guildhall are statues of Charles I and his son Charles II. Both were involved in the civil war, with Charles I leading the first battle here before having his head chopped off a few years later, while Charles II fled the country after his final defeat at Worcester before returning as King about a decade later. Charles I's granddaughter Queen Anne is high above the door as the building was erected just after her death, while above her are numerous weapons fanned out on display around the coat of arms of Worcester.

They are not the only royalty references in Worcester because in the cathedral is

King John rests in Worcester Cathedral

the tomb of King John, of Robin Hood and Magna Carter infamy. In the centre of this cathedral is a statue of him lying on top of his tomb, while throughout this building, there are more religious statues to admire.

Our tour finishes with visiting another Shambles Street with many now-familiar three storey wooden black-and-white vertical striped facade Tudor era buildings.

Tudor era building in Shambles Street

I had hoped following the Severn south to Gloucester would be scenic, but instead, the cycle route is taking many slow dogleg roads which often cross the main road. So as evening approaches, I'm still more than an hour away from Gloucester, my goal for the night.

As I approach the small country town of Ashleworth, I realise that lately I have been staying in built-up areas. So I will stay here instead, especially as the cricket ground on the edge of town looks like a perfect spot for camping.

The only issue is that it's now nearly 6 pm, and I don't have much food for dinner, so I race to the general store. Thankfully, the lady at the general store lets me in just after closing time, allowing me to purchase bacon to add to my pasta. Outside the general store is a red phone box, which is now the town's free book library, making Ashleworth look like a typical English village.

Ashleworth General Store

Children's cricket training is on as I arrive at an oval which appears to have some suitable quiet spaces for me to camp, once everyone leaves.

After dinner, most people have left, but a few are still in the clubhouse. Inside, a handful of locals are watching the England-Kosovo men's football match on a large television. I'm welcomed inside to watch as England wins 5-3 in an entertaining game. We chat about Australia, so naturally, the recent international cricket is mentioned. As the evening winds up, I'm offered the chance to camp inside the change rooms next door.

Unfortunately, the defibrillator inside the change rooms is making a regular beeping noise, so I end up outside in my tent.

Gloucester feels like just another city with a large cathedral, so I'm soon ready to move on. All I really learn is that during the civil war, Gloucester supported the parliamentary forces against the King, whereas Worcester, up the Severn, was a royalist town.

To get to Swindon, I need to cross the Cotswolds, a name that sounds familiar. From a cyclist perspective, it's hilly east of Gloucester. My route involves one particularly steep mile climb before a gradual descent to Cirencester. I do at least briefly see a few of the scenic styles of creamy stone houses with their pointy tiled roofs in the Cotswolds.

Houses in the Cotswold

With more time, I would have explored properly, but with my goal of getting to the railway museum at Swindon for an afternoon visit, I will continue on by using a few short rail trails, which have gaps requiring me to return to road cycling.

Swindon was a large railway town where for 140 years, a large railway workshop operated until 1986. It was initially built by Isambard Kingdom Brunel for his famous Great Western Railway company, whose main line went between London and Bristol via Swindon.

Museum in a former rail building

Today many of these former railway buildings have been converted into shopping centres with a few rail items outside on display.

The Steam Railway Museum is located in one of these former railway repair buildings. It's smaller but more interesting than the National Railway Museum in York as it shows the various industries that worked here to make and repair locomotives, carriages and many other items required by the railways. There are plenty of trains in various stages of being built, which helps explain the various jobs done to keep the railway operating. There is also an overall exhibit of various roles railway staff performed to run a large railway company.

A specific display on the Great Western railway helps explain how it was built and then operated. This company famously used the 7-foot gauge, and an incredibly old steam train *'North Star'* shows just how wide this really is compared to the now universal standard gauge, which is more than two feet narrower. Overall I'm impressed with this highly informative museum.

A 7-foot gauge train

Cooking by a lake

This being a former railway town, there are a few rail trails, including one that loops around to the southern suburbs, where I soon find a man-made lake to cook dinner beside. Once it's dark enough, I find a spot among trees to camp.

In the morning after using a cycle path around the side of the lake, a spiral path takes me up over a motorway before another spiral takes me down to a rail trail which conveys me south to Marlborough, a town with a wide main street and some scenic buildings.

After some quiet roads south of Marlborough through a hilly landscape, I'm crossing over my 2013 self as I cross the Kennet-Avon canal. A café is here beside the canal, while a museum shows that crop circles have been found in this area for 500 years.

Crop circles

My goal of the day is to visit Stonehenge as my English Heritage pass allows me to visit for free. Along the way is Woodhenge, a similar old circular site, which as the name suggests, is made out of wood and has just as many mysteries as Stonehenge.

I'm not surprised that the Stonehenge information centre is busy with a packed car park and café. Despite this, it does have some interesting artefacts on display, including many old tools and weapons. With the actual Stonehenge site a mile away and with no cars allowed, except for the occasional shuttle bus, it's a quiet ride to the site.

I have to leave my bicycle outside the fence to visit a quieter than I expected Stonehenge, but there are still plenty of tourists trying to take their perfect selfies. Thankfully, no one is allowed to touch or go inside these numerous erect stones, allowing me a clear view to admire them from a few metres away on a path that goes around them all. Many still have a horizontal stone on top of two vertical stones, while a few have fallen over. They have tried to hide it, but several still upright stones have been reinforced to stop them from falling over. Helping me on this walk is an informative audio guide on my iPhone.

Stonehenge

I don't have to retrace my route back to the Stonehenge car park because a track takes me to the main motorway, which noisily goes right past. Thankfully after crossing it, I'm able to take a quiet route south to Salisbury.

Along the way is a large mound with castle remains, which has more to see than Stonehenge. With fewer camera-obsessed tourists around, it's a much more relaxing place to explore as I'm allowed to walk all over most of Old Sarum Castle. It was built by the Normans after conquering England following the Battle of Hastings, while apparently, the Doomsday survey book was presented to William the Conqueror here.

What's left of Old Sarum Castle, including the outline remains of the cathedral

The most preserved part of the complex is the main castle in the centre, on its own dirt mound surrounded by its own blackberry-covered moat. Outside the inner moat, mostly only foundations are left, including just an outline of the main cathedral. Thankfully, information panels help show what they assume the various buildings looked like and how busy it was. With plenty of grassy areas to walk around on this mound, on a sunny day, there would be decent views of Salisbury.

As for Salisbury, I don't have much time to explore before catching a train to Woking. I do have a brief look at the cathedral that's infamous for why the Russian spies were supposedly visiting here rather than because they were poisoning people.

Helpfully, my Warmshower host Michael meets me at the Woking station in the evening before guiding me to his home for a relaxing night.

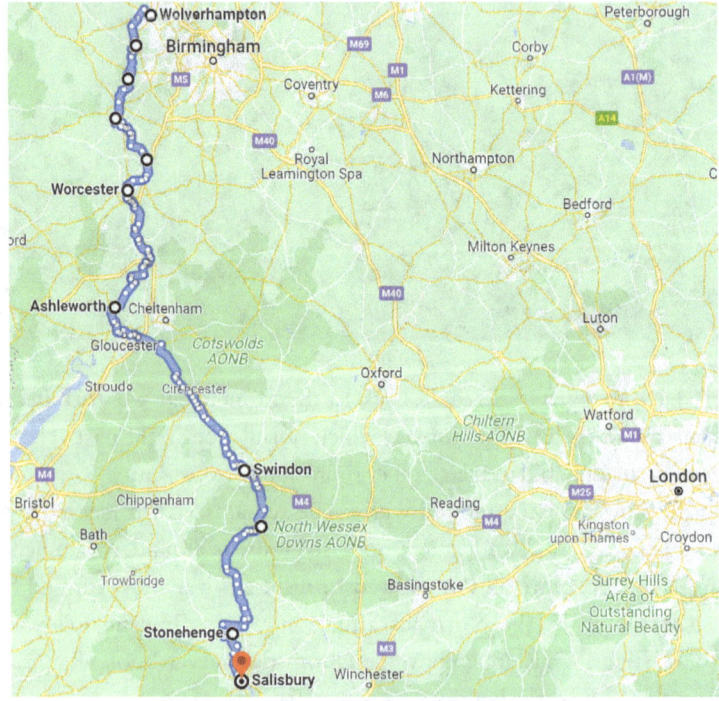

Wolverhampton to Salisbury (Google Maps)

Downs Link

I caught a train to Woking because in nearby Guildford, a rail trail travels south to the English Channel at Shoreham near Brighton.

After yesterday's overcast day, thankfully it's sunny as I make my way to Guildford, where a delightful free guided walk shows me a few sites, including the fancy Guildford gold clock that sticks out of the third floor of the town hall. Our guide explains that when transport was by horse and cart, many travellers stopped here because Guildford is between London and Portsmouth, so there were services like horse stables. Today one of these former stables is a restaurant.

Just off the main street is a tall square Norman era castle which is a short visit. More memorable is the immaculate grass of the open bowling green next door surrounded by a fancy garden with sculptured hedgerows.

After enjoying food at the local street markets, I begin following a canal out of Guildford before joining the Downs Link rail trail on a line that closed in the 1960s. There is still some railway infrastructure on the trail, including white railway gates near the intact double platformed former Bramley Railway Station.

In places it looks like this railway line must have been double-track with two single wide bridges next to each other, but only one is now a rail trail. For the most part, this trail passes through a green landscape with plenty of tree-lined sections, so it's a relaxing ride as I listen to the second day of the fifth and final men's Ashes Test at the Oval in London.

This rail trail is interrupted when an active railway line intersects it near the town of Horsham, the same name of a city close to home in Australia, so I will head in for a look.

Guildford's Clock

Stables turned into a restaurant

Tree-lined rail trail

A castle style town hall and stocks in Horsham

After negotiating some suburbs, the city centre appears smaller than the Australian Horsham, but its population is three times higher, so there must be more suburbs here. Besides the town hall looking like a castle and a wooden stock on the street, there isn't much to see apart from a museum.

Signs and dinosaur fossils in the Horsham museum

Inside are typical items often found in local museums and also dinosaur bones. There are numerous Horsham signs, but none that are relevant to Horsham in Australia. The nearest references are some agricultural items on display as the Australian version is also surrounded by farms.

Back on the rail trail well out west of Horsham, it's a similar decent ride as it continues heading south, with a couple of short diversions around built-over areas.

By the time I'm at Partridge Green, I have had enough cycling. Thankfully, a cricket oval on the edge of town will do for my last night in a tent in the UK.

As I begin cooking dinner at this popular oval, a small dog suddenly starts attacking me. I stick my leg up to defend myself, and at the same time, I flick the

My last camping in the UK

dog away with my foot. I'm then angrily confronted by the dog's owner, who is about the same age as me, so I raise my voice to defend my actions by saying his dog attacked me, and all I did was try to get the dog away from me. He then threatens to punch me. Fortunately, his girlfriend calms him down, allowing me to finish my dinner.

Conflicts between cyclists and motorists are common, but so are those between cyclists and dog walkers. Whenever I have to brake to avoid a dog, I'm sick of hearing "sorry" said by every owner of the dog I nearly cycled over. A small minority don't even try to stop their dog from being in the way. It particularly appears to be a British issue with so many people here walking their dogs unleashed on a cycle path. Compared to Europe, the British have so many more dogs, and for some reason, many museums allow dogs on site.

In the morning, back on the rail trail, once again, another unleashed dog forces me to sharply brake. So I let out all my pent up frustration by yelling at the dog's owner to have her dog on a leash. Since I'm on a bicycle, I'm soon away from her before I can say anymore I will regret.

Close to the sea, I'm back beside a river as this rail trail finishes at the busy seaside town of Shoreham, a place I passed through in 2013, but since it's all a built-up seaside area, I don't recall it. After a Saturday morning street market, I begin going through continuous built-up beachside suburbs to nearby Brighton using cycle paths beside the sea.

I didn't enjoy visiting Brighton last time, and it isn't much better now as it's just too busy with an ugly touristy beach. I briefly see the Royal Pavilion, built in the 1800s with an Indian influence, with its Aladdin style Sultan's Palace bubble towers with pointy tops. Otherwise, I'm glad to get out of Brighton.

Indian influence Royal Pavilion

Thankfully, there is a proper bicycle lane on the route north to the University of Brighton and the nearby football stadium. I'm not the only cyclist as there are plenty of people parking their bicycles outside at the dedicated bicycle parking station outside this stadium, which opened less than a decade ago.

An hour before the game starts, it's a pleasant atmosphere outside this stadium with a band playing on a stage. Alongside Australian goalkeeper Matt Ryan, female and male footballers are being promoted equally outside the stadium, even if the women's team plays most of their games at Crawley, halfway to London.

Bike parking at Brighton Stadium

My only issue with getting into the stadium is that I'm not allowed to take my water bottle inside with its lid on. There even appears to be security staff seemingly employed just to take lids off. Yet I could at other games in Manchester and Sheffield, while there were no issues at the cricket. So I return to my bicycle and swap to a plastic bottle, where I put the plastic lid in my wallet to put back on my bottle once I'm past security.

It's a friendly atmosphere inside this nearly full stadium as Brighton score early in the second half against Burnley. Once again, as time ticks away, hundreds of people leave the stadium early despite Burnley having plenty of chances. Just as injury time starts, Burnley scores. Apart from one section of away supporters celebrating, you wouldn't know this, as the large screen doesn't show any highlights of Burnley's goal, a vastly different experience to the cricket, where Australian highlights are shown as equally as the English ones.

After the match, as I go to cycle to nearby Lewis, I have a flat tyre. So I begin pumping up a new fresh tube while the crowd files past, encouraging me. Once the tyre is full again, to save time, I catch a packed train from the railway station right next to the stadium to nearby Lewes.

At Lewes, I will have to wait an hour for my pre-booked train to London. However, as I leave the football train, an announcement says that my train is cancelled. A train is about to leave for London, but after being kicked off a train between Liverpool and Wolverhampton due to it not being my correct train, I'm unsure what I should do.

As I begin asking railway staff what I'm supposed to do, other passengers encourage me to jump on the train leaving now. So I roll my bicycle on board, and people say I should be fine. Thankfully, no one checks my ticket on this train.

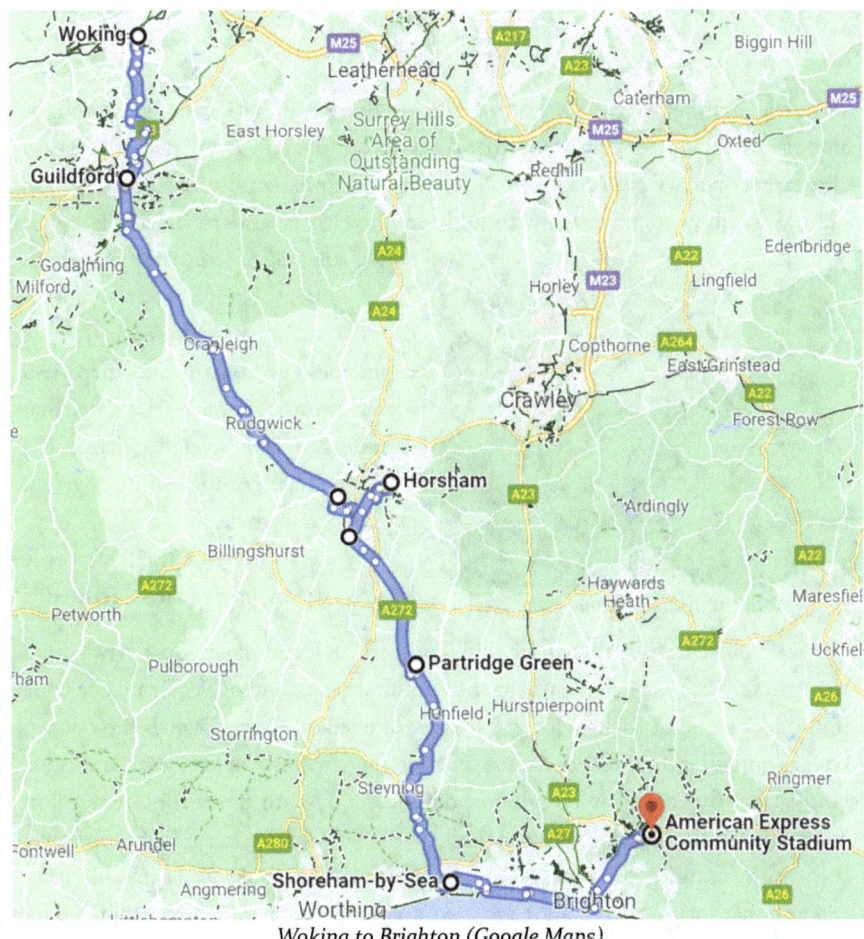
Woking to Brighton (Google Maps)

The Oval

As I make my way to my Warmshower host's home south of the Oval, I pass by supporters leaving the cricket. England is well on top, so we will need to chase a large target once we get two more wickets, hopefully early tomorrow on day four.

My Warmshower hosts Hannah and Greg cycled a tandem bicycle last year across the USA using the Southern Tier route. Their tandem hangs proudly on display in their lounge room below their route map and a few photos. I haven't cycled that route, but I have cycled twice in the USA, so I can compare my American experience to theirs.

Tandem in their lounge room

They are also one of the few people I stayed with who are fans of Brexit.

It's calmer at the Oval than at Old Trafford or Headingley; no party crowd stands here. My assigned seat is in the sun all day, so since I get headaches if I sit in direct sunlight for too long, I search for a shady spot to watch the cricket. After negotiating the packed, narrow outside ring around the back of the various stands, I briefly end up in a high corporate balcony with fancy food where I'm under-dressed. I'm feeling subconscious that I shouldn't be here, so I soon leave. Eventually, an undercover seat behind the bowler's arm looks like a suitable spot.

At entrances to various stands are men dressed in an army uniform, including a black military hat. The man near me also has a well-groomed moustache. At the start of every over, he loudly and firmly tells people in a military tone to sit down.

Military stewards at the Oval

I'm confused as I haven't seen these army men at any other sporting events in England, so during a break in play, I ask him why he is here. He kindly tells me that ex-servicemen were given jobs to be ushers at London cricket venues after the Second World War, and this tradition has continued ever since.

As for the cricket, it doesn't take long for the English tail to depart as they play rash shots due to having a nearly 400 run lead. It's the first time in this series I will be watching Australia's openers bat. Their form has been terrible, so it feels inevitable when they both soon depart, especially when Broad gets Warner for the seventh time in this series.

As we approach the lunch break, as long as our two form batsmen Labuschagne and Smith stay together for a while, there is still hope as there are nearly two days of play left.

Steve Smith has scored an incredible number of runs during this series, while Manus Labuschagne has had a breakout series. However, today is my first proper chance to see them bat because other than at the Oval today, most of my time has been watching England bat.

Unfortunately, a few overs before the lunch break, Labuschagne is stumped and not long after lunch Smith is caught at leg slip. So my hopes are now slipping for an unlikely Australian victory as we still need more than 300 runs.

Thankfully, Matthew Wade steadies the ship with a few around 50 run partnerships, but we need them to be 100 run partnerships as we are just losing wickets too often at the other end. Still, Wade brings up his second century of this series, so maybe this match will at least continue tomorrow.

After taking many chances in his innings, Wade is finally stumped, so now it feels inevitable that we will lose tonight. Less than two overs later, the final two wickets fall in consecutive balls.

It's a strange feeling for everyone here because while England has won this match, Australia has retained the Ashes 2-2 due to having won the last series in Australia. It's a damp celebration by the Australian team, and it feels strange that it's all over after more than two months following all the cricket. So I take a moment to sit in the now-empty stands to soak it all in.

Unfortunately, I don't have Dorothy's red slippers to take me home or even a tornado to take me to Oz, so a plane it will have to be. One disadvantage with flying with a bicycle is finding a bicycle box and then working out how to get to the airport with my bicycle and the box. Ideally, a bicycle box at the airport is the best way, but Qantas say they don't have any available at check-in. I also haven't found any information if they are available anywhere at Heathrow Airport, so on my one free day in London I will have to find one.

Firstly I will see how easy it is to get from Brixton to Paddington Station by the Tube, with the idea being to pack my bicycle at Hannah and Greg's place into a cardboard bicycle box I'm yet to find. Then take it by using the Tube to Paddington Station, where direct larger trains depart to Heathrow.

Along the way to Brixton Tube Station, I stop in at a bicycle shop. They will be able to give me a box.

From Brixton, there isn't a direct tube to Paddington, so I will have to change trains, requiring me to drag the box through narrow busy walkways. After a dry run, it looks too hard with a bicycle in a box, so I need a better idea. I could try to tie the box onto my bicycle and cycle to Paddington, or I could use an Uber to Paddington or all the way to Heathrow, but that is expensive. I will keep thinking and see if there are any bicycle shops near Paddington.

After walking to Paddington via Westminster, Buckingham Palace and Hyde Park, I have found a nearby bicycle shop. They have a box I can reserved for tomorrow.

At the large Paddington Station with its prominent roof, there are a couple of dedicated areas full of bicycle racks on two platforms, with plenty of bicycles locked here.

I now have a plan. Which will involve cycling to Paddington in the morning, locking my bicycle up at the station, before walking fifteen minutes to Evans Cycles to collect the box and then walking back to Paddington.

It's a cold and overcast day, so I will now have a little explore. In 2013 I spent a few days here, especially around the Thames, visiting a few tourist hotspots like the Tower of London and Westminster Abbey, so today is about seeing other places.

After seeing the plain-looking Buckingham Palace again, I stumble on the Wellington Arch, which is only one of a handful of English Heritage sites in London. The English Heritage card has been a valuable purchase as it has saved me a lot of money. As the arch's name suggests, it's related to the Duke of Wellington and Waterloo, with some information on that period inside, along with a nice view from the top of a procession of royal guards marching from Buckingham Palace.

I have been reading an ebook about the development of the Tube, so I end up spending some time just riding the tube and looking at a few of the older scenic stations.

London has many well-used wide cycle lanes, while cyclists can use bus lanes if there isn't a cycle lane. So it's an easy ride past the Oval, through a short cycle tunnel, across the Thames and through Hyde Park to Paddington Station. My bicycle box plan works fine with the help of a double-decker red bus to save time. I'm so efficient that I have to wait ten minutes for the bicycle shop to open.

A short bike tunnel near the Thames, while there are plenty of bicycles at Paddington

There are two train services from Paddington to Heathrow, an express service taking fifteen minutes or a regular service taking 28 minutes. With the regular service £25 cheaper and less busy, there should be more room for my bicycle and the box. It's an empty train, so it's an easy ride to the airport.

My flight home from London will be a direct flight to Perth, Western Australia. This is one of the longest flights in the world but avoids any wasted time changing planes, and there is less opportunity for my baggage to get lost.

I have now got the method for packing my bicycle to a quick process, even if I have to take both wheels off to fit it in this box. I have learned my lesson from Madrid, so this time all my gear is in with my bicycle box, except for a pannier bag I'm taking as carry on. I'm well underweight; I must have lost a few things or sent them home. Let's hope my luggage makes it to Perth.

While taking apart my bicycle, a few male Australian cricketers show up, with a lot more luggage than me. I end up chatting to a few, including Travis Head and his girlfriend Jessica, who are particularly pleasant to chat to and actually show an interest in my ride while we wait to board. However, we take a different route once on the plane as they are in business class and I'm in economy.

Indian Ocean Drive

My sixteen-hour flight from London to Perth was fine, as it's only a couple of hours more than flying Melbourne to Los Angeles, a flight I have done a few times. I particularly like not having to change planes in Dubai, allowing me more time to try to sleep.

I could stay on this plane and continue onto Melbourne, but since it costs the same if I have a layover in Perth, I decided when booking my flights way back in March to spend two weeks cycling a small part of Western Australia. A longer time would be nice, but I need to be home by the start of October. I'm curious to see if I enjoy a two-week cycling trip with flying at both ends. Who knows, maybe one day I will get a full-time job and only have a small amount of time to go cycling, so this is a good rehearsal.

The last time I cycled in Western Australia, I went to the southwest of Perth, so this time, I will head north to Kalbarri via the coastal route before looping back to Perth following an inland railway line.

Two weeks ago, I contacted a few potential Warmshower hosts close to the airport with the idea to stay one night and also to leave a few items I don't need for the two weeks, like my bicycle box. Jane got back to me saying she couldn't host me, but she could pick me up from the airport and look after my bicycle box, which I'm grateful for.

Jane is an older lady, and as we chat for the short drive from the airport, I'm seeing a few familiar shops. However, since this is only my third visit to Perth, it's not quite home.

It takes me about an hour to reassemble my bicycle and decide which items to leave behind. Some items are obvious, like my passport or my UK USB charging plug, while I weigh up if I will need all my cold clothes as I'm expecting it will be warmer in Western Australia than it was in the UK.

Once I knew no one could host me near the airport, I searched for Warmshower hosts near a railway station, preferably in the north-western suburbs of Perth. Luke was kind enough to get back to me.

As I leave Jane's home, I'm feeling jet-lagged, so it's an easy choice to catch a train nearby to the city centre to do some errands. After remembering that I need to purchase an Australian USB plug, I take another train to Glendalough, where Luke has left his home unlocked for me because he isn't going to be home for a few hours. I try to stay awake as long as possible to combat jet lag, but I'm asleep before Luke arrives home.

After somehow managing to sleep right through the night, I finally meet Luke in the morning but he has to soon leave for work. However, he is kind enough to allow me to stay as long as I need today. A few storms are around, so I have considered waiting a while as I'm still tired, but since I only have two weeks before I fly home, I will start cycling.

After catching a suburban train as far north as I can, I begin heading north from Butler towards Yanchep as suburban Perth sort of ends. However, as I pass a few housing estates being advertised as opening soon, suburbia is slowly spreading further north, while there is evidence that the railway line will be extended to Yanchep one day.

Because of a slight headwind on the way north to Yanchep, as soon as I find a road heading east, I take it. I could have stayed closer to the coast longer by going through Yanchep and visiting the smaller town of Two Rocks. However, going inland now, will allow me to visit Yanchep National Park, beside the Indian Ocean Drive, which will be my road for a few days as I head north.

Because I'm on a bicycle, the woman at the entrance gate allows me to enter this park for free. I soon find a small area with a few buildings beside a lake, including a visitor centre. There are several caves I could be guided through, but I'm not feeling like visiting them today. Instead, after lunch, I cycle a short vehicle loop drive through a dry eucalyptus forest before taking a road north out of the national park. Signs say it's a no-through road, but there is just a single metal pole gate for me to duck under as I join the Indian Ocean Drive.

For the rest of the afternoon, this undulating road is away from the coastline with a few gentle climbs but nothing serious. It has a decent road shoulder most of the time, and the traffic is consistent but quiet as the heavier traffic takes the more inland Brand Highway.

A mixed weather day

The Indian Ocean Drive only became a through road in the last decade and is more for holiday traffic heading to a few beachside towns, located just off this road. It's the Western Australian equivalent of the Great Ocean Road, but thankfully not as busy or hilly.

Towns are more spread out than what I'm used to in the UK, so when I actually make a town, it feels special, but I do have to consider what grocery options, if any, are available in each town.

By the end of the day, I'm near the town of Lancelin, but it's a one-way downhill road eight kilometres off the Indian Ocean Drive. Still, with a supermarket, it's worth heading to. It's windy and cold as I look around town, so as I spot a quiet hostel, I will see what they have available.

As I talk to the lovely lady there, she offers a room just for me, which will allow me to get a decent night sleep as I'm still feeling jet-lagged.

While cooking dinner, I watch some Australian TV which feels strange but familiar after six months away. On the news, they are talking about the returning cricketers, which other hostel guests talk about like it was a faraway minor event. All I can think of is that I was at the cricket in London four days ago, and now I'm as nearly as far as I can be from there.

It's spring, so flowers are blooming

Once I climb back up to the Indian Ocean Drive in the morning, it's similar cycling as yesterday, except that it's a beautiful sunny day. At one stage, the road is closer to the sea with some excellent blue views. I'm also seeing plenty of colourful plants flowering as it's Spring here.

At one roadside rest stop, spread out in front of me, is a sea of grass trees; these strange-looking plants have a short, dark, palm tree-like trunk with thin green spiky hair on top, while the male tree has a lengthy appendix sticking up high.

As a large bus with Japanese tourists pulls up, I briefly chat with the local bus driver about where I'm cycling, which he is impressed by.

A sea of grass-trees

One of the reasons for cycling this route is visiting the Pinnacles, a set of outstanding natural features located inland off the main road on a paved road. As I arrive at the visitor centre, the lady at the entrance gate is concerned about me cycling here, so she asks me to tell them when I'm leaving. It's strange to have people be surprised I'm cycling here when in Europe they are so used to cyclists touring around. There are plenty of tourist buses stopped here and a small souvenir shop with ice creams.

So many individual natural features to see as a tracks go around the Pinnacles

Away from the car park, a yellow sandy track goes around numerous natural formations in different shapes and sizes, with the majority being tall and skinny. My bicycle is slipping a few times as I cycle alongside four-wheel drive cars, but I'm still able to cycle for the most part. A mountain bike would be easier, but it's still a great way to see numerous formations. If I wanted to, I could touch them, unlike Stonehenge.

It's strange to think eight days ago, I was looking at Stonehenge, which is regarded as old in the UK, while these features are presumably older.

A couple of hours cycle north is Jurien Bay, the largest town on the Indian Ocean Drive. This time the road actually goes through town, while it's also beside the ocean. It has a decent-sized supermarket and a few hardware stores, cafés, and even a small art gallery with reflective artwork. The visitor info centre has information on campgrounds further north, but instead, I will wild camp behind the local oval.

So far, it has been strange being back in Australia; overall, it feels quieter and more relaxed. Certain things are different, including the noisier birds and the colourful flowering plants. The most significant change has been the longer distances between towns, which means I have to plan more.

With sunset at 6 pm, I have to finish my ride earlier in the day and keep an eye on supermarket closing times, which are much earlier than in the UK. However, I'm enjoying how much easier it is to find water, power and free barbecues in local parks, which allowed me one night to cook some chicken schnitzels.

Free BBQ's are often available in parks

In the morning, after visiting the small town of Green Head with an okay bay to look around, and then Leeman, I know there aren't any towns for the next 90 kilometres. There are a few bush campgrounds along the way beside the ocean, but they are actually not that far from Leeman, so I'm aiming instead to make Port Denison tonight. I have enough supplies to stop along the way if needed, but water could be an issue as it's a semi-warm day, and I doubt there is anywhere to fill up past Leeman.

I'm much closer to the ocean today, so nearly all the time, the sea is visible on my left in an open treeless landscape. While it's a nice view, the road starts to feel repetitive after a while, especially as there are only a few rest stops to break up the afternoon.

The road is beside the coast for 50kms

After 50 kilometres, the Indian Ocean Drive leaves the ocean behind and begins heading inland to join Highway 1, which presumably will have more traffic. As I cross the closed Eneabba railway line, there is a track beside it. With this rail line having gone all the way to Port Denison, I'm assuming this track will allow me to avoid the highway, so I will join it.

A sandy track beside this closed rail line

However, it soon becomes too sandy in places to cycle, so I'm constantly having to walk my bicycle past yellow flowering trees. I should turn around, but every so often, it looks like the track is improving, so I will keep going. When a better-surfaced side-track becomes available, it's an easy decision to take it to the highway.

While it's a lot easier cycling on the highway, the number of semi-trucks and traffic overall means I have to be vigilant all the time. So it's a relief once I can turn off this highway.

Daylight nearly beats me as I arrive into Port Denison, where thankfully, a café is still open to get a cool drink.

After cooking dinner in a park beside the sea, I'm not sure where to sleep as the oval is in the centre of town. After looking at online maps, I spot a golf course on the edge of town.

It's pitch black as I approach the silent golf clubhouse at the end of a road. It's now 10 pm, so this will do for tonight. I could camp right at the clubhouse, but with enough bushland up a hill for me to camp well out of sight, it's probably the more respectful thing to do. I also have no idea if anyone will be playing golf early tomorrow morning.

Between Port Denison and Walkaway, there is only one road, the busy number 1 highway. There are a few small roads beside paddocks, but none that provide a sensible through route.

After briefly cycling on the highway, it's too busy for me, so I try finding a route using secondary dirt roads. They are slower, but are more relaxing. I don't know how people spend months just cycling highways all the time, especially when undertaking the loop around Australia.

A better track beside this rail line

At one stage, I end up in someone's paddock before meeting an active railway line with a faint track beside it to follow. Some sections of this skinny track are covered in grass, but for the most part, it's easier cycling than when I was beside the railway line yesterday. Signs say I probably shouldn't be here, but I'm comfortable with my decision since it avoids the highway. Anyway, with no one around, I should go unnoticed.

Just before Walkaway, I'm able to join a proper paved road to take me into this small town. As the Welcome to Walkaway sign appears, something hard hits the side of my helmet.

As I recover from the shock of being hit, I realise it's a swooping magpie. For anyone not from Australia, during Spring, when Australian magpies are in mating season, they become aggressive about their territory and will viciously swoop people, particularly cyclists. It's just annoying for most people, but they have been known to cause harm to people, particularly their eyes. Some people try putting eyes or cable ties on the back of their helmet, which sometimes works but often doesn't. I find shaking my water bottle in the air often dissuades them. Looking directly at them is the best thing to do. However, sometimes they swoop in pairs, so while you're looking at one, another will come from a different direction.

Along with not missing magpies, I also haven't missed the blowflies. I'm not noticing them when it's been windy, but they have been annoying when the wind dies down. Having been overseas for a while, I can appreciate why overseas visitors struggle with Australian wildlife and the distances between towns.

Today Walkaway is a small quiet town, with a disused cream railway station on an active rail line. A small museum is inside this station, while a train is displayed nearby in a shed.

A private railway company used to run trains from Perth to here to meet the government railway line to Geraldton, so this was an important

Walkaway Railway Station

railway station back in the day. This is a rare example of a private railway company in Australia, which built its own rail line and survived for decades. Most other private lines in Australia in that era went bankrupt while being built and were taken over by their state government. It wasn't until the 1960s, that the government took over this rail line, so today, trains don't have to stop here anymore.

From Walkaway, a secondary paved road follows the railway line to the suburbs of Geraldton, the only city north of Perth. Along the way, I have to be aware of more swooping magpies on the ride in, but thankfully a solid southerly wind helps push me along.

So far on my coastal ride north, the wind has been consistent each day, with mornings usually an easterly sideway wind, while around lunchtime, the wind dies down before strong southerly tailwinds begin in the afternoon. So it has been enjoyable, except when having to occasionally turn south. However, the windy evenings have been quite cool; it has felt colder than it was in the last few days in the UK.

Hopefully, when I begin my return to Perth after Kalbarri, there will be fewer southerly winds inland.

I have a Warmshower in the southern suburbs of Geraldton, which with a strong southerly wind, is a challenging headwind ride to my hosts, as I'm constantly nearly being blown off my bicycle.

Barbara and Tim make me feel welcome, and they share with me route advice. In particular, they recommend going via the Chapman Valley on my way to Kalbarri. Tim also suggests avoiding the Great Northern Highway on my way back south because of the large semi-trailers heading to the mines in the north of Western Australia.

After following the railway line around a headland using a route that only bicycles can get through, I pass a small lighthouse before the rail line ends at an active port. On the other side of the port is a rehabilitated public park beside the beach. Helpfully Geraldton's Visitor Centre is beside the park, allowing me to learn more about the Chapman Valley and of a daily free guided tour at 10:30 am at the Sydney Memorial.

Also near the park is a bicycle shop; it's probably the only one I will see until I'm back in Perth, so I will check my bicycle for any issues that need repair.

With a couple of small holes, my rear tyre is starting to look like it needs to be replaced soon. It should last the final ten days of this trip, but it's probably safer to change the tyre now, just in case it fails in the middle of nowhere.

During the Second World War, the Australian warship HMAS Sydney was off the coast not far from here when it disappeared without a trace, with all 645 lives lost. It had been in battle with the German ship the Kormoran, whose crew mostly survived in lifeboats and were eventually captured. For decades what happened to the Sydney was a mystery. Every so often it was featured on news programs with people searching for it, until both ships were found at the bottom of the ocean in 2008.

Sydney Memorial

The Sydney Memorial was built on a hill overlooking the ocean before the shipwreck was found. The top half-sphere memorial is made out of numerous metal seagulls, with each one representing a sailor lost. Since they found the wreck, they have added an addition to the memorial to show where it was found.

Nearby is a sizeable closed railway station with no rails anymore, instead, buses depart from here. It was one of three former railway stations in Geraldton. With no passenger services here since 1974, the freight-only rail line now bypasses the town by heading to the port directly.

Across the road is the large free maritime museum with a guided tour at 11:30 am on various objects found from various Dutch shipwrecks. The Dutch used to sail from Cape Town to modern-day Indonesia using the Roaring Forties, but they didn't know precisely when to turn north, so a few ships hit the side of Western Australia.

There is also a twelve-minute video showing the Sydney wreck at the bottom of the ocean, along with plenty of information on Geraldton's history, particularly indigenous.

By the time I'm ready to leave Geraldton, it's a warm day as I briefly follow both the ocean and the formation of a railway line that used to head north to both Northampton and Yuna.

Once I leave the ocean and the suburbs of Geraldton, I'm beginning to gradually climb into the Chapman Valley.

About to enter Chapman Valley

Eventually, the road flattens out as I meet the Chapman River and soon, the remains of the former railway line to Yuna is beside the road. Just before Nanson is the remains of a falling-down wooden rail bridge, while at the former Nanson Railway Station, there is still a weighbridge, with an information panel explaining how this station helped develop the European settlement of this area and how the line operated. Nearby is a local museum, but it isn't open today.

Remains of a rail bridge

Further on, the small town of Nabawa has a primary school, a sports oval and a drinking water fountain but all the shops are long closed. From here, I will leave the former railway route to head to Northampton via a quiet road with small gentle climbs. I'm hoping to get there before the supermarket closes.

Northampton is a bigger town than I expected as I make it just before the supermarket closes.

At the former creamy stone Northampton Railway Station, a few rail items, including a couple of carriages and a train, are on display around this complex which last saw a train in 1957.

Near the preserved Northampton Railway Station is a short rail trail

Just south of this former station, a short, less than a kilometre long section of the former rail right of way is now a decent rail trail. Beside the trail are some bus type shelters with brief information on the rail line's history. At the end of the rail trail, the continuing former rail formation back to Geraldton is fenced off and overgrown.

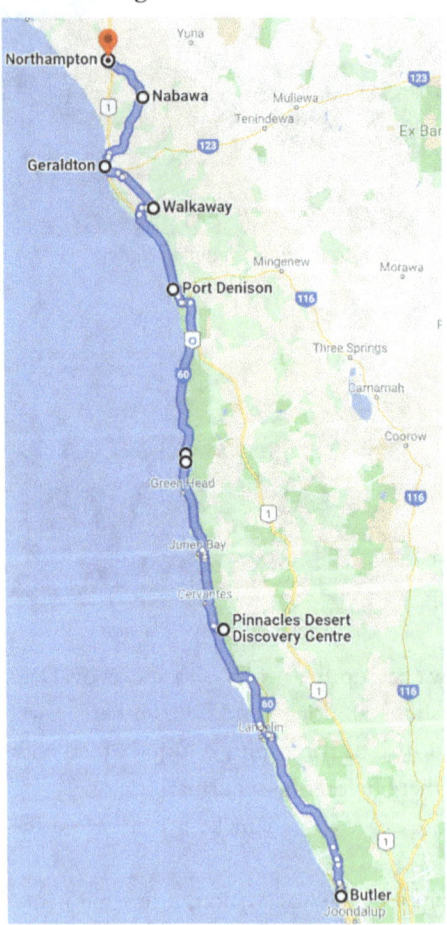

Northampton is on the number one highway and has plenty of services, but the caravan park is closed, and anyway, it's near the highway. Instead, I will head to the oval, on the edge of town.

It's quiet at the oval, and with a scoreboard box open, I will take the opportunity to sleep inside it on my Thermarest mattress, rather than set up my tent.

Butler to Northampton (Google Maps)

Kalbarri

There aren't any towns on the 100-kilometre long direct road to Kalbarri, which is further between towns than I prefer. Still, the scenery is okay, and the traffic is quiet. However, to break up the day, not long after leaving Northampton, I take a slightly longer loop route by heading to Horrocks. As I approach the sea, the only road into Horrocks involves a steep descent.

R U OK awareness tree, on the way to Horrocks

It wasn't really worth the detour as it's just a quiet beachside town with a small general store and I'm still about 90 kilometres from Kalbarri. I soon begin the steep climb back up again.

After re-joining the quiet main road, I'm soon at the remains of a convict hut. Over a small area, there is some information on a failed convict settlement. From here, a sandy track takes me past a farmhouse, where caravaners are staying, while inside a farm shed is some regional historical information.

As the farm track meets the main road, I'm now cycling alongside a pink salt lake for about ten kilometres. With some heavy digging machinery on the water, it looks like salt is collected from the lake. However, with many shrubs in the way, I can't find an access point.

Salt caused trees to fall over and makes lakes pink

Late in the day, as I approach Kalbarri, there are a few lookouts, but I will keep going because I just want to get to town. I'm particularly tired as the wind hasn't been as kind today. It felt like every time I change direction, the wind would as well, usually not in my favour. So I'm glad to finally make it to a larger town than I expected.

Shipwreck memorial at mouth of the Murchison River in Kalbarri

There are plenty of holiday homes here, caravan parks, restaurants, pubs, a supermarket and one backpackers. The backpackers appears to be my best bet for the next two nights.

One disadvantage of using a bicycle for travel is one-way roads, where having to cycle a road twice can make taking that route less advantageous. From the town of Kalbarri, the principal places of interest in the national park of the same name are 35 kilometres away with the majority being a one-way road. In addition, it's twelve kilometres between the two main points of interest, Nature's Window and Z Loop.

Therefore, with Joe's help at the backpackers, I have organised a ride into the park with the local abseil guides Col and Bec in their empty bus.

Just before the park gate, they tell me to get off the bus and cycle in through the gate before I re-board the bus. Apparently, cyclists don't have to pay fees to enter Western Australian National Parks, but bus passengers do.

I'm dropped off at Z Bend carpark, nearby is a lookout of the Z-shape bend the deep Murchison River makes here.

It's less than a two-kilometre easy walk down to the river, with plenty of shade and a couple of short ladders to negotiate through small gaps in the rocks. Besides passing the abseil group, it's quiet down by the river, where the pools of water are only ankle-high among the numerous rocks, allowing a view of many layers in the red rocks.

Z Bend lookout

Not much water in the river, allowing a colourful view of the layers of rock

Nature's Window

In contrast, Nature's Window is less shaded, busier with tourists, and has a nine-kilometre loop walk around the inner part of a long horseshoe bend in the Murchison River that is nearly cutting back on itself. In the high area in between where the Murchison nearly loops back on itself is the natural feature known as Nature's Window. It's a hole in a prominent rock feature that frames the scenery below in the deep Murchison River.

The Murchison River from Nature's Window

Most visitors appear to stop here, so I'm unsure if I should do the loop walk as it feels warm even at 10 am. After seeing and talking to other walkers, I will go.

Initially, the walk is high above the deep river, which has been worn away. Once I descend to the river, a family of four with two pre-teens are here, along with numerous black swans enjoying the river. From here, the signed trail follows the edge of a small cliff, with parts of the path narrow and scenic as I rock scramble for a short section.

As the gorge widens again, for a few kilometres I'm on a more defined path. Besides the warm weather, it's an easy walk until the trail becomes sandy near the end, so it's a slow slog back to Nature's Window.

A narrow path to negotiate beside Murchison River

Colourful plants

While eating lunch in the shade back at the car park, a Park Ranger mentions how the number of tourists in this national park has increased since the roads were paved only in the last two years. Across the river valley, we can see that a new lookout and kiosk is being built to accommodate the increase in visitors.

For my ride back to Kalbarri, clouds have appeared, so it's a bit cooler, but a slight headwind makes it less relaxing than I hoped. Still, the sea of numerous low shrubs in flower on both sides of the road is a pleasant distraction.

Once I'm back on the main road, there is a small climb to negotiate on my way back into Kalbarri, which I know I will have to cycle in reverse tomorrow.

Leaving Kalbarri could be a long day of cycling as I'm on the same road with no towns until Binnu, 80 kilometres away. Even then, I'm unsure if a grocery store is there, and after that, there won't be a town for even longer. So I have plenty of food from Kalbarri, just in case.

After climbing away from Kalbarri, the road is flat and open, with the only tall trees being pines. Other than a few trucks, the traffic is fine, while a sidewind is annoying but not particularly tiring. The larger challenge is that I'm not changing direction for 60 kilometres, so it's becoming repetitive and slow. A few podcasts are helping distract me, but even then, it's challenging to motivate myself after a while.

After about 40 kilometres, there is a short one-way road to a couple of lookouts over the Murchison River, but it's not a better view than yesterday. A few caravaners along with plenty of flies are here, so I don't hang around for long.

As I approach within five kilometres of the number 1 highway, the remains of the town of Ajana appear. This is where the railway line from Northampton terminated until the whole line was closed in 1957.

Today I can just make out where the railway line went. There isn't much of the town left either, just a few houses and a shed on an old platform, where I have lunch while trying to keep the flies away.

South of Ajana, a dirt road follows the railway route to Binnu, so I will take this route rather than the nearby highway.

Not much left of the town of Ajana or the railway formation

Other than regularly having to zigzag to find a smooth surface to get some grip, it's a quiet ride.

Along the way, some wooden signs inform me of the leftover railway infrastructure, including an old railway high-tank and a large in-ground dam with a tin roof. Most of the tin roof is still in place, and it has water in it, which a few ducks are enjoying. It's incredible to see it still exists since the railway line closed more than 60 years ago.

Ajana's railway dam is still in reasonable condition

North of Binnu, the number 1 highway is the only road, so it has plenty of semi-trailer trucks, while towns are even more spread out. From what I have read of other cyclists, it becomes all about cycling as far as you can each day due to the lack of supplies. So I have no desire to cycle this highway, and I'm glad I only briefly have to touch this highway as I head inland.

As for Binnu, there is still a large grain complex where the railway line went through, a tennis court and a small general store, allowing me to buy a cool drink and an ice cream. I need this refreshment break because from here, there isn't a town for 70 kilometres until Yuna, and even then, I'm unsure if there are any facilities there. This isn't an unusual distance in Australia between towns; I'm just thankful each town has had drinking water as it has been warm.

Initially, as I head east, it's okay cycling as it reminds me of being back home with cereal crops, eucalyptus trees, flies, a few utes and relatively flat roads. As I turn in a southerly direction, it's about 3:30 pm, and I'm about two hours ride

Most of the afternoon was like this

from Yuna, so using these flat paved roads I should make it comfortably before sunset.

However, it doesn't take me long to realise I'm now cycling into a strong headwind. While it isn't blowing me off the road, it just makes it a harder, exhausting ride. I have tried cycling on both sides of this quiet road to see if roadside trees offer any protection from the wind, but it doesn't seem to make any difference. It's a dry wind, so every so often, I have to stop just to get out of the wind as it's drying out my face.

There are a couple of side roads, but they are corrugated gravel, so they would be an even slower ride. The only traffic is heading the other way, so there is no opportunity to get a ride out of the wind.

This 34-kilometre section takes me an hour longer than expected, so I'm still cycling during dusk when I can finally change direction. Without the headwind, the final five kilometres following the remains of the Yuna railway line to its terminus is a pleasant semi-dark evening ride.

Yuna has grain silos and a few houses, but all shops have clearly been closed for years. Still it's a place advertised on the CamperMate app as a place to camp.

Thankfully, there is a community centre with tennis courts, which has all I need, including water, picnic tables, power points and lights that I can turn off. After a relaxing evening I set my tent up on the soft surface of a small playground.

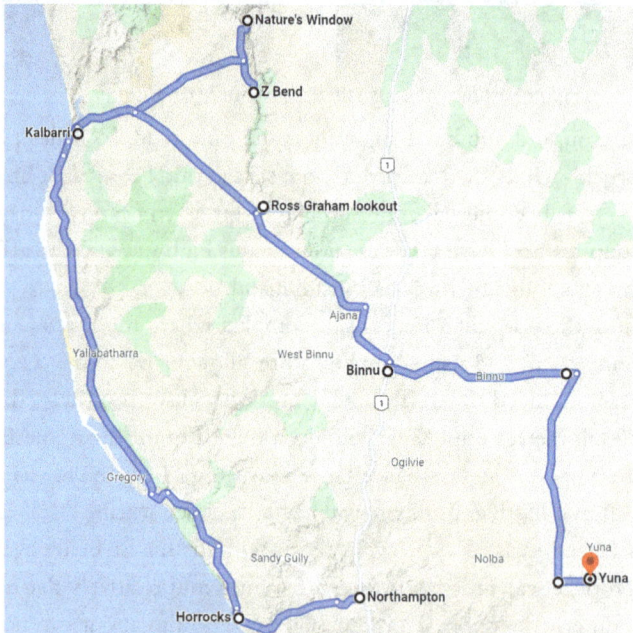

Northampton to Yuna (Google Maps)

Wildflower Country

Camping at Yuna community centre

I sleep so well that I awake to find about half a dozen women doing an exercise class at the tennis courts. They don't appear to care that I slept here, and a few children are interested in my tent. After a relaxing night, I'm more than happy to contribute to the camping donation box.

My Friday morning is a zigzag route on quiet roads past farms affected by salinity, including some with salt lakes. Half the time, I'm cycling into a headwind and other times sidewinds. The only good thing about the headwind is it keeps the flies away, as otherwise, they are vicious when I stop.

A curvy, windy morning ride

Eventually, as I meet a main road and a railway line, there is one abandoned building here with a red mailbox still out the front. It used to be Tenindewa General Store, but apparently is still occasionally used by the community. The only other things left of this town is the remains of the railway siding which established this town in the 1920s and a small section of a former rail bridge on display.

Old Tenindewa General Store

The ride to Mullewa is on the busy main road with mine trucks heading between Geraldton and a few inland mines, while a few mining trains pass me. So after an hour, once the town of Mullewa appears, I'm relieved to get off this road.

The few basic shops in town are expensive, including a small supermarket. While in a small visitor information centre I'm informed that this region is promoted as *Wildflower Country* because of the colourful flowering plants that appear particularly this time of year. However, Mullewa itself feels like it's a town people pass through while heading further out east to the outback, rather than stop to spend time in. I won't be heading any further out from here; instead, I will be making my way south back to Perth following a railway line.

The long yellow wooden Mullewa Railway Station with its pointy red roof is still standing, but it hasn't seen passengers since 1974. Judging by the platform remains on either side of the building, it was once an island station for the branch line out east to Wiluna 700 kilometres away. A short walk around the remains of a few railway infrastructure items like a high water tank shows how busy it must have been.

Mural near the Mullewa Railway Station

Indigenous artwork on the police station

Mullewa has a significant indigenous population, so there is some information on the Yamatji people around town, including a couple of outside gathering places. As well there are many colourful animal-based indigenous artworks around town, notably on the police station and at the skate park.

As I cook dinner in the town's park, I'm asked numerous questions by local indigenous children about my cycling tour.

There is a caravan park, but it doesn't look that inviting, so instead, I set my tent up in the sheep-yards in the showgrounds. Throughout the night, a few mining trains can be heard going past nearby.

As I begin leaving town in the morning, I visit a different looking church that reminds me of similar ones I saw in Russia because it has a few different styles of towers sticking up from this building.

As I approach the church, out of nowhere, I'm attacked by a dog from a nearby house. He actually grabs a bag strap which half pulls a pannier bag off.

A different style of church in Mullewa

Thankfully, its owner comes out behind their big fence and calls the dog back. I don't understand why anyone would want a vicious dog like that.

As I begin heading south I'm following a railway line, mostly on a quiet, paved flat road, except for a section where I have to take a secondary road to keep following the railway. It's a red gravel road, but it can still be comfortably cycled.

The railway is in great condition, and in places, it has clearly been re-laid as the new line is next to sections of the older line. Just before the town of Morawa, a railway line branches off to head to an iron ore mine.

A new rail line built beside the old one, while roads are fine beside the rail line

Throughout the day, I'm passing various colourful plants in flower, along with enjoying hearing and seeing a variety of birds, particularly flocks of red-tailed black cockatoos calling and flying over me.

As part of this wildflower route, every so often, are metal statues representing various aspects of

Wildflowers on the Wildflower Country Route

life in this region, along with information panels that focus on the European settlement. Many have a farming focus, often showing jobs or equipment that no longer exist, like using horses or old farming machinery.

Sculptures along this route

Lunchtime under she-oaks

Some talk about the impact of European settlement on the indigenous population and the impact of land clearing on native wildlife.

All that is left of most towns I'm passing through are just a few houses and run-down town halls that have seen better days. By lunchtime, I'm in the middle of nowhere, so I end up making a sandwich under a she-oak tree while trying to wave away numerous flies.

Compared to other towns, Morawa feels like a metropolis with many houses and operating businesses, while the area around the former railway station in the centre of town is now a scenic public park. However, it's noticeably quiet this Saturday afternoon, with nothing open except for the bowls club.

So I end up bowling a few ends while chatting to a few locals. Steve, the club captain, says he has visited Woomelang, a town near my home, and he knows people from there. Once again, it's a small world.

There is a busy caravan park in town, but with no one around the oval on the edge of town, I will camp there instead. Along with providing a space to camp, sports grounds have been the easiest place to find water and power.

The IGA supermarket is open on Sunday mornings and is my first proper supermarket since Kalbarri. With the Queen's birthday public holiday tomorrow, I'm unsure about supermarket opening times further along, so I will be carrying food for a couple of days. Regarding what food I'm carrying, it's basically a few tins of meat along with pasta, wraps and some fruit.

Numerous windmills in Morawa Museum

The Morawa museum is open for a special weekend display. It's similar to other agricultural museums with various farming machinery alongside local information about local schools, sporting clubs, etc. The main display is an extensive collection of windmill heads with various blades.

There is also a story about how a local person in the 1930s blew up the railway station to hurt Italian migrants camped there. Fortunately, no one died, but people were injured.

For the rest of Sunday, I'm cycling through a few towns, each becoming smaller in size the further south I go. It's sad to see these towns with so many closed shops and abandoned sporting facilities in some cases. It sadly reminds me of similar situations around home. Thankfully, I'm still able to find water on this warm day.

Still, the wildflower tourist route is well marked, and many towns have information panels explaining how these once-thriving towns used to be. All were railway towns when it came through in 1913.

I'm also informed that I'm now in Mallee Fowl territory, a bird I know from home which makes large ground nests in the eucalyptus Mallee landscape.

Along with some towns having various artwork, often on display are old vehicles, mainly farming. Other than a few silos beside the railway line, there isn't much left of the town of Maya, except a steel World War Two Tank that was converted for farm work.

Artwork in Perenjori, while a tank was used by a farmer

I'm not sure why but the railway line between Northam and Mullewa has been split in two due to a 50-kilometre section roughly halfway between the two being abandoned. So all northern traffic goes to the port of Geraldton, which is mainly from a couple of mines, while the less busy southern section mainly carries grain traffic to Perth.

This is really evident in the small town of Buntine, where the railway line is clearly abandoned despite a large silo complex being here. This town feels desolate with a sadly closed bowling green with a

Rail line is closed for 50km

falling apart clubhouse, and from what I can tell, the primary school is also closed, but the buildings are in better condition, and the power is still on. There are remains of a cricket net out the back of the school for me to camp on.

After two days of quiet cycling, as I approach the next town of Wubin, the traffic suddenly increases because this is where my road joins the Great Northern Highway, so there are a few roadhouses and plenty of semi-trailer trucks.

Wubin wheat museum

With the railway line still closed, there is a wheat museum in the former railway complex, and the visitor information centre is in the previous cement block railway station. However, it's too early in the day for either to be open, while I'm unsure if either will be open at all today as it's a public holiday.

My Warmshower hosts in Geraldton, Tim and Barbara, had been concerned about me cycling a 30-kilometre section of the Great Northern Highway south of Wubin because this is the main road between Perth and Port Headland in the north of Western Australia, where there are many large mines.

This highway does have a few road trains, but it's still quieter than many roads I have cycled elsewhere in the world, and there is a decent road shoulder. However, it's still busier than the previous few days. Helpfully there are a few reasonably-sized towns to break up the highway. Along the way, at a locality with nothing but a few grain silos, the rail line suddenly is open again.

Thankfully once I'm off the Great Northern Highway, it quietens down again, with more white salt lakes to admire than trucks to worry about.

One of a few salt lakes on the way to Ballidu

As I approach the town of Ballidu, there are a few painted rusty old bicycles beside the road, while on the way into town off the main road, there are sculptures with either a bicycle or emu theme. I soon learn that there is a bicycle ride every year in March from Wongan Hills to Ballidu, so that is why a few old bicycles are on top of the pub.

Bicycles and emus sculptures on display around Ballidu

I have made decent time to Wongan Hills, so the supermarket is still open.

Since I haven't had the chance to do laundry since Geraldton, I will take the opportunity to stay at the caravan park for $10. It has a decent camp kitchen, and a few caravanners are staying here. However, the downside is the lights at night, which is why I usually avoid caravan parks. After looking around, I have found a dark spot between cabins to set my tent up.

Ballidu Pub

After admiring the well looked after former Wongan Hills Railway Station in the morning, my ride to Goomalling is unremarkable. However, despite it looking on maps as a quiet road, my afternoon ride to Northam is busy with semi-trucks every so often.

Artwork in Goomalling, including reference to a water pipe

I have been to Northam once before, and it feels like a city compared to my previous week with significant supermarkets, a few fast-food franchisers and all services, allowing me a choice of food and the ability to relax in the evening. Once it's dark enough, I set my tent up in an open sports ground beside the Avon River on the edge of town.

Northam is a railway junction town and is on the railway route to the east coast of Australia. However, the original railway route from suburban Perth to Northam was bypassed in 1966 when the standard gauge came through and went a different route using the Avon River Gorge. This changed where railway lines went through Northam, so the old railway station is now disused and not on a current railway route. This sizeable red-bricked station is a rail museum, but it's not open today. I can still walk around the back to see a few rusting trains and the remains of the platform.

Old Northam Railway Station

A railway line still heads south of Northam, so I follow it out of town along with the Avon River before the road, and the railway line both cross the Avon in a westerly direction. The small town of Spencer Brook is in front of me, while the railway line turns left and continues heading south away from Spencer Brook.

Up until 1966, Spencer Brook was a busy railway junction town, with all trains from the east having to cross here. Today I have to look closely to see any remains of railway infrastructure. I can just make out some embankments in a paddock which would have been in the middle of the railway junction; otherwise, it's hard to see anything.

From here, the road and former railway line follow each other. At times, there appears to be a rough track where the railway formation was, but it doesn't last long, so it's easier to stay on this quiet paved road. Not sure why a rail trail hasn't been developed in this section.

Eventually, I can hear traffic and soon, I'm at Clackline, where there is a small park rest stop but not much else. The busy Great Eastern Highway is in front of me, but I can take a track under the highway. Once I'm on the other side of the highway, I'm suddenly on a rail trail with the remains of a couple of platforms while the trail is sandy, especially at the start.

Start of the rail trail at Clackline Junction

The Goldfields Water Supply Pipeline still supplies water to towns between here and Kalgoorlie, more than 500 kilometres away. For the most part, it follows the original rail route all the way to Kalgoorlie. So along with information panels on the railway line, there is information on the history of this water pipeline.

At times I can see that this railway line was double-track, but the rail trail has only been developed wide enough for one train, especially on the bridges. I'm also passing through a few rail cuttings while enjoying seeing the numerous colourful plants in flower, particularly a variety of blue.

Railway was double track

Flowers blooming on the trail

However, I'm not enjoying the swooping magpies, with one particularly vicious.

Closer to Perth, the original rail route was found to be too steep soon after completion, so it was bypassed by using a route nearby in the 1890s, but they still kept the first route as a local rail option for a while. Both former lines make an all rail trail loop, which I rode previously in 2013.

As I meet the loop, the surface improves noticeably, and it's mostly downhill. I'm soon cycling through John Forrest National Park, redoing in reverse what I did in 2013. Along the way, I'm seeing more revitalised rail bridges, while I can tell that one location was a former railway station due to palm trees having presumably been planted there. I'm also encountering a few red-tailed black cockatoos, including one eating in a tree, allowing me a closer inspection of this bird's red tail.

Near the end of this rail trail was the only rail tunnel in Western Australia until the Perth underground was built in 1990. It's not particularly long, compared to the many I went through in Europe.

I'm now seeing plenty of day riders out on this loop part of this trail as we soon meet suburban Perth.

Only rail tunnel in WA until 1990

If you're in Perth, I would recommend doing the loop part of this rail trail as it's a great day ride with the ability to catch a suburban train to Midland. However, I wouldn't bother about further east except if you're looking at cycling out of Perth.

I enjoy cycling in Perth because beside most active railway lines, there is often a wide paved cycle path, so it's easy cycling back to Jane's house before dark. With my flight not leaving until midnight, I have plenty of time to pack my bicycle back into my cardboard box while cooking dinner. Jane doesn't want to drive in the dark, so I order an Uber because the railway line to the airport is still being built.

A bonus with this layover is that this allows me to keep the 30 kilograms of check-in luggage for my flight from Perth to Melbourne. An Australian domestic flight has less luggage included in the ticket.

It feels like there is more security getting luggage through Perth airport for my domestic flight to Melbourne than there was for my international flight from London. At one stage, I thought they were going to take my stove part of my Trangia despite me flying with it from London.

Thankfully, everything went fine, and all bags are accounted for when I land in Melbourne.

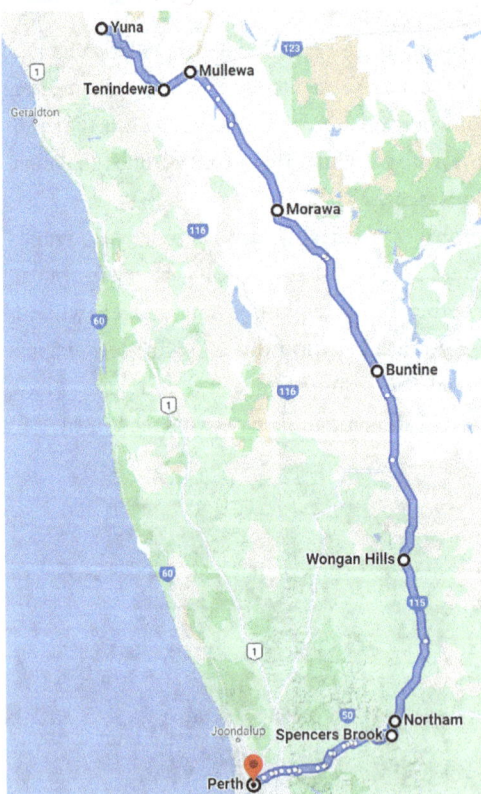

Yuna to Perth (Google Maps)

Overall for this trip, it was the first time my cycle computer has counted up to five digits on the odometer.

Once again, thanks for following my journey, especially to anyone who commented or encouraged me on social media. I'm unsure what's next.

If you wish to follow me on social media including many other cycling trips, including hopefully future trips, search for

Itsnotaboutkms

My First Book

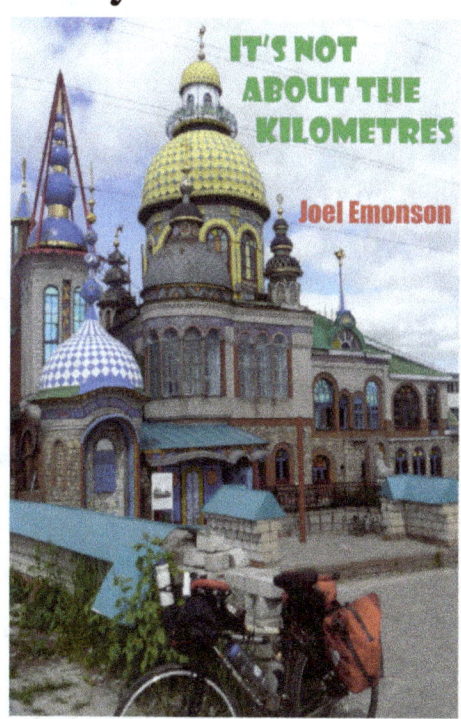

The 31-year-old from Berriwillock, has joined thousands of Australians in Kazan for the 2018 FIFA World Cup opener against France, but none have experienced a journey like his.

Joel Emonson is riding all over Russia on his bicycle during the tournament, going to the Socceroos games in Kazan and Samara.

He won't stop there, saddling up for a further 10 weeks through Eastern Europe.

His journey which started in Vladimir three hours out of Moscow, will take him all over Russia before heading south through Estonia, Latvia, Lithuania, Poland, Slovakia, Hungary, Croatia, Serbia, Bulgaria and Greece before flying home from the Turkish city of Istanbul after visiting Gallipoli.

It's him, his bicycle, a tent strapped to the handlebars and two bags fastened at the back, holding his clothes, food supplies and a portable stove.

He is proudly decked out in the fluoro tradie shirt he wears on the road.

He admits that most people are shocked when he tells them what he's doing, but to him it's the best way to travel.

"Most people can't understand the principle or actually doing it. I don't think about Istanbul. I'm just thinking about tomorrow, where I'm heading the next day"

"You get to see a country. Not just big cities. Cycle touring is such a rewarding way to travel."

The diciest moment so far? "There was a truck coming towards me, overtaking while I was on a narrow shoulder. So two trucks heading towards me at speed. That wasn't fun,"

This is not the first time he has undertaken such a cycling trip.

www.ingramcontent.com/pod-product-compliance
Lightning Source LLC
Chambersburg PA
CBHW051418290426
44109CB00016B/1344